INVESTMENT IN CHINA

A Question and Answer Guide on How to Do Business

Wang Yongjun

amacom
American Management Association
New York . Atlanta . Boston . Chicago . Kansas City . San Francisco . Washington, D.C.
Brussels . Mexico City . Tokyo . Toronto

This publication is designed to provide accurate and authoritative information in
regard to the subject matter covered. It is sold with the understanding that the
publisher is not engaged in rendering legal, accounting, or other professional
service. If legal advice or other expert assistance is required, the services of a competent professional person should be sought.

Library of Congress Cataloging-in-Publication Data

Wang, Yung-tsung
    Investment in China : a question and answer guide on how to do
business / Wang Yongjun.
        p.   cm.
    Includes index.
    ISBN 0-8144-0344-1
    1. Investments, Foreign—China. 2. China—Economic policy—1976-
I. Title.
HG5782.W373   1996
332.6'73'0951—dc20   96-32801
                                                                CIP

Authors: Wang Yongjun, Zhang Quan, He Qu, Zhang Zhishun.
Translators: Cao Jianhai, Chen Denong, etc.
Managing Editors: Anthony Vlamis, He Peihui.

Originally published in Chinese under the title Zhongguo Xishou Waizi
Wunda.

©1997 CITIC Publishing House (English version).
© 1995 CITIC Publishing House (Chinese version).
All rights reserved.
Printed in the United States of America.

Printing number

10   9   8   7   6   5   4   3   2   1

Contents

Preface

The reforms and open policies established in China since 1979 have invigorated this ancient state and appealed to a surge of overseas investors. With a sustained growth in its national economy, China is clearly on an upturn.

Since the implementation of these reforms and open policies, China's policy has been to encourage direct foreign investment through a series of preferential policies designed to attract foreign investment and a continuing effort to enact legislation in regard to investment, improve the investment environment, and hasten the process of entering the world economy. Especially since the 1990s, the Chinese government has pinpointed the construction of a socialist market economy as its goal. It seeks to attract foreign investment and guide it particularly to infrastructure facilities, basic industries, technological renovation of enterprises, and capital- or technology-intensive industries; secondary targets are financing, retailing and wholesaling, tourism, and real estate.

China has made outstanding accomplishments since the 1980s in attracting and utilizing foreign investment. The number of enterprises with foreign investment established with the approval of the Chinese government has increased tremendously even since 1990. In 1991, 12,978 such enterprises were established, a 78.4% increase over 1990; 48,764 in 1992, or 275.7% over 1991; and 83,473 in 1993, or 71% over 1992. In 1993 alone, a total amount of US$27.5 billion was actually utilized, which is 1.45 times the cumulative amount of the 12 years before 1990. In 1994, because of a shift of investment from the coastal areas into infrastructure facilities, basic industries, and capital- or technology-intensive industries while labor-intensive processing projects gradually moved farther inland, the total number of foreign-invested projected dropped a little compared to 1993. Nevertheless, because of the continued placement of capital by projects approved in 1993, the actual amount of foreign funds utilized increased 22.8%.

In general, China's situation in attracting foreign investment has greatly improved. Open regions have gradually expanded from coastal areas into their neighboring and inland areas. Areas for foreign investment have gradually moved and expanded from mainly labor-intensive industries into infrastructure facilities, basic industries, and capital- or technology-intensive industries as well as service industries such as financing, retailing, wholesaling, and real estate. Foreign investment has diversified, to include the stock market and securities, apart from attracting governmental or nongovernmental commercial credit and direct investment. The number of large high-tech projects has gradually increased as transnational groups become even fonder of the Chinese market. And with further deepening of reforms, major laws and regulations have been or are being modified or adopted, among them, the labor law, the law on competition, the tax law, the law on foreign trade, patent and copyright laws, the law on the protection of intellectual property rights, and regulations on a unified exchange rate system, a sign of an improved environment for foreign investment.

In order to satisfy the need for potential investors to understand issues related to China's introduction of foreign investment, we wrote this book based on our knowledge of China's laws and regulations and our own experience over a dozen years in introducing foreign investment. For easy reference, this up-to-date guide is short, clear, and to the point. It uses a question-and-answer format to clarify the major issues. The appendixes contain the legislation relevant to foreign investment in China.

Wang Yongjun, Vice Chairman of China Association of Enterprises with Foreign Investment

Zhang Quan, Board Director and Specially Invited Consultant of China Association of Enterprises with Foreign Investment

He Qu, Consultant of China Association of Enterprises with Foreign Investment

Zhang Zhishun, Assistant Secretary-General of China Association of Enterprises with Foreign Investment

1.

General Information on China's Attracting Foreign Funds

1. When did China start utilizing foreign funds?

After the founding of the People's Republic of China (PRC) on 1 October 1949, China used loans from other countries to speed up the construction of its socialist industrialization, based on the principles of equity, mutual benefit, and codevelopment. A few joint venture firms were established with foreign governments; of these, the China-Poland ocean shipping company lasted the longest. In the 1970s, the Chinese Government used export credit from foreign commercial banks, and some Chinese enterprises initiated economic cooperation projects with foreign banks or firms, such as processing against supplied materials. By the 1960s and 1970s, China had stopped utilizing foreign government loans. Thus, over the first 30 years after the founding of the PRC, China had not attracted much foreign capital.

It was not until the general policy on reforms and opening to the outside world was ascertained at the Third Plenary Session of the 11th Committee of the Communist Party of China in 1978 and the Law of the People's Republic of China on Chinese-Foreign Equity Joint Ventures was adopted by the state on 1 July 1979 that attracting foreign investment, particularly from the private sector, began in earnest.

2. What is the relationship between the reforms and open policies and utilizing foreign investment in China?

Reforms and opening to the outside world and utilizing foreign investment are complementary. Reforms and open policies establish the necessary conditions for utilizing foreign investment, and utilization of foreign investment promotes China's reforms and opening. The reforms and open policies, establish a good investment environment that attracts foreign business. Thus, the reforms and open policies signal a fine environment for foreign investors, and the influx of foreign capital requires that China develop its economic system in the direction of a better fit with international practices.

3. What advantageous conditions have been offered for foreign investment since the reforms and open policies?

Reforms of China's economic system are gradually turning a planned economy into a socialist market economy, and in the course of this change, some internationally common economic management methods are gradually absorbed. The centralized financing system is being gradually replaced by one in which various financing organizations compete with one another under the leadership of the Central Bank, with a foreign exchange swap market established and developed. The same is true of the pricing of commodities, which is now being adjusted by the market instead of by the state. Currently 85% of the means of production and 95% of the means of livelihood are priced by the market. Successful reforms have established a fine environment for production and operations by enterprises with foreign investment, with more and more investment opportunities available for foreign investors; additionally, the establishment of tens of thousands of enterprises with foreign investment has resulted in an influx of advanced foreign managerial expertise and new competitive mechanisms, breaking up the previous monopoly by state-owned enterprises, changing people's values and standards, and speeding up the course of reforms in China.

The reforms and open policies have also increased China's foreign trade and economic cooperation with foreign countries throughout the world. China's foreign trade rose from 9.86% in 1978 to 35.9% in 1993, an annual increase of 14.2%, which is 5.3% higher than the growth of its gross national product. The development of its foreign trade has led to a yearly increase of foreign exchange reserves, thus solidifying China's ability to balance international revenues and expenses. Under the banner of reforms and open policies, China has so far opened to the outside world almost all of its regions, including the coastal, border, and riverside regions as well as inland provincial capital cities, and adopted a series of preferential policies in various regions according to their respective economic strengths. China has produced a fine environment for foreign investment;

it now has a number of infrastructure facilities and has adopted a group of foreign economic laws and decrees, while on the way to perfecting various services as called for by foreign investment.

Without these reforms and open policies, China would not have arrived at its present position for utilizing foreign investment or developing a socialist market economy. At the same time, the incorporation of thousands of enterprises with foreign investment from all over the world has promoted the development of China's foreign economy. The advantages of the Chinese economy have been brought into play via renewal of products and upgrading of quality, tying China closer to the world market, and hence greatly improving the extent and depth of China's openness.

4. What is China's progress in attracting foreign investment?

China has made world-recognized achievements in attracting direct foreign investment since the adoption of reforms and open policies. Between 1980, when the first Sino-foreign joint venture enterprise was established; and the end of 1994, China approved the establishment of over 220,000 enterprises with foreign investment (140,000 are Sino–foreign equity joint ventures, over 35,000 are Sino–foreign cooperative joint ventures, and over 45,000 are wholly foreign-owned enterprises and 105 projects in offshore petroleum prospecting and exploitation. The total contracted foreign investment amounted to over US$302.7 billion, with over US$93.9 billion actually invested.

Exhibit 1-1 details the annual number of approved enterprises with foreign investment, their respective foreign investment amounts by contract value, and amounts of actual foreign investment.

5. What stages has China undergone in attracting foreign investments?

Since 1979, China has gone through three stages in attracting foreign investment.

1. *The initial period, 1979–1986.* In July 1979, the National People's Congress passed and issued the Law of the People's Republic of China on Chinese–Foreign Equity Joint Ventures, the first law regarding foreign investment. During 1979 and 1980, the State approved special policies for the provinces of Guangdong and Fujian regarding their foreign economic activities and established on a trial basis four special economic zones, in-Shenzhen, Zhuhai, Shantou, and Xiamen in South China. Preferential

Exhibit 1-1. Foreign Investment in China, 1980 to 1994

Year	Number of Foreign Investment Projects	Amount of Foreign Investment by Contract Value (billion U.S. dollars)	Amount of Foreign Investment actually Placed (billion U.S. dollars)
1980–1982	921	6.010	1.166
1983	471	1.732	0.636
1984	1,851	2.649	1.258
1985	3,073	5.932	1.658
1986	1,662	2.834	1.875
1987	2,233	3.709	2.314
1988	5,786	5.297	3.190
1989	5,784	5.595	3.392
1990	7,237	6.596	3.487
1991	12,978	11.977	4.366
1992	48,764	58.123	11.007
1993	83,473	110.852	25.759
1994	47,490	81.406	33.800
Total	221,723	302.712	93.906

policies were granted in the special economic zones in order to attract foreign investment.

During these early years of implementation of open policies, China took its first steps to attract foreign investment. Due to incomplete legal legislation, insufficient preparation in all areas, and concerns of foreign business regarding investment in China, progress was slow.

In May 1983, the first nationwide conference on attracting foreign investment was held by the State Council, summarizing China's initial experience after implementing the open policies and seeking feedback on its progress. On the basis of this conference, more flexible foreign investment policies were adopted. In May 1984, the State Council decided to open fourteen more coastal port cities, including Shanghai, Tianjin, Dalian, Qingdao, and Guangzhou, and still more preferential policies were implemented. In February 1985, the State Council established coastal economic development areas in such regions as the Yangtze River Delta, Pearl River Delta, and South Fujian-Xiamen-Zhangzhou-Quanzhou Delta. In addition, it undertook a series of new measures (e.g., decentralizing review and approval rights, offering tax deductions, and offering market shares) and passed enabling legislation. Finally foreign business became interested in investing in China, and China undertook new measures to attract direct foreign investment. Between 1980 and 1986, the contract value of foreign investment reached US$19.157 billion, for an average of US$2.737 billion per year; of this amount US$6.593 billion was actually placed, for an annual average of US$0.942 billion.

The bulk of the direct foreign investment during this period was from Hong Kong and Macao, most of it in labor-intensive processing enterprises and tertiary-sector projects like hotels and recreational facilities. Most of these enterprises and projects were located in Guangdong and Fujian provinces, close to Hong Kong and Macao.

2. *Steady development, 1987–1991.* In October 1986, the State Council issued the Regulations on Encouraging Foreign Investment (generally known as 22 Articles), in response to some difficulties that enterprises encountered. It also offered more preferential treatment for enterprises that manufactured products for export and those that engaged in advanced technology. Related departments of the State Council adopted over a dozen detailed implementation regulations that had the effect of improving the environment for attracting foreign investment even more. Foreign investment reached another high tide. Between 1987 and 1991, foreign investment by contract value amounted to US$33.174 billion, for an annual average of US$6.635 billion; actual foreign investment was US$16.749 billion, for an annual average of US$3.35 billion. These two average figures meant an increase over the 1980–1986 period by 242.2% and 355.6%, respectively.

During this period, China's structure for attracting foreign investment was improved, and it saw an increase of manufacturing enterprises, enterprises manufacturing products for export or using advanced technologies, and foreign-invested regions and industries.

3. *Fast development, since 1992.* After Deng Xiaoping's speeches were published in early 1992, an upsurge of foreign investment swept across the country, and the introduction of foreign investment underwent a new, substantial development, both in breadth and depth. In 1992, the total amount of approved foreign investment reached US$58.123 billion by contract value, which is equal to that of the prior 13 years. In 1993, the figure shot up to US$110.852 billion. There was a drop in 1994 in both the total number of approved enterprises with foreign investment and the total amount of foreign investment by contract value, yet the amount of actual foreign investment surpassed that of 1993. China has thus entered into a new stage in attracting foreign investment.

During this stage, the areas of direct foreign investment have expanded, including sectors previously closed to foreign business, such as finance, insurance, and foreign trade, which were opened with conditions or on a trial basis. More large transnational corporations began to enter

China, and foreign investment moved into inland China and some large cities.

The direct foreign investment introduced into China centers mainly in the coastal regions in southeast China. Guangdong Province holds first place, in number of approved enterprises with foreign investment, amount of foreign investment by contract value, and actual amount of foreign investment. Following Guangdong are Shanghai, Beijing, Fujian, Jiangsu, and Shandong.

There has been growth as well in foreign investment in China's inland provinces and cities and an increasing diversity of areas that enterprises with foreign investment engage in; they include such sectors as petroleum, coal, communications, telecommunications, metallurgy, machinery, automobiles, electronics, chemicals, building materials, light industry, textiles, pharmaceuticals, and real estate. The areas of foreign investment continue to expand to such tertiary sectors as finance, insurance, consulting, accounting, and law. Some areas previously closed to foreign business, such as aviation and cargo shipment, are now open to foreign investment. China's foreign investment structure has been improved constantly over the past dozen years. Of the cumulative amount of foreign investment by contract value during the period 1980–1983, industrial projects took up 55.8% (or 77.6%, when calculated by the number of projects), agricultural projects, 1.5%, and tertiary-sector projects, 38.9%. Development in infrastructure projects, technology- or funding-intensive projects, and tertiary-sector projects has been picking up speed, and increasing numbers of large transnational corporations seek to invest in China.

In general, most foreign investment in China is directed to small or medium-sized labor-intensive, general processing projects, and organizations manufacturing products for export or using advanced technologies remain a comparatively small percentage. Nevertheless, as China's economy develops and living standards improve, the Chinese market has become increasingly more attractive to foreign business.

China now has over 100,000 enterprises with foreign investment in production or open for business, and most of them enjoy a sound operation, yielding better and better economic results. Enterprises with foreign investment already boast a fair production capacity. In 1993, the total industrial output value of enterprises with foreign investment reached RMB 302 billion yuan, employing a total workforce of 12 million. Revenues from taxes levied on these enterprises have increased over the years too; the figure stood at RMB 20.6 billion yuan (excluding tariffs and land fees). Enterprises with foreign investment in 1994 made up over 36% of the total export of China's foreign trade. As China's reforms and openness continue to develop, enterprises with foreign investment will become larger and inevitably will play an increasingly important role in China's modernization.

6. What are the characteristics of foreign investment in China?

1. Today 133 countries and regions are investing in China. The top ten countries and regions in investment amount are Hong Kong and Macao, Taiwan, the United States, Japan, Singapore, the United Kingdom, Thailand, Canada, Germany, and Australia.

2. Increasingly foreign investment is moving from China's coastal regions to its inland provinces and cities. In 1993, the number of organizations with foreign investment and the amount of foreign investment in inland China increased from the previous 7 or 8% to nearly 20% of the national total.

3. The size of foreign investment projects has grown. In 1992, the average amount of foreign investment by contract value stood at US$1.19 million per project. In 1993, the figure rose to US$1.33 million, and in 1994, it reached US$1.64 million.

4. Many transnational corporations have turned their attention to China as a potential market. Of the 500 largest industrial enterprises in the world (according to rankings by *Fortune* magazine), 80 have invested in China. Among them are Motorola, General Electric, Shell, IBM, Ford, Dupont, and Xerox from the United States; Volkswagen, Lufthansa, and Siemens from Germany; Philips from the Netherlands; Citron from France; Northern Telecom from Canada; TPL from Italy; Bell from Belgium; Mitsubishi, C. Itoh, Mitsui, Toshiba, Panasonic, and Sony from Japan; and Sande from Singapore. These organizations have either invested in projects in China or tremendously increased their China investment. Many of them have medium- to long-term plans for investment.

5. The foreign investment structure has been strengthened. There are highway, port, power station, subway, and tunnel projects and large raw material projects, as well as a number of funding- or technology-intensive projects urgently needed for national economic development. By the end of 1993, China had approved over 3,000 large projects of over US$10 million each.

6. Areas for foreign investment have been expanded. Investment in tertiary-sector projects in particular has seen fair growth. There are enter-

prises with foreign investment now in such areas as finance, insurance, real estate, retailing, consulting, accounting, and advertising.

7. There are developments in organization structure. Over 20 Sino-foreign joint stock companies have been established, and over 20 companies have appeared in the listing for special RMB shares (Category B shares) transactions at the Shenzhen and Shanghai stock markets. In the past two years, China has approved, on a trial basis, the establishment of two shareholding companies engaging mainly in investment while providing comprehensive services to their invested enterprise. China is also examining various other forms, such as foundations and trusts. Such new methods have provided new means of investment to overseas investors and added sources of funding for enterprises with foreign investment.

7. What is the situation in regard to China's borrowing from foreign financing?

An important part of China's strategy is to borrow a fair amount of foreign funds for economic development from international capital markets. Between 1979 and 1993, it signed a total of US$85.948 billion worth of loan agreements with foreign financing organizations, of which US$71.404 billion was actually drawn.

China began borrowing foreign capital after the implementation of the reforms and open policies. In December 1979, the Japanese Government committed itself to loaning long-term, low-interest facilities to three large projects in China. In April, China and Japan signed a loan agreement under which Japan was to provide China with 50 billion Japanese yen annually.

During the first few years after implementation of the reforms and open policies, when China was still exploring international financing, it had few foreign debts, and the average annual increase was only about US$800 million between 1979 and 1983.

Between 1984 and 1988, China's foreign debts grew rapidly, with an average annual increase of 58.5 percent and foreign debts in arrears increasing US$7.2 billion per annum, nine times over that of the prior five years. By 1988, foreign debts reached US$40 billion. The large influx of foreign capital somewhat eased the difficulties of a foreign exchange shortage in China.

After 1989 and the period of rapid increase of foreign debts, China entered a relatively stable development stage in borrowing foreign capital, with the increase of foreign debts slowing, though still at a net inflow status. The rate of increase of foreign debts in 1989 and 1990 fell to 14.6%, over 40 percentage points less than the 58.5% of the prior period. At this time, China began to repay the huge amounts of foreign debts it had accumulated. After 1987, China gradually established a fairly effective foreign debts surveillance system while continuing to complete the foreign debts control system and legal legislation. A sound system of foreign capital circulation has finally been established and put into practice. To sum up, the growth of foreign debts has become an increasingly more important means of China's national economic development.

During the first few years after China began borrowing foreign capital, 85% of foreign debt came from a few Asian countries and regions like Japan and Hong Kong, with an insignificant portion from Europe and America. That situation has now changed, with a substantial increase in funding from Europe and America, though Japan remains in the top place. Hong Kong and Macao are still the major regions from which China obtains international credit funds, but their portion of China's foreign debts has fallen. This diversity in source of funds is a favorable change because it reduces China's foreign debts risk.

China has followed a fairly healthy structure in the term of foreign debts. The majority of foreign debts are of medium to long term, with repeated extensions. Before 1984, China's foreign debts were basically fixed-rate loans. With the increase in commercial loans came floating interest rates, with the rates relatively low. Debts are owed in US dollars, Japanese yen, deutsche marks, Hong Kong dollars, and others, though the yen is still a large proportion, and the fluctuation of exchange rates of the Japanese yen versus other currencies has an important influence on China's repayment of foreign debts.

Drawing lessons from other countries that fell into a debt crisis, the Chinese Government has been very cautious. Since 1987, it has gradually strengthened its administration of loans from foreign sources and designated special agencies for such international loans. By some international indexes, China's foreign debts are within affordable limits, and when China's economic strength and size are taken into consideration, there is room for additional foreign capital.

Closely related to the economic results the borrowed foreign capital will bring about and the repayment schedule is how the international loans will be used. From the standpoint of industrial allocation, China has applied its long-term loans mainly to transportation, energy, mining, machinery, and chemical industrials and short-term loans mainly to light and textile industries, commerce, and civil service. Generally long-term loans are used mainly to resolve bottlenecks in China's economic development, and short-term loans are basically applied in foreign exchange earning and fast profit-making industries and projects such as light and textile industries. China has used the majority of its borrowed capital in manufacturing and construction projects. The industrial application orientation, under which the domination by infrastructure projects has gradually given way to these projects plus export and foreign-exchange-earning projects, is fairly rational; it will relieve the vulnerable links in China's national economy, strengthen its staying power for economic development, and improve capabilities for export and foreign exchange earning.

8. What countries provide government loans to China?

Japan, France, Germany, Spain, Italy, Canada, the United Kingdom, Austria, Kuwait, Australia, Sweden, Finland, Denmark, the Netherlands, Belgium, Russia, the United States, Luxembourg, and the Republic of Korea, among others, are providing government loans. Following is a breakdown of the size of the loans to China:

> One country loaned US$10–13 billion
> Seven countries loaned US$1–2.9 billion
> Ten countries loaned US $0.1–1 billion
> Three countries loaned US$10–100 million

9. Which international financing organizations have made loans to China, and what is the situation like?

There are two types of international financing organizations: truly international financing institutions, such as the International Monetary Fund, the World Bank, and the United Nations Development Programme, and regional financing institutions, such as the development banks of Asia, Africa, Oceania, and the Americas, the World Liquidation Bank, and the North European Investment Bank. After the 1960s, foundations were set up for political and economic reasons in developed and OPEC countries, among them, the Joint Foundation of Japan, the Development and Assistance Foundation of Kuwait, and the Development and Assistance Foundation of Saudi Arabia.

After resuming its seat in the World Bank and the Asian Development Bank in the 1980s, China obtained loans from the World Bank and the Asian Development Bank of, respectively, US$15.9 billion (for 131 projects) and US$3 billion (for 30 projects). Some key projects are now under implementation.

The North European Investment Bank has provided China with US$280 million for project financing.

Since 1979, China has borrowed US$13 billion from the Joint Foundation of Japan (the Japanese Government) and US$490 million from the Development and Assistance Foundation of Kuwait.

Many funds from various developed countries (pension funds, welfare funds, development funds, etc.) are being used for investment in China.

The China Foundation for the Old Liberated Areas once issued US$60 million in "nonrecoverable" loans to finance projects for relieving poverty and enriching the old liberated areas,* with not only a prime interest rate but also a term dependent on project results. Repayment of loans is encouraged only when profits are generated, and the repayment time can be extended until the projects yield profits.

The former Ministry of Aviation authorized Tienli International Investment Co., Ltd. of Hong Kong to sign a contract using US$96 million from the Aviation Foundation in the development of aviation industry and science and technology. This is a cooperative method of financing.

10. When did China start its international financing business, and what is its status?

China started its international financing business in 1981 and has thus far approved the establishment of 32 Sino-foreign joint venture leasing companies, which, together with other leasing firms, have played a tremendous role in the development of China's aviation and communications industries, using US$15 billion over the past 15 years in financing the technological renovation of 6,000 enterprises. This means nearly half of the total amount of funds China has spent on technological renovation in this period (US$30.5 billion) and 33% of 18,000 enterprises with technological renovation.

11. What is the impact of foreign investment on China's economic development?

1. *Making up for China's shortage of funds.* Shortage of funds has been a major factor inhibiting the development of China's economy. Therefore,

---

*"Old liberated areas" refers to the old base areas of the Chinese Communist revolution, such as the Shaanxi-Gansu-Nigxia (Province) Border Region in northwest China and the Jinggangshan Mountain areas in Jiangxi Province in southeast China, places where the economy is comparatively underdeveloped.

in addition to utilizing domestic funds fully and improving the effectiveness of such fund usage, China, since the beginning of implementation of the reforms and open policies, identified a long-term strategy of using foreign investment make up for a shortage of funds. By the end of 1993, China had put into use US$71.404 billion in foreign loans and US$60.108 billion in direct foreign investment. The influx of so much foreign capital has effectively eased the fund shortage situation.

China's fast economic growth owes a lot to the increasing amounts of foreign capital, and the foreign investment actually put into use every year is also an increasingly larger proportion of the total completed fixed assets investment in China. In 1985, foreign capital was 5.35% of the total fixed assets investment, with 2.26% in direct foreign investment, and 1993 saw a rise of these two ratios to 17.9% and 12.6%, respectively. By 1993, over 80,000 enterprises with foreign investment had entered the production stage or opened to business, bringing about a total output value of industrial enterprises at RMB 302 billion yuan, a 46.2% increase over the year before.

Foreign capital also serves as China's main source of financing in certain industries. Of China's seas, for instance, over 600,000 square kilometers hold promise of petroleum or gas. Petroleum prospecting is highly risky and calls for huge investments, but China, with outmoded technologies and not enough money, has been unable to prospect. After 1979, China started to introduce foreign investment in offshore oil prospecting by means of Sino-foreign cooperation. By 1987, seismic testing of 360,000 kilometers had been completed, 179 prospecting wells and assessment wells drilled, 128 structures prospected, and 39 oil and gas containing structures discovered. China has since opened oil prospecting in the mainland to foreign investment. Frequent reports of success from South China have verified the correctness of China's foreign investment policies.

2. *Promoting changes in China's industrial structure and better products.* The difference in economic development between China and developed countries lies mainly in China's backward industrial technology. After implementation of the reforms and open policies, China devoted itself to introducing advanced technologies. Over the course of a few years, Shanghai Volkswagen and Beijing Jeep have upgraded the technology incorporated in China's sedan car industry from that of 1950s into that of 1980s; joint venture enterprises in elevators (Tianjin Otis, China Schindler, and Shanghai Mitsubishi, etc.) have advanced China's elevator industry from manual operation to computer control. Currently organizations with foreign investment are in the mainstream in many industries in China, such as television, motors, automobiles, elevators, and pharmaceuticals.

Joint venture enterprises have not only introduced new technology and new equipment but also promoted technological advancement in related industries, with the result that their products are moving into the international marketplace. The Taiwan-invested Ji'an Bicycle Factory in Kunshan Development Zone exports a majority of its products, bringing with them the products of some 40 other domestic enterprises into the international market. To supplement Shanghai Volkswagen's Santana model, China's automotive industry has improved the overall technological level in parts manufacturing.

Borrowed capital has also played an important role in renovating domestic industries with imported technologies. In 1991, transactions for technology introduction into China stood at US$3.459 billion, 33.2% of it (US$1.15 billion) in foreign loans to finance the renovation of a large group of enterprises. Importation of technologies and equipment bought using foreign loans has also brought about a number of additional key industrial projects in China, such as the large-scale iron and steel industry, thermal power equipment, and nuclear power stations. Such investments center mainly around infrastructure industries and infrastructure facilities areas, hence strengthening China's industrial power and laying a solid foundation for the development of domestic industry.

Through market competition, business transactions, and personnel exchange, foreign-invested organizations with relatively advanced technologies have produced modeling effects in technology and production upgrading for other enterprises in China, thus promoting the technological progress of domestic industries and narrowing the gap in technological level between China and the world's advanced countries.

3. *Importing advanced managerial expertise.* Modern management theories and technologies are the fruit of human civilization and a common spiritual wealth of all humanity. Following direct foreign investment and foreign loans are not only capital and technologies but also advanced management methods. The Yunnan Lubuge Hydropower Station, built with foreign loans, is an example of how managerial expertise has been disseminated across the country. The most typical example is the hotel industry; first-class hotel management and staff have been brought in by equity and cooperative joint ventures. Within a short period of time, China's hotels, with a reputation for backward operations and service, have reached the world's first-class level, contributing substantially to the development of China's rich tourist industry.

Enterprises with foreign investment have applied advanced means in production, sales, and personnel and accounting control, setting a good example for other Chinese enterprises. The "mimic foreign-invested enterprises" reforms sought in part to find new ways to reform state-owned or collective enterprises by drawing on the experience of advanced means of management practiced in enterprises with foreign investment.

Enterprises with foreign investment have also built up a group of new types of management personnel. A strategy of localizing management personnel—that is, hiring a large number of medium- to high-level management personnel from the local market—has been implemented in most enterprises with foreign investment. These employees, having participated in the management and operation of the enterprises, have thus had the opportunity to learn at firsthand advanced theories of management and are becoming experts. These people are contributing to the spread of international management experience in China.

Since opening to the outside world, China has sent personnel overseas for training and has invited international management experts to introduce their management philosophy and experience. These methods are paying off; a large number of Chinese management personnel have been thus trained, the result being a substantial improvement in the quality of China's personnel and management.

4. *Promoting the formation and development of China's socialist market economy.* Economic system reform and the reforms and open policies are mutually complementary. The 14th Committee of the Communist Party of China set out the establishment of a socialist market economy as its goal. Reforms over more than a dozen years are designed to convert China's highly centralized economic planning mechanism into one of a socialist market economy. As these reforms have promoted China's opening to the outside world, the opening, in return, has promoted the economic reforms. For example, the special economic zones and enterprises with foreign investment are promoting the market orientation of economic system reforms and speeding up the development of China's market economy.

Along with the establishment of a large number of enterprises with foreign investment, China's traditional ownership structure has given way to a new system of mutually supplementary and developing state-owned, collective, private, and foreign-invested economic units, with the state owned remaining in the majority. Modern enterprises under the domination of public ownership form the foundation of the socialist market economy, and foreign investment is a helpful supplement to this economy. The flow of foreign capital has brought with it the restructuring of property ownership. The industrial production output value of enterprises with foreign investment in Fujian Province reached RMB 32.574 billion yuan in 1993, 38.1% of the total by enterprises at or above the level of township. Enterprises with foreign investment have also brought into the

Chinese economy such modern property ownership mechanisms as joint stocks and cooperation, promoting property ownership reforms in China.

The State issues no mandatory planning figures to enterprises with foreign investment regarding their production or sales; all necessary input and labor for the production of such enterprises is to be obtained from the market, and so all sales of their products realized in the market. Market-oriented enterprises with foreign investment have introduced international competition mechanisms (including competition of commodities and services in price, quality, technological level, and so forth) and stimulated the growth of markets in domestic financing, means of production, labor, real estate, technology, and information.

The influx of foreign investment has made Chinese economic life more complex. Because of the flow of funds and goods, the government is learning to develop the required interest rates, taxation, exchange rates, and so forth. As a result, the shift of government functions has quickened.

5. *Promoting the development of China's open economy.* The birth and development of large numbers of enterprises with foreign investment have greatly stimulated the construction of China's open economy.

First, enterprises with foreign investment have a relationship with the world economy. Foreign investors in China come from more than 100 countries and regions in the world, and as they arrive in China for investment, they have brought into the country such various economic relations as sales and supply channels, and connections in technological development, marketing, and credit. All Chinese enterprises are learning to take advantage of these economic relationships with the international community and are gradually penetrating the international market.

Second, enterprises with foreign investment have become the major source for the increase in China's exports. Calculating by the official exchange rate, in 1993 the export volume of enterprises with foreign investment stood at 48% of the total, while other enterprises stood at only 7.67%. The export volume of enterprises with foreign investment was only 9.12% of the national total export volume in 1989; in 1994 it reached over 36%, an annual increase of 5%.

China has been increasing its portion in world trade since the 1990s, from 0.75% in 1978 to 2.5% in 1993, and it has become the eleventh largest trading country in the world, an achievement directly related to the fast growth of its import and export trading business by enterprises with foreign investment.

Third, enterprises with foreign investment have rationalized China's export products structure. During the initial period after opening up, China exported mainly raw materials and primary-level products, such as petroleum, coal, and agricultural products. Since the mid-1980s, China has gradually improved its export commodities structure, with the portion of finished products rising from less than 50% in 1980 to 81.8% in 1993. In a position of increasing importance in China, the export business of enterprises with foreign investment is an increasingly important influence on China's structure, which is quickly shifting to a structure in which finished products become the majority.

6. *Creating employment opportunities.* The introduction of foreign investment has resulted in the creation of new employment opportunities. By the end of 1994, enterprises with foreign investment employed approximately 12 million people. This figure would be much higher if it included the employment opportunities created by enterprises and units incorporated to supplement or provide services to those with foreign investment. In addition, large infrastructure facilities and infrastructure industry projects have been undertaken in China, contributing also to the increase of employment opportunities.

2.

China's Investment Environment and Preferential Policies

12. What laws, decrees, regulations, and so forth has China adopted to attract foreign investment? What conventions and international treaties has China signed?

Over the past 15 years, China has strengthened its economic legislation in order to improve its investment environment. The National People's Congress or its Standing Committee and the State Council alone have adopted over 500 foreign economic decrees, including 50 laws directly related to foreign investment. They include the Law of the People's Republic of China on Chinese–Foreign Equity Joint Ventures, the Implementing Regulations of the Law of the People's Republic of China on Chinese–Foreign Equity Joint Ventures, the Law of the People's Republic of China on Chinese–Foreign Cooperative Joint Ventures, the Law of the People's Republic of China on Enterprises with Foreign Investment, the Law of the People's Republic of China on Economic Contracts Involving Foreign Interests, and the Income Tax Law of the People's Republic of China for Enterprises with Foreign Investment and Foreign Enterprises. China has attached great importance to protecting intellectual property rights and endeavored to complete its legislation in this regard by adopting the Patent Law of the People's Republic of China, the Trademark Law of the People's Republic of China, and Regulations of the People's Republic of China on the Protection of Computer Software and by joining in the World Intellectual Property Rights Organization Convention, the Paris Convention for the Protection of Industrial Property Rights, the

Madrid Agreement for International Registration of Trademarks, the Berne Convention for the Protection of Literary and Artistic Works, and the Universal Copyright Convention.

Moreover, China has signed mutual investment protection agreements with over 50 countries, including Sweden and Rumania, and investment insurance agreements with the United States and Canada. In addition, China has entered into agreement with 33 countries, including Germany, on avoiding double taxation.

13. How did China implement the expansion of open regions to improve its investment environment?

Between 1979 and 1980, in order to attract foreign investment, the Chinese Government designated Guangdong and Fujian provinces as entitled to special preferential policies and flexibility in their economic activities and on a trail basis opened four special economic zones (Shenzhen, Zhuhai, Xiamen, and Shantou). In May 1984, China opened 14 coastal cities: Dalian, Qinhuangdao, Tianjin, Yantai, Qingdao, Lianyungang, Shanghai, Ningbo, Wenz-hou, Fuzhou, Guangzhou, Zhanjiang, Haikou, and Beihai. In May 1985, the State Council decided to turn the Changjiang (Yangtze) River Delta, Pearl River Delta, and South Fujian Delta into three coastal open economic regions and turned Hainan Island into the largest special economic zone. In the 1990s, Shanghai Pudong New Area was opened. In 1992, approval was given to open five more cities along the Changjiang (Yangtze) River, 18 provincial capital cities, and 13 border towns in China's northeast, northwest, and southwest regions. The opening of these areas has had a great impact on inland China and border areas. Thus far China has established special economic zones, economic and technological development zones, coastal open cities, coastal open economic regions, riverside open cities, and tourism and vacation zones—in all, 10 different types of open regions where preferential policies are granted for foreign investment. China has thus posed itself as a multilayered, full-dimension open nation, with coastal open cities on the east, Changjiang (Yangtze) River-side open regions headed by Shanghai's Pudong New Area, border regions, and inland regions centering around provincial capital cities.

Within these regions, a large number of infrastructure and service facilities have been established—communications, electric power supply, telecommunications, water supply, and industrial facilities—rendering a sound environment for foreign investment and good living conditions for foreign staff working in China.

The recently opened inland regions have unique strengths. In addition to a rich supply of natural resources and labor, these regions have lower costs than the coastal areas. Furthermore, they enjoy a well-established industrial and agricultural base, with a group of key enterprises, of large and medium size, staffed by strong technical forces, thus rendering a huge potential for development. Quite a number of projects programmed in China's Eighth Five-Year Plan and Ten-Year Development Plan will be implemented in these regions, most of them aimed at either expansion or renovation of existing enterprises, although there are new projects, too. The development of these industries calls for various types of international cooperation in funding, technology, and equipment, hence providing a huge market for investment and a great number of investment opportunities the world over.

14. What preferential taxation policies are applicable for investment in China's development zones?

The corporate income tax for enterprises with foreign investment is 30% on a taxable income basis, plus a 3% local corporate income tax. However, a 15% deduction of this tax will be granted to those located in the following regions or engaged in the following projects:

1. Enterprises with foreign investment located within the special economic zones
2. Manufacturing enterprises located within the economic and technological development zones
3. Manufacturing enterprises located within the Shanghai Pudong New Area or enterprises engaged in such energy or communications construction projects as airports, seaports, railways, highways, and power stations
4. Enterprises assessed to be in new or high-tech business and located within the national new and high-tech development zones
5. Manufacturing enterprises engaged in the following projects and located within the coastal economic development zones, the special economic zones, or old urban downtown areas where there is an economic and development zone:
   —Technology-intensive projects
   —Projects with foreign investment of over US$30 million and a long projected time for return on investment
   —Construction projects of energy, communications, or seaport facilities

6. Sino–foreign equity joint ventures engaged in the building of harbors or seaports
7. Financing institutions such as foreign banks or Sino–foreign equity joint venture banks located within the special economic zones or other regions approved by the State Council, provided that the investment amount by the foreign investors or the operating fund transferred from the headquarters exceeds US$10 million and the term of business exceeds 10 years
8. Enterprises with foreign investment engaged in projects encouraged by the State and located in other regions designated by the State Council

Manufacturing enterprises with a business term of over ten years are entitled to a corporate income tax exemption for two years starting from the first profit-making year and to a further 50% corporate income tax deduction from the third to fifth years.

15. What has China done to decentralize and otherwise simplify administrative approval procedures to attract foreign investment?

To improve efficiency and simplify the formalities, the Chinese Government has decentralized the approval process, increasing the power of local governments in this regard. Thus far, coastal provincial and municipal governments are entitled to approve manufacturing projects with an investment of up to US$30 million and inland provincial and municipal governments up to US$10 million. Local governments also have the power to examine and approve all nonmanufacturing projects, regardless of the size of projects, except in the case of energy, communications, raw materials, or other projects that require a nationwide overall balance or are restricted by the State.

Many provinces and municipalities have set up a single examination and approval organization, tremendously reducing the time required for review and approval. Various special organizations have been established in most coastal provinces and cities, such as foreign investment service centers, raw materials supply and procurement companies, exchange swap centers, law firms, accounting firms, and economic and trading consulting firms, all providing various services to enterprises with foreign investment.

16. What additional measures has China taken in recent years to enlarge areas for foreign investment?

In addition to opening more regions to foreign investment, the areas for such investment have also been expanded. In the 1980s, foreign investment was mainly in manufacturing enterprises, with foreign investment in the tertiary sector greatly restricted, and some areas were strictly forbidden for foreign investment, such as trading and aviation. Since 1992, China has lifted a lot of its restrictions on foreign investment in the tertiary sector and adopted encouraging attitudes toward gradually opening a number of other areas for foreign investment (e.g., financing, insurance, merchandise, foreign trade, aviation, harbor and shipping, real estate, tourism, accounting, and consulting).

17. What new developments are there in the structure of foreign investment enterprises?

Since 1992, China has approved the establishment of 20 Sino-foreign joint stock companies, over 20 firms are licensed for the Shenzhen and Shanghai stock exchanges dealing in special RMB stocks (Category B), and over 30 shareholding companies are providing comprehensive services for their investment enterprises. This has led to new structures for foreign investment, adding new funding sources for enterprises with foreign investment, and providing new means for transnational companies to increase their investment in China.

18. What is being done to encourage investment from Taiwan?

In order to encourage Taiwan to make investments in the mainland, the State Council adopted the Regulations of the State Council on Encouraging Investment by Taiwanese Compatriots on 3 July 1988, which states that plants in the mainland with investment by Taiwan compatriots are entitled to the same treatment as enterprises with foreign investment as detailed in relevant economic laws, decrees, and regulations. It is also reemphasized that the State will not nationalize investment or other assets from Taiwan investors. In the case of a takeover of Taiwan-invested enterprises by the State to meet social or public interests, compensation will be made according to an established legal procedure. Additionally, more flexibility is reflected in some articles of the regulations compared with laws for enterprises with foreign investment, mainly as follows:

1. *Larger areas for investment.* Taiwan investors are allowed, for instance, to purchase shares or securities of enterprises, housing properties, and land usage rights as well as development and operations of land according to law.
2. *Ascertained inheritance rights of properties.* Taiwan investors' investment, purchased properties, industrial property rights, profits gained from investment, and other legitimate rights are under the protection of the State laws and decrees and transferable and inheritable according to law.
3. *No limitation on term of business of enterprises.* The term of business is purely up to the investors in enterprises wholly owned by Taiwan investors or the joint decision by all parties to equity or cooperative joint venture enterprises. Or it may not be specified in some cases.
4. *Rights to authorize relatives or friends as agent.* Taiwan investors can authorize their relatives or friends residing on the mainland to act as their agent for their investment in the mainland by legal proxy.

19. What is China doing to encourage investment from overseas Chinese and from Hong Kong and Macao?

The State Council issued the Provisions of the State Council Concerning the Encouragement of Investments by Overseas Chinese and Compatriots from Hong Kong and Macao on 19 November 1990, which states that plants in mainland China with investment from overseas Chinese or from Hong Kong or Macao are entitled to, in addition to what is stipulated under the regulations, treatment applicable to enterprises with foreign investment as detailed in relevant laws, decrees, and regulations. It is also reemphasized that the State will not nationalize investment or other assets of overseas Chinese investors or those from Hong Kong or Macao. In the case of a takeover of their invested enterprises by the State to meet the needs of social or public interests, compensation will be made according to an established legal procedure. Other articles of the regulations are identical to those under the regulations for encouraging investment from Taiwan, containing clear stipulations on the rights of investment in the mainland by overseas Chinese or those from Hong Kong or Macao, their areas of investment, means of investment, applicable preferential treatment, application for investment, resolution of disputes arising from investment, and so forth.

20. Has the implementation of the 1994 reform policies in taxation and exchange control had an impact on foreign investment?

China's laws, decrees, and policies have proved successful and effective after 15 years of implementation, having stimulated a large influx of foreign investment into China. However, there have been changes in the domestic and international environment and the new situation occasioned by recent domestic economic structural reforms. As a result of these reforms and the need to attract still more foreign investment and in view of the need to move closer to stipulations of the General Agreement on Tariffs and Trade (GATT) so as to enable China's economy to become mutually supplementary to the world economy, conditions are to be created gradually to grant national status to enterprises with foreign investment. During this transition, the foreign investment policies will remain consistent and stable so that China's investment environment will remain sound.

With regard to China's exchange system reforms, for example, an issue of widespread concern both inside and outside China, the People's Bank of China has stated, "Current modalities of exchange control system will be maintained in enterprises with foreign investment." This announcement is positive in two ways in relieving investors' concerns and continuing to attract foreign investment. First, eliminating dual exchange rates (the official exchange rate and the exchange rate at the exchange swap market) will benefit not only foreign trade enterprises but also enterprises with foreign investment; under one unified market exchange rate of 8.6 (the state exchange rate used to be 5.57 US dollars to RMB yuan), enterprises with foreign investment will gain nearly 50% more over the money exchange, a beneficial change for foreign investors. Second, by eliminating the previous foreign exchange quota system, both state-owned enterprises and enterprises with foreign investment may acquire the foreign currency necessary for their production and operations at the exchange swap markets at the market exchange rate announced by the Bank of China, thus the supply and demand of exchange is satisfied through market transactions. This is a great step toward a market economy. Enterprises with foreign investment are allowed to maintain their bank accounts in existing currencies to control their own exchange proceeds (a policy more preferential than that which China's foreign trade enterprises enjoy) and allowed to maintain their own exchange swap market for conducting supplies or sales of their exchange.

Taxation reforms are being made mainly in four areas:

1. Domestic enterprises pay corporate income tax rate closer to that levied on enterprises with foreign investment, the rate for the latter remaining unchanged.

2. The consolidated industrial and commercial tax adopted in the 1950s has been replaced by a unified value-added tax, consumption tax, and business tax, thus unifying tax laws, standardizing the taxation system, relieving double taxation, and creating a fair tax environment for all types of enterprises. As an allowance to enterprises with foreign investment already approved, a policy with a guaranteed validity of five years has been adopted so that these enterprises may apply for tax refunds of any extra tax paid because of the new tax laws.

3. A land increment tax has been created, mainly aimed to avoid rising land prices driven up by random buying and selling of land, which has previously had a negative effect on China's investment environment.

4. The import tax rates for 2,898 taxable items have been lowered. The general tariffs continue to fall, resulting in lower costs for enterprises with foreign investment that need to import raw materials, parts, and accessories to sell their products in the domestic market.

Reforms of the financing system have been threefold:

1. Administration and management are separated to strengthen control by the Central Bank.
2. Several major policy-oriented banks are designated to support State key construction projects (including those with foreign investment) in satisfying funding needs and loans for purchasing equipment.
3. All other previous State specialized banks are to become commercial banks. They will conduct their own financing businesses under the market mechanism, which is favorable for a more flexible environment for enterprises with foreign investment that have good economic results and are seeking loans.

Reforms in several other areas have been designed to reflect consistency and stability of the existing policies and to create a flexible environment for enterprises with foreign investment.

No major problems have occurred during the implementation of these reforms. These have been some minor problems, and suggestions from various organizations are being investigated by the government departments concerned in the hope of addressing and resolving them in the detailed implementation clauses and specific regulations yet to be adopted.

21. What are China's preferential policies for attracting foreign investment?

In recent years, and especially since the spring of 1993, China's foreign investment laws, decrees, and policies have become increasingly complete to meet the challenge of speeding up reforms and further opening to the outside world. These laws and decrees have produced the following specific stipulations with regard to foreign investment in China:

1. Foreign businesses may invest with such tangible instruments as money, machines, equipment, or other materials or also intangibles such as industrial property rights or specialized technologies.

2. No import tax is to be levied on equipment or other materials imported by foreign business as investment instruments.

3. There is no limit on the percentage of subscribed capital by foreign investors for joint ventures, and registration is allowed for enterprises wholly owned by foreign investors.

4. Enterprises with foreign investment are allowed to purchase raw materials or parts and accessories for their products directly, encouraging exports and permitting selling of their products in both international and domestic markets.

5. Enterprises with foreign investment are encouraged to recruit local staff but are also allowed to employ technical specialists and senior management personnel from outside China.

6. Low-taxation policies have been adopted for enterprises' with foreign investment, with still further preferential policies for enterprises investing in state-encouraged businesses and regions. Depending on their location and the business they engage in, a 15%, 24%, or 30% corporate income tax will be levied on them, plus a two-year exemption and a three-year deduction of this tax calculated from the first profit-making year for manufacturing enterprises with a term of over 10 years of business operation.

7. Enterprises of advanced technologies or exporting their own manufactured products as well as those engaging in infrastructure facilities or key materials are encouraged to register.

8. The Chairman of the Board of Directors of an enterprise with foreign investment can be appointed by the foreign investor.

9. An undetermined time of joint venturing is allowed for state-encouraged investment projects.

10. No nationalization or takeover of enterprises with foreign investment will be effected by the State. If such takeover does occur under special circumstances and to meet needs for social or public benefit, this is to be done according to laws, and compensation will be made.

22. What is China's investment environment like?

China's investment environment is good, say foreign investors, mainly for the following reasons:

1. Stable political situation, social harmony, consistently speedy and healthy economic growth, and availability of clear medium- or long-term economic development plans.
2. Rich resources, vast land, and availability of an industrial base, and technical strength supplementary to foreign investment.
3. Huge population and huge market potential.
4. Ample supply of high-quality, low-cost of labor, as well as low cost of other production elements.
5. Relatively complete foreign investment laws and decrees, sufficient legal protection for foreign investments, and consistency of preferential policies.

In the course of China's rapid development in absorbing foreign investment, problems did occur. In some regions, for instance, there is a shortage of working capital, some operating enterprises suffer from either poor management and operation or poor relations between labor and capital, and there has been a negative impact on the operation of enterprises when new policies are adopted and while moving from old to new policies. These problems are typical in economies that are growing and developing and have been noted by both the central government and local governments at all levels, which are investigating, studying, and resolving them.

3.

The Formation and Development of China's Opening

23. When did China start to open to the outside world?

In December 1978, the 11th Central Committee of the Communist Party of China decided at its 3rd Plenary Session that China should focus on economic construction, take on reforms and opening as a state policy, strive to be free from old ideas, be practical, seek experience, be keen on forging ahead, and implement opening up to the outside gradually, from south to north and east to west. China now has a multilayered opening, with certain key regions at its center.

24. What special policies did the State offer to Guangdong and Fujian, the first two provinces opened to the outside world?

In order for the provinces of Guangdong and Fujian to make full use of their cultural and geographical advantages, being the home of many overseas Chinese and those from neighboring Hong Kong, Macao, and Taiwan, to seize the opportunity of a favorable international situation, to use foreign funds in the development of foreign economy and trade, and to take a pioneering step in the building of China's modernization and economic development, the State in July 1979 granted these two provinces special policies and flexibility in their foreign economic activities:

- Increased local power to invigorate their economic development
- More flexibility in opening, developing the foreign economy and trade, attracting foreign investment, and introducing technology, under the guidance of state planning
- More financial support, with the two provinces free to utilize most of the added revenues produced in the locality over 10 years

25. When were the special economic zones established, and what policies were adopted?

Deng Xiaoping proposed in 1979 that four special economic zones—Shenzhen, Zhuhai, Shantou, and Xiamen—be established. In August 1980, the Standing Committee of the National People's Congress approved the bill from the State Council to establish special economic zones, after which the State Council approved the four. Then the four zones began official development and construction. In April 1988, the 7th National People's Congress at its first session approved Hainan to be China's largest special economic zone.

Setting up special economic zones is an important part of a series of measures in the implementation of China's reforms and open policies. These zones are located at the frontier of China's opening up to the outside world; they serve as a special channel to use foreign funds, introduce advanced technology, and head toward the international marketplace. Also, they are one of the comprehensive experimental locations of China's reforms.

The Chinese government applied special economic policies in these zones, which are different from the economic administration system for inland regions in the following areas:

1. They establish an economic structure in which there are multiple economic sectors, with foreign investment playing the major part.

2. Mainly they use market regulation under the economic guidance of the State.

3. They are convenient to overseas businesspeople in entering or leaving the zones because they simplify formalities for entry and exit.

4. The local governments are granted provincial-level power in economic administration. Also, the Central Government has tailored its regulations for these zones in the areas under its control (e.g., foreign affairs, public security, border defense, customs, foreign exchange, harbors, railways, and post and telecommunications).

5. There are specific favorable policies, such as increased credit loans, retaining all newly increased revenues, including foreign exchange revenues, for a certain period of time, and exemption from tariffs for materials needed for the construction within the zones.

6. Comparatively more preferential treatment is granted to enterprises with foreign investment established within the zones:

—a reduced 15% tax rate on corporate income tax

—exemption of the income tax for the first two years and a 50% reduction of income tax during the third to fifth years, starting from the first profit-making year, for manufacturing enterprises with a term of business over 10 years, upon application by such enterprises and approval by tax authorities

—an extended three-year 50% deduction of corporate income tax for enterprises using advanced technology

—a reduced rate of 10% of income tax for enterprises exporting their own products, if their yearly export volume reaches 70% or more of the total output value

—exemption from export tariffs and value-added tax on exporting products manufactured by the enterprises (with the exception of petroleum, finished oil products, and others specified)

—exemption from import tariffs and value-added tax on importing equipment or raw materials needed in the manufacturing of exporting products by the enterprises or office equipment for use by the enterprises themselves

—favorable land usage and other fees for enterprises with foreign investment

26. When were the 14 coastal port and industrial cities opened, and what policies were adopted?

At the suggestion of Deng Xiaoping, the state held a forum of some coastal cities in April 1984, and, on the basis of the experience in opening up to the outside world during the prior five years, decided to open 14 coastal port cities: Tianjin, Shanghai, Dalian, Qinhuangdao, Yantai (including Weihai), Qingdao, Lianyungang, Nantong, Ningbo, Wenzhou, Fuzhou, Guangzhou, Zhanjiang, and Beihai. The cities were given more autonomy in their foreign economic and trade activities in order to provide a more favorable investing environment for foreign business and policy support for technological renovation of old enterprises. Since then,

China has formed a pattern of an open coastal line threading from the south to the north.

Foreign businesses investing in the open coastal cities are entitled to the following preferential treatment:

1. Only a 24% corporate income tax will be levied on manufacturing enterprises with foreign investment located in the open coastal cities.
2. Only a 15% corporate income tax will be levied on enterprises with foreign investment engaging in the following projects:
   —technology-intensive projects
   —projects with over US$30 million of foreign investment, and a long anticipated time for return on investment
   —energy, communications, and ports construction projects
   —Sino–foreign equity joint venture enterprises engaging in port construction
   —financing institutions (e.g., foreign banks, Sino–foreign joint venture banks) with over US$10 million of foreign investment or operating funds transferred into a branch bank from the headquarters, plus a business term of over 10 years
   —enterprises with foreign investment engaging in state-encouraged projects
3. Fifty percent reduction of the 24% corporate income tax will be levied on enterprises exporting products should their annual export volume reach 70% or more of the total output value.
4. Fifty percent deduction of the corporate income tax will be extended to a further three years for enterprises of advanced technology when they remain such after the period during which they have enjoyed an exemption from or a deduction of corporate income tax according to law.
5. Manufacturing enterprises with foreign investment with a business term of over 10 years are entitled to a two-year exemption from and a subsequent three-year 50% deduction of the corporate income tax, starting from the first profit-making year.
6. Sino–foreign equity joint venture enterprises engaging in the construction of ports and with a business term of over 15 years are entitled to a five-year exemption from and a subsequent five-year 50% deduction of the corporate income tax, starting from the first profit-making year.
7. Enterprises are entitled to exemption from tariffs and value-added tax for equipment imported for production or business operations and construction materials imported as a means of in-

vestment or increased investment, and vehicles and office equipment for use by the enterprises themselves.

8. Enterprises are entitled to exemption from value-added tax for their exporting products, unless the products are limited by the State for export or are to be sold in the domestic market.

9. Enterprises are entitled to exemption from the value-added tax for the portion of imported raw materials, parts and accessories, elements and devices, and packaging materials used for production of export products, except for those imported to produce products for sale in the domestic market.

10. Business personnel working or residing in enterprises are exempt from tariffs and value-added tax on personal belongings for setting up a home or vehicles for transport purposes, for use by themselves only and within reasonable quantities.

27. When were the economic and technological development zones established, and what policies were adopted?

As an important measure in implementing the opening policies, the State set up economic and technological development zones to serve as the base for China's international economic and technological cooperation and export-oriented economy. The purpose was to concentrate within designated regions the building of infrastructure, complete legislation of economic laws and regulations concerning foreign interests, establish highly efficient management structures, create a fine environment for foreign investment, introduce advanced industrial production projects, and speed up the economic development of the city where the zone is located. Since 1984, the State has approved the establishment of the following 32 economic and technological development zones:

Dalian Economic and Technological Development Zone
Qinhuangdao Economic and Technological Development Zone
Tianjin Economic and Technological Development Zone
Yantai Economic and Technological Development Zone
Qingdao Economic and Technological Development Zone
Lianyungang Economic and Technological Development Zone
Nantong Economic and Technological Development Zone
Caohejing Economic and Technological Development Zone
Minhang Economic and Technological Development Zone
Hongqiao Economic and Technological Development Zone

Ningbo Economic and Technological Development Zone
Fuzhou Economic and Technological Development Zone
Guangzhou Economic and Technological Development Zone
Zhanjiang Economic and Technological Development Zone
Weihai Economic and Technological Development Zone
Yingkou Economic and Technological Development Zone
Kunshan Economic and Technological Development Zone
Wenzhou Economic and Technological Development Zone
Rongqiao Economic and Technological Development Zone of Fuqing
Dongshan Economic and Technological Development Zone of
    Zhangzhou
Shenyang Economic and Technological Development Zone
Hangzhou Economic and Technological Development Zone
Wuhan Economic and Technological Development Zone
Changchun Economic and Technological Development Zone
Harbin Economic and Technological Development Zone
Chongqing Economic and Technological Development Zone
Wuhu Economic and Technological Development Zone
Xiaoshan Economic and Technological Development Zone
Nansha Economic and Technological Development Zone of Panyu
Dayawan Economic and Technological Development Zone of
    Huizhou in Guangdong
Beijing Economic and Technological Development Zone
and Urumqi Economic and Technological Development Zone

Enterprises with foreign investment located in an economic and technological development zone are entitled to the following preferential treatment:

1. A 15% corporate income tax will be levied on manufacturing enterprises with foreign investment. Should they have a term of business of over 10 years, they will be entitled to a two-year exemption from and a subsequent three-year 50% deduction of corporate income tax, starting from the first profit-making year.

2. A 10% corporate income tax will be levied on enterprises exporting products, after the period during which they have enjoyed an exemption from or a deduction of corporate income tax, should their annual export volume reach 70% or more of the total output value.

3. A 50% reduction of the 15% corporate income tax will be levied during an extended period of three years for enterprises of advanced technology when they remain such after the period during which they

have enjoyed an exemption from or a deduction of the corporate income tax according to law.

4. Enterprises are entitled to exemption from tariffs and value-added tax for the portion of building materials, production equipment, raw materials, parts and accessories, elements and devices, vehicles for transport, office equipment, and management equipment, all imported for their own use.

5. Enterprises are entitled to exemption from export tariffs and value-added tax on their own exporting products, except for those products otherwise specified or products manufactured with imported tariff-free raw materials or parts and accessories for sale in the domestic market.

28. When were the open coastal economic zones established, and what policies were adopted?

In February 1985, the State approved the establishment of the open coastal economic zones of Pearl River Delta, Changjiang (Yangtze) River Delta, and South Fujian-Xiamen-Zhangzhou-Quanzhou Delta, covering 51 cities and counties.

In March 1988, the State further approved Liaodong (East Liaoning) Peninsula, Shandong Peninsula, and certain cities and counties in other coastal regions as open coastal economic zones. By then, a total of 426 square kilometers of coastal regions, covering 293 cities and counties with a population of 280 million, had been opened, inclusive of the special economic zones and open coastal cities. In other words, basically all coastal cities and counties had been opened.

To expedite the development of an export-oriented economy in the coastal regions, the State Council issued the Additional Regulations on the Development of an Export-Oriented Economy in Coastal Regions, with clearly defined stipulations on increased foreign economic and trading authorities of local governments, renovating old enterprises by means of Sino–foreign equity or cooperative joint venturing, development of processing businesses with both raw materials supplied and finished products exported, a more flexible foreign exchange swap, setup of funds for export risks, strengthening of transportation for the development of an export-oriented economy, and provision of science and technological support.

China has adopted the following preferential policies applicable to the open coastal economic zones:

1. The corporate income tax will be levied at a rate of 24% on manufacturing enterprises with foreign investment.
2. The corporate income tax will be levied at a rate of 15% on enterprises with foreign investment engaging in the following projects:
   —technology-intensive projects
   —projects with over US$30 million of foreign investment and an
   anticipated long time for return on investment
   —energy, communication, and ports construction projects
   —other state-encouraged projects
3. Favorable corporate income tax, tariffs, value-added tax, and
other rates will be levied on enterprises exporting their own products, enterprises using advanced technology, and enterprises with
foreign investment, according to the preferential policies applicable to the open coastal economic zones.
4. Foreign businesses are allowed to invest in the development and
operations of tracts of land.

29. When was the decision made to open Shanghai Pudong New Area, and what policies were adopted?

In order to quickly build Shanghai, the largest industrial and commercial
port city in China, into an international economic, trade, financial, and
shipping center, and hence to bring about an economic upsurge of the
Changjiang (Yangtze) River Delta and the whole Changjiang (Yangtze)
River Valley, the State Council decided in April 1990 to develop and open
the Pudong New Area of Shanghai, an important economic development
region in China.

The Shanghai Pudong New Area is a triangular area to the east of the
Huangpu River, southwest of the Changjiang (Yangtze) River mouth, and
next to downtown Shanghai, with an area of 518 square kilometers and a
population of 1.38 million. Bordering on the East Sea and nestling with
the Changjiang (Yangtze) River on the north, Pudong New Area is situ-
ated at the joint of the so-called golden seacoast and golden waterway of
China, overlooking the center of downtown Shanghai across the sea. A
flat terrain, the area enjoys a mild and humid climate all year, and it has
a river coastline of 65 kilometers.

In order to attract foreign investment and speed up the construction
of Shanghai Pudong New Area, the municipal government of Shanghai
issued on 10 September 1990 the Regulations of the Shanghai Municipality on Encouraging Foreign Investment in Pudong New Area.

China has granted a number of preferential policies for opening

Shanghai Pudong New Area. Such policies have certain notable features:

1. Foreign enterprises are allowed to set up tertiary-sector projects such as department stores and supermarkets.
2. Shanghai is allowed to establish a stock market and authorized to review and approve the issuance of RMB stocks and Category B stocks for the development of Pudong.
3. A bonded area or a free trade zone is to be established in Waigaoqiao of the Pudong New Area, with the greatest amount of openness in China. Within this area, special preferential policies have been implemented, such as tariff-free and import-export–free treatment, permission to establish domestically or foreign invested international trade organizations, 100% retention of foreign exchange earnings by enterprises, and free circulation of various foreign currencies.
4. Foreign investors are allowed to set up financial organizations such as banks, accounting firms, and insurance companies, in any part of Shanghai.
5. The Central Government gives Shanghai greater review and approval power with regard to establishing manufacturing or nonmanufacturing enterprises within the Pudong New Area and enterprises applying for import and export businesses.

Preferential policies for Pudong New Area extend to tariffs and value-added and income taxes, with the most preferential system applicable in the bonded areas.

The development objectives of Pudong are to establish in China by early in the next century the best municipal infrastructure facilities, the largest commercial activities center, a comprehensive free trade zone with the greatest openness, an advanced export processing base, modernized suburban agriculture, and high-quality living quarters with complete service facilities. Within the decade after that, Pudong is to be built into a world-class modernized new area with international dimensions and multiple functions.

Following are the preferential policies applicable in Pudong New Area, with approval by the State Council:

1. The corporate income tax will be levied at a rate of only 15% on manufacturing enterprises with foreign investment located within the area, which are to enjoy a two-year exemption from and a subsequent

three-year deduction by 50% of the tax rates starting from the first profit-making year, if their term of business is above 10 years.

2. No tariffs or value-added tax will be levied on imported machines and equipment, vehicles, and building materials needed for construction; on equipment, raw and auxiliary materials, vehicles for transport, office equipment for self-use, or personal belongings for setting up a home or vehicles for transport for foreign expatriates, imported by enterprises with foreign investment; or on products being exported when they satisfy the state regulations.

3. Manufacturing enterprises with foreign investment located within the area are to engage mainly in the export business but are allowed to sell in the domestic market their import-substitution products upon approval by the department in charge, after retroactively paying tariffs and value-added tax.

4. Foreign investors are to enjoy a five-year exemption from and a subsequent five-year deduction by 50% of the corporate income tax, starting from the first profit-making year, when they invest in energy and communication projects such as building of airports, harbors, railways, highways, and electric power stations.

5. Foreign businesses are allowed to engage in the tertiary-sector projects within the area and, with approval and on a trial basis, in businesses that according to prevailing regulations are restricted or prohibited by the state, such as financing or commercial retailing.

6. Foreign businesses are allowed to open additional banking organizations with foreign investment in Shanghai, including its Pudong Area, which will approve the opening of accounting firms and then a certain number of branches of foreign banks, according to actual needs for the development of Pudong, while appropriately lowering the income tax rate for banks with foreign investment and implementing differential tax rates for different banking organizations, the details of which will be further specified in related laws and regulations that Shanghai is to issue soon in order to ensure the normal operation of banks with foreign investment.

7. Within the bonded area of Pudong New Area, foreign trading organizations are allowed to conduct entrepôt trade or act as an agency for enterprises with foreign investment located within the area in importing raw materials or parts and accessories for use by these enterprises, as well as in exporting their products, while key business or management per

sonnel working in the area enjoy convenience in entering or leaving China since these people may obtain a multiple entry-exit visa.

8. Enterprises with domestic investment, including those with investment from other parts of China, located within the area, will be treated on a case-by-case basis regarding the industrial policy of Pudong New Area and will be entitled to a deduction of or even exemption from income tax if deemed as conforming to the industrial policy and benefiting the developing and opening of Pudong.

9. Paid transfer of land use right is permitted within the area, while the term of land use right can be 50 to 70 years, and foreign business may contract for the development of tracts and land.

10. Increased revenues of Pudong New Area will be retained for further development, in order to speed up the construction of the area and provide the necessary infrastructure called for by development and investment.

To promote the development and opening of Shanghai Pudong New Area, the Shanghai Municipality has worked with state authorities to establish certain regulations and administration methods—for example:

Industrial Orientation and Investment Guide for Shanghai Pudong New Area

Interim Administration Methods on Planning and Construction in Shanghai Pudong New Area

Review and Approval Methods for the Establishment of Enterprises with Foreign Investment in Shanghai Pudong New Area

Regulations on Exemption from and Deduction of Corporate Income Tax and Value-Added Tax for Encouraging Foreign Investment in Shanghai Pudong New Area

Regulations on Land Control in Shanghai Pudong New Area

Administration Methods of Shanghai Municipality on the Waigaoqiao Bonded Area

Administration Methods of Shanghai Municipality on Foreign-Funded Financial Institutions and Sino–Foreign Equity Joint Venture Financial Institutions

Administration Methods of the Customs House of the People's Republic of China on Goods, Vehicles for Transport, and Handcarried Personal Materials Entering or Exiting the Waigaoqiao Bonded Area of Shanghai

30. When were the new and high-tech industrial development zones established in China, and what policies were adopted?

Upon approval by the State Council, the first of China's new and high-tech industrial development and experimental zone was established in Beijing in May 1988. Developed on the basis of the "electronics street" of Zhongguancun of Beijing's Haidian District, this industrial park of science and technology covers an area of 100 square kilometers. After six years of reforms and development, the Beijing Experimental Zone has become not only an industrial park in China for the development of new and high technologies but an important base for the development of science and technology industries utilizing foreign investment.

In order to promote the commercialization and industrialization of new and high-tech achievements, actively attract foreign funds, introduce advanced technologies, and establish and develop new and high-tech industrial zones, the State Scientific and Technological Commission adopted in March 1991 the Conditions and Methods of the State for the Recognition of Enterprises with New and High Technologies in New and High-Tech Industrial Development Zones. Since then, China has approved the establishment of over 50 such zones, located in the following cities:

Beijing	Zhengzhou	Zibo
Wuhan	Lanzhou	Kunming
Nanjing	Shijiazhuang	Guiyang
Shenyang	Jinan	Nanchang
Tianjin	Shanghai	Taiyuan
Xi'an	Dalian	Nanning
Chengdu	Shenzhen	Urumqi
Weihai	Xiamen	Baotou
Zhonghai	Hainan	Xiangfan
Changchun	Suzhou	Zhuzhou
Harbin	Wuxi	Luoyang
Changsha	Changzhou	Daqing
Fuzhou	Foshan	Baoji
Guangzhou	Huizhou	Jilin
Hefei	Zhuhai	Mianyang
Chongqing	Qingdao	Baoding
Hangzhou	Weifang	Anshan
Guilin		

Authorized by the State Council, the State Scientific and Technological Commission is responsible for reviewing and determining the geographic scope and area of all national new and high-tech industrial development zones and exercising administration and providing detailed guidance.

The establishment of new and high-tech industrial development zones will promote the commercialization and industrialization of high-tech results by relying on China's own forces of science and technology, with great impact on the readjustment of the industrial structure, promotion of renovation of traditional industries, improvement of labor and production efficiency, and strengthening of international competitiveness. Foreign businesses investing in a plant in a new and high-tech industrial development zone will enjoy even more favorable treatment than that offered by preferential policies in the economic and technological development zones, according to the Interim Regulations on Certain Policies of the State New and High-Tech Industrial Development Zones, compiled by the State Scientific and Technological Commission, and Regulations on Taxation of the State New and High-Tech Industrial Development Zones, compiled by the State Tax Bureau.

31. When were bonded areas established in China, and what policies were adopted?

For the convenience of production by enterprises with foreign investment and the speedy development of major regions, China approved in 1990 the establishment of a bonded area in Shanghai Pudong New Area—the Waigaoqiao Bonded Area—followed by 14 other such areas:

Tianjin	Ningbo
Futian of Shenzhen	Fuzhou
Shatoujiao of Shenzhen	Zhuhai
Dalian	Hainan
Guangzhou	Shantou
Qingdao	Xiamen
Zhangjiagang	

Bonded areas serve mainly to initiate entrepôt trade and processing services for export and develop such businesses in the service of trading, such as processing, packaging, storage, and commodities exhibition to promote the growth of the economy with foreign interests. Taxes for enterprises within the areas will be in accordance with preferential tax policies applicable in the regions where such areas are located.

The following favorable treatment is granted to bonded areas:

1. Foreign organizations located in a bonded area are allowed to act as the agency for enterprises with foreign investment also located in the area in importing raw materials or parts and accessories for use in their production and in exporting their products.

2. Enterprises are not required to obtain import or export permits for, and are free from tariffs and value-added tax on, imported machines, equipment, and materials for the construction of infrastructure facilities and production in the zone, vehicles for manufacture and transport, and office equipment, and importing raw materials, parts and accessories, instruments and devices, and packaging materials for use by processing of exporting commodities, as well as transit goods in storage and exporting products processed in the area.

32. What are the state-approved tourism and vacation zones, and what are the policies?

In order to expand the opening to the outside world, to use China's rich heritage, and to promote the transition from sightseeing tourism to sightseeing plus vacation tourism for speedier growth of the tourist industry, the Chinese Government opened on a trial basis national vacation zones, encouraging enterprises and individuals from foreign countries, as well as Taiwan, Hong Kong, and Macao, to invest in and operate tourist facilities and projects. The Chinese Government has so far approved the establishment of the following zones:

Dalian Jinshitan National Vacation Zone
Qingdao Shilaoren National Vacation Zone
Jiangsu Taihu Lake National Vacation Zone
Shanghai Hengsha Island National Vacation Zone
River of Hangzhou National Vacation Zone
Fujian Wuyi Mountains National Vacation Zone
two national vacation zones on Meizhou Island
Guangzhou Nanhu Lake National Vacation Zone
Beihai Yintan National Vacation Zone
Kunming Dianchi National Vacation Zone
Sanya Yalong Bay National Vacation Zone

The national vacation zones are comprehensive tourist areas, up to international standards for vacation tourism, and catering mainly to overseas tourists.

The State has issued a series of preferential policies since tourism is a foreign exchange–earning industry, and its development is encouraged:

1. A corporate income tax will be levied at a rate of only 24% on enterprises with foreign investment located within a national vacation zone. For manufacturing enterprises with foreign investment with a term of business of over 10 years, there is a two-year exemption from and a subsequent three-year deduction by 50% of the corporate income tax starting from the first profit-making year.

2. Enterprises with foreign investment located within a vacation zone enjoy exemption from tariffs and value-added tax on imported building materials, equipment for production and business operation, vehicles for transport and office equipment, with a total value of less than the overall investment amount and to be used by enterprises themselves, as well as on imported settling-in materials and vehicles for transport for use by resident foreign expatriate business or technical personnel, within reasonable quantities. Relevant regulations applicable for bonded areas will be used by the Customs House with regard to raw materials, parts and accessories, elements and devices, auxiliary materials, and packaging materials imported for the production of exporting tourist commodities.

3. Machines, equipment, and other construction materials imported for the construction of infrastructure facilities in the vacation zones will be exempt from import tariffs and product (value-added) tax.

4. Foreign exchange stores are allowed to open within a national vacation zone.

5. Sino-foreign joint venture tourist taxi companies using China-made vehicles may be established. Within designated quantities, the purchased vehicles are exempt from the state infrastructure provision charge, the vehicle purchase surcharge, and the special consumption tax. This policy also applies to taxi companies within the zone established by domestic investors; however, such vehicles are to be used by the taxi companies themselves only, and are not allowed for resale.

Sino-foreign joint venture Category A tourist agencies can be established in the zones, conducting the zones' overseas tourism businesses.

33. How did China implement the opening of the riverbank areas, coastal and border regions, and inland areas to the outside world?

In spring 1992, the state issued Advice on Endeavoring in Faster and Better Upgrading of Economy for Speedier Reforms and Expanded Openness in order to promote an overall nationwide opening to the outside world.

1. *Opening of riverbank areas.* Approval has been given to open six port cities—Wuhu, Jiujiang, Huangshi, Wuhan, Yueyang, and Chongqing—along the Changjiang (Yangtze) River, where related policies for open coastal cities are applicable.

2. *Opening of border regions.* Approval has been given to open 13 mainland Chinese border cities:

Hunchun of Jilin Province
Suifenhe and Heihe of Heilongjiang Province
Manchuli and Erlianhot of the Inner Mongolia Autonomous Region
Yining, Tacheng, and Bole of the Xinjiang Uighur Autonomous Region
Ruili, Wanting, and Hekou of Yunnan Province
Pinxiang and Dongxing of the Guangxi Zhuang Autonomous Region

Expanded authority has been granted local city governments in developing border trade and foreign economic cooperation, encouraging inland enterprises to invest in border cities, and permitting the establishment of border economic cooperation zones.

3. *Opening of inland provincial capital cities.* Approval has been given to open provincial (autonomous regions') capital cities where policies for open coastal cities are applicable. They include:

Hefei	Taiyuan	Yinchuan
Nanchang	Hohhot	Xining
Nanning	Changchun	Urumqi
Changsha	Harbin	Chengdu
Zhengzhou	Xi'an	Kunming
Shijiazhuang	Lanzhou	Guiyang

4. Approval has been given to the establishment of bonded areas including the following:

Futian and Shatoujiao of Shenzhen
Tianjin Harbor
Cities of Dalian, Guangzhou, Zhangjiagang, Ningbo, Fuzhou, Xiamen, Shantou, and Haikou.

5. Approval has been given to 63 foreign-owned or Sino-foreign joint venture banks or financing institutions to conduct foreign exchange businesses in the five special economic zones and the following eight cities:

Shanghai	Fuzhou
Tianjin	Ningbo
Dalian	Qingdao
Guangzhou	Nanning

6. Areas for foreign investment have been expanded to include merchandising, financing and insurance, trading, transportation, real estate, tourism, and others.

In summary, China has gradually formed over 15 years an all-dimensional, multilayered open pattern with specific regions.

4.

Orientation of Foreign Investment in China

34. Why has China identified certain areas for foreign investment, and how is the investment guided?

China is a developing country with a socialist market economic system, or a market economic system, under the national government's guidance. Its purposes for introducing foreign investment are mainly to promote social development and economic growth and to reach the State-determined goal of raising living standards into the next century. Therefore, the introduction of foreign investment is to be accomplished according to this strategic goal and is to serve the needs to reach this goal. The government has determined areas for foreign investment in order to ensure that investments are made in areas in compliance with the State plan for national economic growth and social development and gradually to advance in step with world economic development, thus extending protection to foreign investors. The guidance for foreign investment is usually done through relevant laws and regulations in relation to areas for foreign investment adopted and announced by the government and through periodically compiling and updating the *Orientation Directory of Industries for Foreign Investment*, with specific implementation by various levels of related government departments in charge of investment projects.

35. In what areas does the Chinese Government encourage foreign investment?

According to regulations stipulated by the Chinese Government, foreign investment is sought mainly in the areas of infrastructure facilities, basic

industries and technological renovation of enterprises, as well as funding-
or technology-intensive industries; financing, merchandise, tourism, and
real estate are moderately encouraged for foreign investment.

Following are the areas or projects in which the Chinese Government
encourages foreign investment:

1. New agricultural technologies, comprehensive agricultural development, and energy or communications and key raw materials industries urgently needed for development.
2. New or high or advanced technologies urgently needed by the
   State or new equipment or materials that can improve product
   performance, conserve energy and raw materials, upgrade enterprises' technological level or economic interest, or result in manufacturing import-substitution products that meet market needs.
3. Projects generating more foreign exchange revenues in answer to
   international market needs, which improve product levels, open
   new markets, or increase product export volume.
4. New technologies or equipment projects that comprehensively
   utilize resources, recycle resources, or reduce environmental pollution.
5. Other projects stipulated in State laws, decrees, or regulations.

36. In what areas does the Chinese Government restrict foreign investment?

The Chinese Government restricts foreign investment in the following
areas:

1. Areas in which China has already developed or introduced advanced technologies and where production capacity is already ca-
   pable of satisfying domestic needs.
2. Industries in which the State is implementing a trial introduction
   of foreign investment or businesses monopolized by the State in
   selling, transacting, or operating.
3. Exploration or mining of rare or valuable mining resources.
4. Other projects stipulated in State laws, decrees, or regulations,
   such as those with quota or permit restrictions.

The projects restricted for foreign investment are classified into Restrictive Categories A and B, with a complete list compiled and modified,
and announced and implemented, by related Government departments.

37. In what areas does the Chinese government prohibit foreign investment?

Foreign investment is not allowed in the following areas:

1. Projects that do not contribute to China's national security, national economy, social development, or social or public interest.
2. Projects that pollute the environment, destroy natural resources, or endanger human health.
3. Projects that manufacture products using technologies uniquely owned by China.
4. Other projects stipulated in State laws, decrees, or regulations.

38. What are the areas allowed by the Chinese Government for foreign investment apart from those listed as encouraged, restricted, and prohibited?

All areas apart from those encouraged, restricted, and prohibited are within the scope in which the Chinese Government allows for foreign investment, whereby foreign businesses have the flexibility to select projects for investment.

39. What areas has the Chinese Government newly opened for foreign investment in recent years, and what is the extent of openness?

Since 1992, the Chinese Government has opened certain new areas for foreign investment:

- In *energy*, inland petroleum prospecting and mining, power generation, and energy recycling.
- In *communication and telecommunications*, highways, harbors, railways, civil aviation, and telecommunications facilities.
- In *raw materials*, exploration and mining of low-grade gold.
- In *forestry*, forest planting on barren hills or wasteland to develop forestry, in the form of either equity or cooperative joint ventures with Chinese partners.
- In *merchandising* and *foreign trade*, commodity retail business in some major or central cities, in the form of either Chinese-foreign

joint ventures or wholly foreign-owned ventures, and foreign trade business in designated development zones.

- In *financing*, banks in some open coastal cities, in the form of either Chinese-foreign joint ventures or wholly foreign-owned ventures.
- In the *tertiary sector*, real estate development and management of downtown renovation projects in large- or medium-sized cities.

Because China does not have sufficient experience with these areas and they pose a considerable degree of complexity, their opening is still in the trial stage, to safeguard the interests of investors.

40. What are China's regulations in attracting foreign investment by build-operate-transfer means?

Since the 1980s, developing countries have been applying for build-operate-transfer (BOT) means for introducing foreign investment in projects for highways, railways, power stations, and wastewater treatment, among others, and achieving sound results. China is exploring how to use BOT to attract foreign investment in infrastructure facilities. There are not any specialized laws or regulations; rather, the prevailing laws and regulations concerning enterprises with foreign investment, as well as the approval mechanism, apply. Foreign businesses may set up BOT project firms by means of either equity or cooperative joint ventures with Chinese partners or wholly foreign-owned ventures. According to regulation, the procedure and approval process for BOT project firms will be guided by the prevailing policies relating to foreign investment.

41. What are the policy regulations for foreign investment in civil aviation?

In order to speed up the development of China's civil aviation industry and improve management levels, the State Council has approved conditional investment from foreign businesses, with the bulk of investment to be financed by the State. According to existing regulations:

1. Foreign businesses are allowed to invest in the civil aviation industry in the form of either equity or cooperative joint ventures.
2. Foreign businesses are allowed to invest in the construction of airport flight areas (including runways, sliding ways, and aircraft parking area) or in the construction of airport supplementary proj-

ects, such as terminal buildings, air cargo warehouses, land services, aircraft maintenance, air catering, airport hotels, airport
restaurants, and air fuels; or in establishing air transportation enterprises or aviation enterprises in service of agriculture or
forestry.

3. Enterprises with foreign investment engaging in the construction
   of airport flight areas may expand their scope of business, with approval, to include managing airport supplementary projects, such
   as terminal buildings, air cargo warehouses, land services, aircraft
   maintenance, air catering, airport hotels, airport restaurants, and
   air fuels.

4. Foreign businesses, especially foreign air cargo shipment enterprises, are allowed to purchase shares of Chinese air cargo shipment enterprises or exchange shares with their Chinese
   counterparts, or to set up air cargo shipment enterprises.

5. Stipulations have been made with regard to foreign businesses'
   share of investment in civil aviation industry and nomination of
   the Board Chairman and the General Manager.

Foreign investment in China's civil aviation industry is still in the
trial stage and will be gradually expanded as the business matures.

42. What preferential measures has the Chinese Government devised for investment in areas listed as encouraged for foreign investment?

Following are the preferential policies for foreign investment in areas the
Chinese Government encourages, in addition to those stipulated in relevant State laws, decrees, and regulations:

1. Regardless of where they are located, projects with a total foreign
investment of over US$30 million, upon approval by the State tax author-
ities, are entitled to the preferential taxation treatment applicable in economic and technological development zones.

2. Enterprises engaged in the building and operation of energy or
communications infrastructure facilities (coal, electric power, local railway, highway, or harbor), with a large investment and a long projected
time for return on investment, may expand their business scope in relation to their business, subject to approval.

3. Enterprises introducing new, high, or advanced technologies ur-

gently needed by the State, or new equipment or materials to manufacture import-substitution products, with the capability of self-balancing their own foreign exchange, may be free from a set ratio of product sales in the overseas and domestic markets.

4. When the total investment amount exceeds US$100 million, the percentage of the registered capital against the total investment may be appropriately lower than that stipulated by the regulations, subject to approval.

5. Priority will be given to enterprises requesting export quotas when their products involve such quotas.

43. What restrictive measures has the Chinese Government devised for investment in areas listed as restricted for foreign investment?

Projects with foreign investment in restricted areas, with approval, are entitled to preferential treatment according to laws and regulations but are subject to the following stipulations:

1. The length of business operations of Chinese-foreign joint ventures should be specified in the joint venture contract.

2. For projects falling within the Restrictive Category A (e.g., wristwatch chips or assembly, refrigeration boxes, cans, aluminum materials, photocopiers, one-time syringes, cassette recorders, ordinary antibiotics, a luxury office buildings), 100% of the total investment is to be the registered capital if the total investment is below US$10 million; 70% of the total investment is to be the registered capital if the investment is between US$10 and US$30 million; and 60% of the total investment is to be the registered capital if the investment is above US$30 million. Further, the Chinese partner(s) to such projects must use their own funds for investment in fixed assets, while project review and approval rights are to be handled according to relevant regulations by the State Council with quota limitations.

3. For projects falling within Restrictive Category B (e.g., offshore or inland fishing, table salt, cigarettes, cotton or woolen textiles, chemical fibers, film, sedan cars, air-conditioners, color television sets, video recorders, arterial railways, aviation and water transportation, foreign trade, luxury hotels, banks, insurance, publishing, printing) when within quota limitations, the project proposals are to be reviewed and approved by the government departments in charge (of concerned trades) directly

under the State Council and filed with the State Planning Commission or the State Economic and Trade Commission. When the projects are outside quota limitations, the review and approval shall be handled according to current procedures and methods.

4. Projects falling within Restrictive Category A, upon approval, may be regarded as ones in allowed areas and thus free from restrictions, should either of the two following specified conditions be satisfied: (a) the export value takes up over 70% of their production value or (b) the existing manufacturing capabilities are used to improve the level of their products, so that the export value is increased by over 30%.

5.

Measures of the Chinese Government for Protecting the Legitimate Rights and Interests of Foreign Investors

44. How does China protect the legitimate rights and interests of foreign investors?

In developing its foreign trade and international economic cooperation, China has always followed the principle of "respecting contracts and keeping promises," as well as equality and mutual benefits, and has endeavored to put this principle into practice. Since the implementation of the reforms and open policies, China has consistently respected and protected the legitimate rights and interests of foreign investors. While working to bring overseas investment into active roles and to promote the economic development of the country, China has allowed benefits for overseas investors and applied legal legislation for their protection. For this purpose, Article 2 of the Law of the People's Republic of China on Chinese–Foreign Equity Joint Ventures, the first investment law of China, issued in 1979, clearly stipulates: "The Chinese government protects, by the legislation in force, the resources invested by a foreign participant in a joint venture and the profits due him pursuant to the agreements, contracts and articles of association authorized by the Chinese government as well as his other lawful rights and interests."

China has enacted legal measures to protect the legitimate rights and interests of foreign investors mainly by the following three means:

1. *Domestic investment laws.* China's fundamental law the Constitution of the People's Republic of China, states: "Foreign enterprises or other foreign economic organizations as well as Chinese-foreign joint venture enterprises in the People's Republic of China shall abide by the laws of the People's Republic of China, while their legitimate rights and interests are protected by the laws of the People's Republic of China" (Article 18) and, "The People's Republic of China protects the legitimate rights and interests of foreigners in the People's Republic of China" (Article 32). In addition to the clear stipulations under the Law of the People's Republic of China on Chinese–Foreign Equity Joint Ventures, subsequent investment laws (such as the Law of the People's Republic of China on Enterprises with Foreign Investment, the Law of the People's Republic of China on Chinese-Foreign Cooperative Joint Ventures, and Regulations of the People's Republic of China on Cooperation with Foreigners in the Development and Exploitation of Offshore Oil Resources) have all contained clear stipulations concerning protection of the legitimate rights and interests of foreign investors.

2. *Signed investment protection agreements with foreign governments.* After bilateral negotiations, China has signed intergovernmental investment protection agreements (or treaties) with more than 50 countries, providing protection for the legitimate rights and interests of enterprises or individuals of the other country gained through investment in China.

3. *Laws on the protection of intellectual property rights and other investment in nontangible instruments.* On 1 March 1983, the Chinese Government issued and implemented the Trademark Law of the People's Republic of China; on 1 April 1985, the Patent Law of the People's Republic of China; on 1 November 1987, the Law of the People's Republic of China on Technical Contracts; and on 1 June 1991, the Copyright Law of the People's Republic of China. These laws have stipulations on measures of protection of trademarks and inventions registered, cultural and movie and television works, technical confidentiality (including development, transfer, consultancy, and services thereof), and computer software. On 4 June 1991, the State Council adopted Regulations of the People's Republic of China on the Protection of Computer Software, with detailed stipulations on the implementation methods for the protection of computer software. In addition, China joined the World Intellectual Property Rights Organization in 1980, the Paris Convention for the Protection of Industrial Property Rights in 1984, the Convention for the Protection of Intellectual

Property Rights of Integrated Circuits in 1990, and the Berne Convention for the Protection of Literary and Artistic Works and the Universal Copyright Convention in 1992. Along with the development of world economy and technologies and changes in intellectual property rights systems, China has modified its patent law and trademark law to expand the scope of protection and provide more severe penalties for violations. In 1994, China's national coordination and guidance organization for the protection of intellectual property rights held a working meeting on the subject. As a result, the State Council adopted the Decisions on Further Strengthening Protection of Intellectual Property Rights; it requested all open coastal provinces and municipalities to organize within the year a large-scale inspection on legal enforcement with regard to the protection of intellectual property rights, to halt the production and sales of copyright-violating laser cassettes and disks, endeavoring to reach the target of preventing all types of violations against intellectual property rights within one or two years. By September 1995, local trademark administration organs had investigated and dealt with some 1,000 trademark violation cases, nearly 100 of them concerning foreign interests, with 531 cases in Shenzhen, Guangzhou, and Shanghai alone, resulting in the confiscation of over 2 million pieces of illegal trademark logos and fines of RMB 4.33 million yuan.

45. What is the definition of the "legitimate rights and interests" of foreign investors that the Chinese Government protects?

The legitimate rights and interests of foreign investors stand for the investment made in China, profits gained, and other legal rights and interests, in accordance with contracts, articles of association, agreements, and so forth, compiled according to Chinese laws and approved by the Chinese Government, including rights for entry into and exit from China, the right of residing in China, and the right to business operation in order to undertake investment activities, and all types of intellectual property rights used as a form of nontangible investment instrument or provided for technological transfer.

46. Will the Chinese Government take over foreign investors' properties?

Legal stipulations on takeover or nationalization of foreign properties exist in many countries, even in developed countries, as an inalienable

right of a sovereign state. However, in order to encourage foreign investment in China and protect the legitimate rights and interests of foreign investors, China has a special stipulation under Article 5 of the Law of the
People's Republic of China on Enterprises Operated Exclusively with Foreign Investment: "Except under special circumstances, the state shall not
nationalize or expropriate wholly-owned foreign enterprises. Should it
prove necessary to do so in the public interest, legal procedures will be
followed and reasonable compensation will be made." The same stipulations are also seen in relevant regulations adopted by the State Council on
encouraging investment from compatriot Chinese from Hong Kong,
Macao, and Taiwan and from overseas Chinese.

47. What is meant by "reasonable compensation"?

Reasonable compensation is the compensation at a value equivalent to the
invested assets taken over. In bilateral negotiations for investment protection agreements, governments of some developed countries request "fair"
and "sufficient" compensation for the invested assets taken over, with
due consideration given to ideal operational profits if the takeover would
not occur (so-called projected high business value). This is certainly unreasonable, so such expressions do not appear in any of investment protection agreements China has signed with foreign governments.

48. How does the Chinese Government protect the patent rights obtained in China by a foreigner?

Article 60 of the Patent Law of the People's Republic of China stipulates:
"For any exploitation of the patent, without the authorization of the
patentee, constituting an infringing act, the patentee or any interested
party may request the Administrative Authority for Patent Affairs to handle the matter or may directly institute legal proceedings in the people's
court. The Administrative Authority for Patent Affairs handling the matter shall have the power to order the infringer to stop the infringing act
and to compensate for the damage. Any dissatisfied party may, within
three months of receipt of the notification, institute legal proceedings in
the people's court. If such proceedings are not instituted within the time
limit and if the order is not complied with, the Administrative Authority
for Patent Affairs may approach the people's court for compulsory execution."

49. How does China respect the intellectual property rights of a foreign investor? What is the legal support? How does a Sino-foreign joint venture enterprise protect the technical confidentiality of an investor?

According to Chinese laws, foreign investors may invest in China with intellectual property rights (industrial property rights), or intangible assets, and China respects and protects their intellectual property rights by legal legislation on intellectual property rights and by joining international conventions (treaties) and organizations concerning intellectual property rights. Since 1993 the Chinese Government has compiled and issued specialized laws and decrees on trademarks, patents, technical contracts, copyrights, and protection of computer software, and has become a member of the World Intellectual Property Organization Convention, the Paris Convention for the Protection of Industrial Property Rights, the Convention for the Protection of Intellectual Property Rights of Integrated Circuits, the Berne Convention for the Protection of Literary and Artistic Works, and the Universal Copyright Convention. In recent years, the Chinese Government has also made necessary amendments to its patent law, expanding its scope of protection to include drugs, chemical products, foodstuffs, seasonings, and drinks, in order to provide protection to investors.

In order to strengthen the protection of intellectual property rights, the State Council issued in 1994 the Decision on Further Strengthening Protection of Intellectual Property Rights, established a national coordination and guidance organization on intellectual property rights, and held a working meeting on the subject. By the State's Council's decision, the General Administration of Customs has worked out and promulgated a special proclamation on the implementation of protection of intellectual property rights and on the prevention of entry or exit of goods violating such rights. In the meantime, Chinese judicial departments tightened their cases concerning violations of intellectual property rights. The Intellectual Property Rights Court of the Intermediate People's Court of the Beijing Municipality since 1994 has tried and closed as many as 90 cases concerning violation of intellectual property rights, of which over 40 are related to foreign interests (Europe, America, and Hong Kong, Macao, and Taiwan regions), including commercial software cases.

50. What international treaties has the Chinese Government signed in relation to the protection of royalties of technical patents and trademarks?

International treaties or agreements China has joined relating to intellectual property rights include the following:

World Intellectual Property Rights Organization Convention (WIPO), in March 1980

Paris Convention for the Protection of Industrial Property Rights, in December 1984

Madrid Agreement for International Registration of Trademarks

Berne Convention for the Protection of Literary and Artistic Works and the Universal Copyright Convention, in July 1992

Convention for the Protection of Gramophone Records Producers from Unauthorized Duplication of Their Records, on 7 November 1992

Patent Cooperation Treaty, in August 1993

Treaty on Trademark Laws and Its Implementing Regulations, in October 1994

6.

Business Structures in China for Foreign Investment

51. What business structures are used in China for foreign investment?

There are two means of foreign investment that China attracts: indirect investment and direct investment.

Indirect investment is a means of international credit, by which loans are obtained from foreign governments and international financing institutions, via bilateral or multilateral agreements between governments or financing institutions, for designated projects.

Direct investment is mainly investment from international private sectors, usually referring to direct investing of funds by overseas investors (companies or individuals) in enterprises of the investment recipient countries, via the signing of investment cooperation agreements. This form contains more flexibility and diversity. According to the actual Chinese situation and international practices, the Chinese Government has decided on four ways to attract direct foreign investment: (1) Sino–foreign equity joint venture enterprises, (2) Sino–foreign cooperative joint venture enterprises, (3) wholly foreign-owned enterprises, and (4) Sino–foreign cooperation projects for the exploitation of natural resources. In addition, in projects of compensatory trade, processing or assembly for export, and leasing trade, foreign businesses usually have technical or equipment input, and therefore such flexible trading structures are also regarded as a means of direct foreign investment. Also belonging to means of direct foreign investment is the issuance of securities or stocks in international capital markets for the direct use of construction projects or the issuance of the securities or stocks directly by enterprises so that such enterprises with foreign investment. Investment in stocks and securities will occupy an increasingly important position in all means of direct foreign investment.

52. What is the difference between indirect and direct investment, and what is the relationship between them?

There are two major differences between indirect and direct investment: (1) a direct investment is not a liability, assuming only investment risks with no liability risks involved, while an indirect investment is a liability; and (2) a direct investment entails on the investor(s) powers of management and control over the invested projects, while the investing country providing an indirect investment has only the creditor's rights entitled to collection of interests, with no management or control over the projects. However, when the foreign investor to a direct investment project applies and obtains some funding from the government or financing institutions of the home country to support the investment, this would be a combination of indirect and direct investment.

53. What is a Sino–foreign equity joint venture, and what are its characteristics?

A Sino–foreign equity joint venture is a means of cooperation by which one or several foreign companies, enterprises, or other economic organizations, together with their Chinese counterpart(s), jointly invest in and manage a venture enterprise in China while sharing risks and profits in proportion to their share(s) of investment. The nature of such a venture is a limited liability company, which becomes, upon approval, an independent legal corporation governed and protected by China's laws. If the venture obtains approval after application to issue stock to the public, it becomes a joint-stock limited liability company.

The Chinese and foreign parties to a Sino–foreign equity joint venture enterprise may invest with such instruments as cash or goods in kind (factory premises, equipment, etc.) or industrial property rights. Shares of investment are to be determined by the joint venture parties, but the subscription(s) by the foreign investor(s) shall normally not be below 25% of the registered capital. The venture shall have a Board of Directors, who shall decide on the nomination of the General Manager and Deputy General Manager(s) to be responsible for the management and operations of the venture. The Board may also authorize the Chinese or foreign partner(s) to be responsible for management and operations. The Law of the

People's Republic of China on Chinese–Foreign Equity Joint Ventures, the first foreign investment law in China, adopted in July 1979, and the Implementing Regulations of the Law of the People's Republic of China on Joint Ventures Using Chinese and Foreign Investment, issued later, contain clear stipulations regarding a Chinese–foreign equity joint venture enterprise and its nature, formation, management and operations, distribution of profits, term of joint venturing, termination and liquidation, and so forth.

The characteristics of a Chinese–foreign equity joint venture are as follows:

1. The principle of equal and mutual benefit has been fully reflected since losses, risks, management authorities, termination, liquidation, and so forth are all to be shared in proportion to the investment made by the investors, and the initiatives of investors can be brought into full play, serving to introduce advanced international science and technology and prompt the upgrading or renewal of products as well as the improvement of China's industrial structure.

2. Foreign investors' sales channels and managerial expertise can be utilized to improve accessibility to market information and increase product exports.

3. China can draw on the experience of foreign investors' management and operations, to further China's socialist market economy.

4. Since benefits and risks are to be shared, there is no added liability for the State, which is favorable to the development of China's economy.

The negative part of Sino–foreign equity joint venturing is the existence of certain restrictive factors in the joint management by the investors and their counterparts because of the variety of strict and complex regulations and procedures. A lot of improvement has been made in these areas with the development and growth in number of equity joint venture enterprises.

54. What is a Sino–foreign cooperative joint venture, and what are its characteristics?

A Sino–foreign cooperative joint venture is also called a contractual joint venture. According to the Law of the People's Republic of China on Chinese–Foreign Cooperative Joint Ventures, for matters such as investment by investors or terms of cooperation, distribution of profits or products, share of risks or losses, means of management and operations, and ownership of assets at the termination of the venture, the investment parties will negotiate with each other and reach an agreement, which is set down in a contract. The cooperative joint venture is established after approval of the contract and articles of association and business registration. When conforming to conditions for a legal corporation according to Chinese laws, such cooperative joint ventures can be of a Chinese legal corporation.

The investment by investors or terms of cooperation can be in the form of cash or goods in kind, or land use rights, industrial property rights, nonpatent technologies, or other property rights.

In comparison with equity joint ventures, cooperative joint ventures are more flexible and are more popular for medium- or small-sized enterprises that may not have the capability to form an equity joint venture (lack of funds, for instance). However, since all details are subject to stipulation in the contract, a good cooperative joint venture contract is of utmost importance in running the enterprise.

55. How does a wholly foreign-owned enterprise operate in China?

Foreign enterprises or wholly foreign-owned enterprises are ones established in China according to Chinese laws, all of whose capital comes from foreign investors. When conforming to conditions set for a legal corporation by Chinese laws, such enterprises can be of a Chinese legal corporate status. Foreign enterprises are to abide by the laws and decrees of China, doing no harm to China's social or public interests, and, in return, their legitimate rights and interests are protected by Chinese law. Management or operational activities of foreign enterprises within the scope of approved articles of association are free from any interference, but such enterprises are to accept the supervision and inspection by related Chinese departments (of industry and commerce, taxation, etc.).

Branch organizations set up in China by foreign companies or other economic organizations are not regarded as foreign enterprises.

56. What is Sino–foreign cooperative development?

Sino–foreign cooperative development projects approved by the Chinese Government in the early stage are mainly those prospecting for and developing offshore petroleum, resorting to contracts of risks as the means of cooperation. A contract is signed between a Chinese department in charge of the petroleum industry and a foreign company, by which, unless otherwise specified by the Chinese department in charge or by the contract itself, the foreign (oil) company is to make investments during the prospecting stage, assuming any risks, with no funds from the country owning the natural resources, which may participate in investment during the development stage according to the conditions of the oil field, while the foreign investor shall, according to the contract, gain return on investment, recover expenses, and obtain the share of proceeds from the petroleum produced by the project. During the development stage, the foreign partner may ship outside China the petroleum due it or bought, and remit any legitimate proceeds outside China. This business structure has two advantages. First, in case of failure of prospecting, the country owning the natural resources does not share the risk, and so it suffers no losses. Second, since the foreign partner has to identify the oil field quickly and participate in the investment and development in order to gain profits, it will apply advanced technologies during the stages of prospecting and development in order to speed up the process while endeavoring to lower costs. The country owning the natural resources thus benefits from the introduction of advanced technologies, so the natural resources can be developed more quickly.

57. How is compensatory trade conducted?

As a means of direct foreign investment, compensation is a means by which the foreign partner invests in technology or equipment and gets repaid for the investment in-kind by receiving products produced with the technology or equipment or other products agreed on by the parties. Matters such as the quantity and pricing of the invested equipment and products repaid, timing for such compensation, responsibilities, and resolving of disputes, among others, are to be specified in the contract between the parties. The contract is to be submitted for approval by the government department in charge. Repayment by means of products produced with the invested equipment is terms *direct compensation*; repayment by means of other products is termed *indirect compensation*. When the indirect compensation involves products under license control or quota limitations, prior approval shall be obtained from the government department in charge. In foreign countries, compensation trade is also termed *back purchase* or *exchanged purchase*. This is a flexible and advantageous means of investment and trade, for faster development of natural resources and upgrading or renovation of old enterprises in circumstances of lack of funds (especially foreign exchange) and advanced technology and equipment.

58. How is processing against supplied materials or assembly of supplied parts conducted?

Processing against supplied materials or samples, assembly of supplied parts, and compensation trade are often put together in China and termed *three supplies and one compensation businesses*. By the "three supplies," the foreign business provides certain raw materials, elements or instruments, or parts, auxiliary materials, packaging materials, or sample drawings, for the Chinese partners to process or assemble according to the requirement of the foreign business, with finished products sent to the foreign party for sales, and the Chinese party charging only processing fees and cost of raw materials consumed in the course of processing against samples. Because of high costs and not enough labor in developed countries today, some labor-intensive industries have been moved to developing countries, where labor is less expensive, by means of processing against or assembly of supplied materials or parts. The developing countries can use this industrial shift to improve the operating capacity of their own enterprises and their employment rate, for the benefit of economic development. This method is simple and flexible, calling for simple technology and equipment, and is therefore appropriate for developing countries. As a result, this method is popular among medium and small enterprises.

When requested by the processing party, foreign businesses often provide some technology and equipment to help in introducing suitable, relatively advanced technology and equipment and hence in improving product quality and level. The cost of this technology and equipment are usually paid by a deduction of processing fees.

59. Does China encourage international leasing in attracting foreign investment? What is the present situation, and what are the future prospects in this area?

International leasing, which originated in the United States after World War II, is a fast-growing method of international investment and trade. World trade conducted by this method stands for over US$30 billion worth of transactions. It enjoys fast growth particularly in Asian countries (Japan, Republic of Korea, Singapore, etc.).

International leasing is a method of investment and trade that combines a commodity credit with a financing credit. The leasing firm provides funds to purchase the technology and equipment needed, negotiated, and ordered by a lessee enterprise and leases to the lessee for use; the lessee periodically pays to the lessor (the leasing firm) rental and interest. At the end of the lease, the lessee may renew, purchase, or return the leased technology and equipment according to the contract. Three basic types of lease are commonly practiced:

1. *Funded lease.* The funds of a leasing company are mainly provided by international financing institutions or banks as credit loans, with the payment of interest and capital effected from rentals collected by the leasing company. Usually a leasing firm has investment from domestic or foreign financing institutions or banks and for certain functions is concurrently a financing institution. This type of lease is suitable for the introduction from overseas of large, new, and durable advanced technologies and equipment. A funded lease constitutes the bulk of international leasing businesses.

2. *Lever lease.* When the leasing company is unable to raise funds for expensive equipment to be ordered and leased, it applies for a mortgage loan from a bank or consortium against such equipment ordered, providing guarantee by transferring the right to collect rental fees (creditor's rights) to the bank or consortium. After the provision of guarantees for the mortgaged loan, the equipment is leased to the lessee. This is the main method of lease China uses in its civil aviation industry in introducing aircraft for the development of its aviation industry.

3. *Other types of lease.* This covers the following kinds of leases:

—general lease: directly leasing equipment from a foreign business

—specialized lease: a leasing firm or a group of companies leasing their own products

—lease of services: provision to the lessee of such services as technical maintenance, parts, raw materials, fuel, training, and operations

—comprehensive lease: rentals to be paid in products

From the beginning of implementation of its reforms and open policies, China has used international leasing as a means of investment. It established the China Oriental Leasing Company, the first leasing firm in China joint venturing with Japan. During the past 15 years, China has approved the establishment of over 30 Sino-foreign joint venture leasing companies in international leasing businesses. The total number is over 300 when taking into account domestically funded leasing firms, with a total value of lease amounting to over US$10 billion. When taking into consideration the lease of aircraft by means of a lever lease, the leasing businesses have been valued at more than US$20 billion. Notwithstanding the occurrence of delayed payment of rentals due to current transit or operational mechanisms by lessee enterprises, international leasing is a promising business in China with bright prospects since this is a method by which a lessee enterprise can acquire comparatively advanced equipment and technologies with a lower-than-usual investment and by a convenient means. What is more, there are a great number of state-owned enterprises in China requiring investment and renovation.

60. How is investment in stocks or securities assessed? What are the prospects in this area?

The issuance of international bonds and stocks is a common means of fund raising and financing in the world today. International bonds are documents pertaining to the assumption of liabilities in repaying capital and interest issued by the government or enterprise or other economic organization in acquiring foreign loans; such documents are called *bonds* when the repayment is due over one year later and *promissory notes* when the repayment is due within a year. International bonds can be broken into government bonds and private bonds, the former being able to be in the listing of stock markets with a lower interest rate and longer time for repayment, while the latter, not for stock markets with a higher interest rate and shorter time for repayment but a simpler and more flexible procedure for purchase. Bonds can also be divided into ordinary company bonds and transferable company bonds; the latter can be changed into stocks, whose price floats along with stocks. Depending on the issuer, there are government bonds, civil construction bonds, enterprise bonds, and financial bonds.

Stocks are documents issued by a joint stock enterprise and raising funds, pertaining to the rights and liabilities assumed by its shareholders according to their shares in the enterprise. Stocks can be transacted at the stock market upon approval.

Both bonds and stocks are negotiable securities, with this major difference: bonds represent the creditor's rights, with a fixed time for repayment and a fixed interest rate; stocks represent stock holding rights, with no determined time for repayment, but whose holder is entitled to profits per these stocks at a rate dependent on the profit-generating situation of the enterprise.

In order to speed up the process of joining the world economy more fully and to promote national modernization, China, since its reforms and opening, has actively undertaken preparations and experiments in issuing international bonds and stocks. It first approved the China International Trust and Investment Corporation (CITIC) to take the lead in issuing overseas international bonds, followed by approvals for this corporation and financial institutions in Guangdong and Fujian to issue international bonds. At the end of the 1980s, along with the implementation of changes of operational mechanisms of state-owned enterprises, a joint stock system was allowed for dissemination. At the end of 1990, the State set up China's first stock market, in Shanghai, and another in Shenzhen in 1991. Agencies of these two stock markets have been established all over the country. So far, 283 joint stock enterprises have issued RMB stocks (Category A stocks) with State approval, 53 joint stock enterprises have issued foreign currency stocks (Category B stocks) with domestic circulation, and over 30 have issued overseas stocks and stocks in listing (Category H stocks). Issuance of bonds and stocks, as well as administration of stock markets, are standardized and growing into maturity.

Currently, funds raised by China through issuing bonds and stocks occupy only 10% of total financing, a great difference in comparison with developed countries. The securities industry is still in the ascendant in China.

61. Is BOT an encouraged method?

Short for "build-operate-transfer," BOT is a guarantee-free method of cooperation by which an investor identifies a project in an investment recipient country, assumes sole responsibility in investing in the construction and operation of the project, and, after recovering the investment and obtaining compensation, returns the project to the possession and management of the investment recipient country. This is a new means of international capital investment, applied usually in projects concerning infrastructure facilities calling for huge investments and a great length of time, and popular in underdeveloped countries short of funds and technologies. The first BOT project has been implemented in China on a trial basis: the Beijing-Tongxian Expressway, by Beijing civil construction departments and an American company. Construction started in September 1994, with 20 months as the projected time for completion, when the expressway will open for traffic. The approved term for operation is 20 years, after which the expressway will be returned to China.

Along with China's economic development and expansion of construction, the building of infrastructure facilities has a long way to go. This type of investment will undoubtedly be welcomed and encouraged if the BOT trial project is successful.

7.

China's Channels for Attracting Foreign Investment, Public Notary, and Arbitration Organizations

62. What are China's channels for attracting foreign investment?

To attract foreign investment, there have to be certain channels and a set of compatible organizations and departments providing various investment opportunities and services. Over the past dozen years, China has gradually opened such channels and set up such departments:

1. *Government administration system for foreign investment.* Along with the adoption of the first foreign investment law of China—the Law of the People's Republic of China on Chinese–Foreign Equity Joint Ventures— the Chinese Government set up the Foreign Investment Administration Committee, under the jurisdiction of the State Council. In 1982, it was replaced by the Ministry of Foreign Economic Relations and Trade and in 1993 by the Ministry of Foreign Trade and Economic Cooperation, which has under it commissions (bureaus, offices) of foreign economic relations and trade of local governments, forming a government organization responsible for review and approval of enterprises with foreign investment. Planning commissions at all levels are responsible for review and approval of project proposals and feasibility study reports. Foreign invest-

ment administration committees (bureaus) are set up in provinces and cities with massive foreign investment. Business registration is the responsibility of the State Administration for Industry and Commerce, with local bureaus at different levels of governments. These bodies also have the power to supervise the operations of enterprises with foreign investment, including revoking business licenses of enterprises engaging in illegal activities. Also providing guidance and supervision for foreign investment are taxation departments, customs houses, state commodity inspection departments, exchange control departments, and foreign affairs offices at all levels of governments.

2. *Foreign investment service centers.* The first foreign investment service center was established in the mid-1980s in Guangdong Province. The Guangdong Center provides foreign investment services and is granted partial approval for import and export rights. By the end of 1980s, foreign investment services centers had been established in most provinces and cities in China. There are basically two types of such centers. The first category is of concurrent administrative functions, responsible, for instance, for business invitations when authorized by the government and handling all formalities for project review and approval, plus business registration and opening. Some are designated as the government department in charge of enterprises with foreign investment (wholly foreign-owned enterprises), acting as a specialized department for enterprises with foreign investment. In the second category are purely service organizations, which also maintain ties with government departments in charge of introduction of foreign investment and providing accurate guidance and direct services to overseas investors.

3. *Associations of enterprises with foreign investment.* Social organizations enjoying the status of a legal corporation, they are jointly set up by enterprises with foreign investment (Sino–foreign equity joint ventures, cooperative joint ventures, and wholly foreign-owned enterprises) and registered with government approval. These associations seek to provide services to enterprises with foreign investment, to Chinese and foreign investors, and to the government in attracting foreign investment, and they watch out for the legitimate rights and interests of Chinese and foreign investors. According to their scope of services, they explain China's foreign investment policies, laws and decrees, and environment; provide overseas investors with investment consulting (including recommending investment projects); inform the government of comments and suggestions made by investors; assist enterprises with foreign investment in opening sales channels and exchange; and make presentations on the business management and operational experience of enterprises with

foreign investment. The China Association of Enterprises with Foreign Investment was established in November 1987; since then, such associations have been established in all provinces of China, except in the autonomous regions of Inner Mongolia and Tibet, and even in some cities and counties. These associations have had a wide impact both inside and outside China.

4. *International trust and investment corporations system.* At the same time as the adoption of the first foreign investment law of China—the Law of the People's Republic of China on Chinese–Foreign Equity Joint Ventures—the State Council officially approved the incorporation of the China International Trust and Investment Corporation (CITIC), the first such organization in China engaging in international trust and investment business. Provincial-level international trust and investment corporations have since been established in all provinces, autonomous regions, and municipalities. Such corporations mainly engage in financing, the introduction of technologies, and investment or participation in investment in domestic and overseas projects; recommending investment projects while providing investment consulting, legal, accounting, and credit advice; issuing, or issuing on behalf of the issuer, bonds outside China; handling import and export businesses on behalf of investment projects of the corporation; and establishing China representation facilities for and on behalf of foreign firms that have business relations with the corporation. CITIC has made great progress and is ranked among the world-renowned international corporations, enjoying high credit and a fine reputation. International trust and investment corporations have formed a network in China, serving as an effective channel for China in business and investment invitation.

5. *Returned overseas Chinese associations system.* China has more than 50 million overseas Chinese and citizens of Chinese origin outside China, and a large number of returned overseas Chinese and their relatives in China. Overseas Chinese have a history of patriotism—doing their best to provide financial support to the construction of China, as well as the livelihood of their relatives. Remittances from overseas Chinese have been a part of China's foreign exchange revenue. Since the reforms and opening, overseas Chinese have actively engaged in investing in the development of their home country. Investment from overseas Chinese, together with investment from Hong Kong and Taiwan, has been important to China. Therefore, the State has issued even more preferential policies for investment by overseas Chinese and those from Hong Kong, Macao, and Taiwan. A large group of enterprises with foreign investment approved in the early 1980s have seen many of them established through in-

troduction by China's government departments in charge of overseas Chinese affairs and the returned overseas Chinese associations, an indication of the great importance of fully utilizing and promoting the role of the overseas Chinese system as the main channel of business and investment introduction.

6. *China representation facilities of foreign firms.* Representation facilities of foreign firms (including companies, banks, and other economic organizations) resident in Beijing have reached more than several thousand in number; a great number of such facilities are also found in China's coastal and inland cities. On behalf of their overseas companies or industrial or commercial circles, they identify investment partners and handle all China business of their companies. They constitute a direct and effective channel for foreign investment in China.

7. *Public relations organizations and departments.* Public relations and international public relations activities are new to China, and they are for promoting international investment and developing world's economic and technological exchange and cooperation. The Public Relations Association of China has been established in China, with quite a number of public relations companies with foreign investment or wholly owned by foreign businessmen. Along with the continued development of foreign investment, public relations departments will play an even greater role in China's business and investment climate.

8. *Trade and investment talks, seminars, commodity fairs, and exhibitions.* With assistance and participation from the United Nations Industrial Development Organization, China opened its first international investment talks in Guangzhou in 1982. Promoted by governments and nongovernmental organizations at all levels, talks and seminars since then have been an important channel for investment talks. In addition, some commodity fairs, shows, and domestic and overseas exhibitions have developed from the traditional trade only into a comprehensive economic exchange place including investment talks.

9. *Other channels for international activities and liaison.* Currently an investment promotion organization has been established between the governments of China and Japan. Consisting of representatives designated by the governments, the organization holds regular talks to discuss investment projects and the investment environment. Exchange visits of experts and academic workshops are also some of the appropriate means to promote economic exchange and international investment.

63. What public notary, appraisal, and arbitration organizations in China assess the validity of foreign investment?

Using public notary, appraisal, and arbitration organizations has been a popular and effective practice in developed countries, as well as a reflection of economic and social development, in standardizing and ensuring investment and economic intercourse.

After the founding of the PRC, the China Foreign Trade Arbitration Committee was established as the authoritative arbitration institution. Since the implementation of reforms and open policies, China has actively engaged in the development of all types of public notary and appraisal organizations. Public notary sections have been set up in all legal and administrative departments, with authoritative personnel familiar with all laws and decrees to act as notaries. Foreign experience has been drawn upon also to set up various types of appraisal organizations consisting of certified public accountants, auditors, lawyers, and responsible persons of different levels of authoritative organs, who appraise by scientific means State properties and foreign-invested properties to safeguard the legitimate rights and interests of investors. In order to strengthen the management of appraisal organizations and appraisers in self-restraint and justice and to promote property appraisal of China in accordance with international rules, the China Association of Property Appraisal was established at the end of 1993, with over 500 members at present. A system of certified appraisers has also been proposed to certify that documents after notarization and appraisal in relation to project investment are valid after approval by government bodies in charge and are protected by laws of the country.

64. What roles do China's legal and accounting organizations play in foreign investment?

Registered with government departments in charge, a group of law firms, accounting firms, and auditing firms have been established in China. Various types of law firms are allowed to be established, including State-run firms that take up approved administrative staffing, firms of lawyers in cooperation or partnership, joint stock firms, and firms named after an individual, but concepts of ownership, type of administrative organization structure, and the terminology of administrative officers are not applied to law firms or lawyers.

China's various types of law and accounting firms are extremely important and indispensable to foreign investment, since a foreign business's investment in a Chinese enterprise is governed by Chinese law, as are investment and operational activities. Law and accounting firms play an authoritative role in determining whether investment and operations are in accordance with Chinese law and in determining what rights and interests are legitimate under the protection of Chinese law. They confirm and guarantee investment validity; without them, investment and operational activities would not be guaranteed. These are the reasons that such law and accounting firms have been established in China.

65. Does the Chinese Government allow foreign attorneys, accountants, auditors, and others to participate in appraisal and auditing of foreign investment in China?

Immediately after the implementation of reforms and open policies, China drew on foreign experience and greatly strengthened its legal and accounting systems. Efforts have been made to increase the exchange of personnel from legal and financial circles while allowing branches of overseas law firms and accounting firms to be established in China, and allowing lawyers, accountants, and auditors employed from overseas by foreign investors for enterprises with foreign investment to participate in the appraisal activities of the investment and operations of the enterprises. Once foreign nationals satisfy certain conditions, they can participate in qualifying examinations for lawyers and certified public accountants in China; those who pass the examinations are granted qualification certificates. Since 1994, over 350 people from Taiwan, Hong Kong, and Macao have applied to take the qualifying examinations for lawyers, and over 480 from Taiwan, Hong Kong, Macao, the United States, the United Kingdom, Canada, Australia, New Zealand, Singapore, and Malaysia have applied to take the examinations for certified public accountants. Eighty-eight applicants have acquired the certificate for a Chinese certified public accountant.

8.

Preparations for the Application of Establishing an Enterprise With Foreign Investment

66. What needs to be done in preparation for the establishment of an enterprise with foreign investment?

The following steps are indispensable for establishing an enterprise with foreign investment:

1. project selection
2. partner identification
3. negotiations on and signing of the letter of intent for cooperation on a project
4. drafting and signing of a feasibility study report by both parties
5. drafting and signing of the joint venture contract and articles of association
6. submission of documents for review and approval

Depending on the size of the project, some of the steps may be combined or simplified.

67. How are projects selected?

Potential projects should first be in compliance with Chinese regulations concerning foreign investment. Projects can be selected when they are of advanced technologies or manufacturing products for export, which the State grants priority for development, while taking into consideration such basic information as conditions for construction, funding for supplementary parts of the projects, size of production, technological level, sales market, economic results, and foreign exchange balance (of revenues and expenses) capability. Projects will not be selected if they do not meet all criteria or if they are restricted by the State unless prior consent by relevant government departments is obtained. These are the principles for project selection for both Chinese and foreign investors. In addition to conformity to State foreign investment criteria and industrial policies, a potential investor should regard as the first priority for consideration whether he meets the basic conditions for cooperation. Also important for consideration by a foreign investor is whether he has strengths in the project, such as in funding, advanced technologies, or sales markets inside and outside China.

68. How are partners identified?

Along with the deepening of China's reforms and opening, foreign trade and economic exchanges are continually increasing, rendering a wide range of opportunities and various channels for contacts, for the benefit of Chinese and foreign investors in identifying partners.

Various types of economic and trade talks, investment talks, commodity fairs, shows, and exhibitions held in China by the State foreign economic and trade departments and organizations in charge of the business or by local foreign economic and trade organizations provide a number of selected projects for discussion by Chinese and foreign investors.

There are many means and channels for China to invite business and introduce investment, and for overseas investors to identify partners in China:

- The United Nations Industrial Development Organization and its over a dozen country or regional investment promotion offices in Vienna, Paris, New York, Tokyo, Beijing, and other cities.
- Intergovernmental investment promotion organizations, such as the Sino-Japanese Investment Promotion Committee and Sino-German Investment Promotion Organization
- Foreign organizations whose portfolio includes recommending partners to China, or even participation in investment, such as the Foundation for the Industrialization of Developing Countries, Industrial Alliance Association, and Foreign Trade Association, es-

tablished in northern European countries; the Council of Commerce and Foreign Trade Association in Italy and France; the Japan-China Economic Association; the Trade Promotion Society of Japan; and the Trade Promotion Commune of the Republic of Korea.

For purposes of identifying partners or investment consultancy, foreign businesses inclined to invest in China may contact the following:

- Foreign Investment Department of the Ministry of Foreign Trade and Economic Cooperation
- China Association of Enterprises with Foreign Investment
- China International Trust and Investment Corporation (CITIC)
- State-level specialized corporations, such as the Huaneng Group (in electric power), petrochemical corporation, coals corporation, medical drugs corporation, tobacco corporation, and automobile industry corporation
- foreign economic and technical cooperation corporations in machinery, electronics, light industry, and textiles
- foreign economic and trade departments
- foreign investment service centers
- associations of enterprises with foreign investment
- trust and investment corporations of all provinces, autonomous regions, municipalities directly under the jurisdiction of the Central Government, and specialized cities by State planning.

Foreign investors may directly visit these units, get in touch with them by cable, or contact Chinese domestic units through business sections of Chinese embassies, China's business representation facilities resident in foreign countries, overseas organizations of the Bank of China, and representative offices of trust and investment corporations.

69. How are negotiations done and a letter of intent signed for a project?

After an investment project has been selected and a partner identified, the rest of the work should be carried out quickly: conducting mutual visits and investigations regarding the project and direct discussions and negotiations. Project discussions and signing of the letter of intent on the project are the basis of project application and approval. These steps must be followed:

Step 1: Ascertain each other's credit situation through meetings and investigations, with both parties providing legal documents and notarized materials on corporate status and identification certifications and proxies of the legal representative certifying authority in signing legally authentic documents.

Step 2: Through mutual visits and investigations, acknowledge each other's financial strengths and technological levels, domestic and overseas development levels, and market demand and supply situation. In the case of a project of advanced technologies, notarized documents certifying technological validity and exclusive ownership should be provided.

Step 3: Negotiate the contents of the project proposal, and sign the letter of intent.

Project negotiations are necessary not only when the project is selected and a partner identified, but all the way through the preliminary feasibility study, feasibility study report, draft agreement, contract, and articles of association.

Those participating in negotiations should be familiar with laws, decrees, and regulations; the business involved; the technologies concerned; accounting; and management and operations. For negotiations of key projects, a chief negotiator should be appointed to lead a negotiation team, with a letter of authorization issued by the legal representative. Legal consultants may be invited during negotiations and representatives from supervising government departments in charge of the business may be invited for participation and coordination.

In the course of negotiations, both parties should, on the basis of friendly discussions, undertake to handle differences appropriately. Focus should be placed on honesty, credit and reputation, and friendship, always resorting to friendly consultation to resolve differences. Whatever is said should count; fewer commitments should be made even if it means to speak less; and promises should always be honored.

70. What does a project proposal contain?

A project proposal is the primary stage of the project feasibility study and the basic document with which the Chinese and foreign partners apply for project approval. It states the necessity and viability of the project from the macro standpoint. Its contents should address preliminary estimates and suggestions regarding domestic and overseas markets, production levels, levels of technology, expected economic results, and foreign exchange balance (of revenues and expenses). These are basically identical to the contents of a study on investment opportunities and a preliminary feasibility study.

A preliminary feasibility study should be done at the same time as the project proposal in cases of large or medium size or key projects, with rough estimates and analysis on the following components:

- market demand and supply
- input of raw materials
- accessories and energy
- selection of plant area and location
- project design (technology, equipment, civil construction)
- management cost (management cost in workshops, administrative expenses, and cost of sales)
- project progress
- financial analysis (investment amount, fund raising, cost of production, and taxes)

The accuracy of the investment amount and cost of production should normally be within plus or minus 20%.

71. How should a feasibility study report be compiled?

The feasibility study is the key stage of the preinvestment period of a project. In the case of a construction project, the feasibility study should provide technical, economic, and business support. Multicase comparison, comprehensive analysis, and scientific proof should be made regarding key factors of a construction project before the best scheme is selected.

A feasibility study report should be compiled in a realistic manner, providing correct and reliable data and in compliance with relevant State regulations. All calculations should be scientific and reasonable, and a systematic analysis should be made, with reservations, of the construction, production, and operation of the project. Any problems should be recognized, with measures proposed for resolution.

A feasibility study report contains the following items:

- outline of the project implementation
- background and history of the project
- plant area and location
- project design
- market and production capacities

- materials and inputs
- plant organization and management cost
- labor and plan for construction progress
- financial analysis and projected economic results

Estimates of investment and cost at this stage should be accurate with a plus or minus 10% margin.

72. What are the basic requirements for drafting and signing a foreign investment project contract and articles of association?

The contract and articles of association are the basic legal documents in an enterprise with foreign investment; they determine the rights, obligations, responsibilities, and interests of the parties. Once approved by the Chinese Government, the contract and articles of association are in force, and all signing parties are required to perform, fully and seriously, according to the terms and conditions set out in the contract and articles of association. Government bodies at different levels exercise lawful supervision and inspection of all parties in their execution of the contract and articles of association, aiming to protect the legitimate rights and interests of all investors and the enterprise. Therefore, the drafting and signing of the contract and articles of association must be dealt with in a careful and serious manner. Joint venturing parties must appoint personnel to draft the documents or employ a lawyer familiar with foreign investments to do the work. Comments and suggestions should be sought from experts before signature, and prior consultation made with consulting organizations and supervising government departments in charge of the business. The documents should be signed by the legal representatives or their authorized persons with proxies.

Negotiations on a Sino–foreign equity joint venture enterprise should be a step-by-step approach, especially when working on a project with a large investment and with agreements signed between stages. The final contract should contain the major terms and conditions contained in previously signed agreements. Therefore, the final contract always applies in case of any discrepancies between the contract and agreements. With the consent of all parties concerned, they may sign only the contract and articles of association, leaving out the agreements. For wholly foreign-owned enterprises, only articles of association need to be submitted for review and approval.

73. What are the basic characteristics of a Sino–foreign joint venture contract and articles of association?

A *contract* is an agreement regarding the establishment, alteration, and termination of rights and obligations of all parties concerned; its formation is a legal activity reflecting the unanimity reached by all parties and is binding on all signing parties. The signing parties to the contract normally do not disclose its contents.

Articles of association are compiled on the basis of basic principles according to the contract and as determined by the enterprise, with detailed stipulations on the aims of the enterprise, organization structure, principles of organization, form management and operation, basic systems, and rules of procedures. The articles are often disclosed to the public, to help the public exercise its supervision over the enterprise, so that the enterprise may better assume social obligations.

The contract and articles of association have the following common basic characteristics:

1. Contents are complete and detailed, and are of legal effect and can be executed.
2. All terms and conditions are unanimously agreed on by all parties.
3. Signing of the contract and articles of association is a legal activity and is of legal force over all parties concerned.
4. The contract and articles of associations are in force only when all terms and conditions contained in it are in compliance with the laws of the country where the enterprise is located.

74. What are the basic requirements for the contents of a joint venture contract and articles of association?

The contract and articles of association should include the following:

1. General information on the parties and the enterprise: legal addresses, legal representatives, nature and aims of the enterprise, scope of business, size of production, major products, and major economic targets.
2. Investment amount, registered capital, subscriptions to the registered capital by each and all investing parties, means of payment and timing of payment, loans of the enterprise, method of financing, guarantee(s), and counterguarantee(s).

3. Responsibilities of each and all parties, including those during construction, business start-up, and production and operation.
4. Technology transfer, technical service, and royalties for use of technologies as well as means of payment.
5. Organizational structure of the enterprise, including the Board of Directors, the management structure and its duties and responsibilities, scope of authorities, and rules for procedures.
6. Preparation and construction, such as the construction design, the construction itself, and acceptance of construction.
7. Means of product sales and ratio of sales in domestic and overseas markets, as well as the items, quantities, sales channels, sales price, means of balancing foreign exchange revenues and expenses, and measures to be taken in this respect.
8. Principles for profit distribution, reserves of the three funds, and share of risks.
9. Accounting, taxation, labor management, terms of business, liquidation and termination, insurance, arbitration, responsibilities in case of default, and applicable laws.

75. What are the issues of importance to parties to a joint venture enterprise in drafting the contract, articles of association, and other related documents?

1. The contract and articles of association should be carefully worded to avoid ambiguity in expression that could lead to misunderstanding. Every effort should be made to minimize the probability of future disputes' arising from the terms or terminology.

2. There should not be an article on "freezing of laws," an expression meaning that the investor(s) must comply only with laws and regulations adopted before the contract or application is approved, not with laws passed later.

3. There should be no articles setting out responsibilities to be assumed by any government body. Not permitted either is the listing in the document of all laws and decrees (or taxation laws) of the country, which implies that the parties are not required to abide by any laws, decrees, or regulations not already passed.

4. There should be no articles on the obligations of a third party without its signed consent. Such articles are invalid from legal and commercial point of view.

5. The documents are to specify the investment amount, means of

payment, and timing of payments by each and all parties, specifying also the currency and unit applied, with currency conversion by the exchange rates as announced by the State exchange control organs. In specifying means of payment, a breakdown should be made stating the respective amounts by means of cash, goods, facilities, and/or intangible assets, and in the case of payment in intangible assets (e.g., patents, specialized technologies), the documents should describe the basis of technical evaluation, principles for such evaluation, and formulas for calculations, in addition to legal responsibilities to be assumed by the investor in the validity and exclusive ownership.

6. Articles on responsibilities in case of default should be clearly stated and specific, using no ambiguous terms, to avoid legal problems in the future in case of default.

9.

Application, Review and Approval, and Registration of an Enterprise With Foreign Investment

76. What is the procedure for establishing a Sino–foreign equity or joint venture (JV) enterprise?

The basic application procedure for approval of the establishment of an equity or JV enterprise is as follows (see Exhibit 9-1):

Step 1: Submission of the project proposal for review and approval. First, the Chinese and foreign parties sign a letter of intent on the project; then the Chinese partner submits the project proposal for working with a foreign partner in the establishment of a JV enterprise and the preliminary feasibility study report to the government department in charge of the Chinese partner. These documents are reviewed and approved by this department, which then submits them to the review and approval authorities. They will approve or disapprove it based on State development plans, regional distribution of production capabilities, and industrial policy.

Step 2: Submission of the feasibility study report for review and approval. Upon approval of the JV project proposal, the parties jointly prepare the feasibility study report, to be reviewed and signed by both parties before

Exhibit 9-1. The Review and Approval Procedure for an Equity or Cooperative Joint Venture Enterprises

Steps for review and approval	*Documents to submit*
Step 1: approval of project proposal	a) preliminary feasibility study b) letter of intent c) project proposal for equity or cooperative joint venture d) comments by supervising government departments in charge of the Chinese party
TO STEP 2 WHEN APPROVED BY REVIEW AND APPROVAL AUTHORITIES	
Step 2: Approval of feasibility study	a) approval letter by review and approval authorities on the project proposal b) feasibility study report signed by Chinese & foreign parties c) copies of all documents submitted during step 1
TO STEP 3 WHEN APPROVED BY REVIEW AND APPROVAL AUTHORITIES	
Step 3: Approval of contract and articles of association acquiring approval certificate business registration banks customs house tax bureau others	a) copies of documents submitted during steps 1 and 2 b) approval letter by review and approval authorities on the feasibility study report c) business registration papers and credit statements of Chinese and foreign parties d) contract and articles of association e) list of nominated board members from both parties

submitting it to the review and approval authorities. The review of a feasibility study report is a serious job and carefully follows established procedures. The review and approval authorities will, in the case of a large- or medium-sized project, send the document to a qualified construction consulting firm, for it to prepare an appraisal report and make recommendations for the decision.

Step 3: Approval of the contract. On the basis of the feasibility report, the parties draft and sign the contract and articles of association, and submit them to the review and approval authorities for approval and issuance of the approval certificate.

These three steps must be followed one by one, with no leaping over permitted, except in the case of a small project, when the first two steps can be combined with the consent of the review and approval authorities.

77. What is the application procedure for approval of the establishment of a wholly foreign-owned enterprise?

In applying for the establishment of a wholly foreign-owned enterprise, the foreign investor need only submit a preliminary project report to the review and approval authorities. When written approval is obtained, he can start compiling articles of association, to be submitted for approval (see Exhibit 9-2).

According to the Law of the People's Republic of China on Enterprises with Foreign Investment, the approval or disapproval shall be decided by the review and approval authorities within 90 days upon receipt of the application, and an approval certificate shall be issued in case of approval.

78. What are the review and approval authorities for the establishment of an enterprise with foreign investment, and what are the regulations on their approval authorization?

According to Chinese law, applications for the establishment of enterprises with foreign investment will be reviewed and approved by government bodies authorized by the Ministry of Foreign Trade and Economic Cooperation or the State Council, or local governments of provinces, autonomous regions, municipalities directly under the Central

Exhibit 9-2. Review and Approval Procedure for Wholly Foreign-Owned Enterprises

Steps for review and approval	Documents to submit
1. review and approval of project proposal and preliminary feasibility	a) project proposal b) preliminary feasibility study c) business registration papers and credit statements of the foreign investor

TO STEP 2
WHEN APPROVED
BY REVIEW AND
APPROVAL
AUTHORITIES

2. review and approval of articles of association and feasibility study report	a) approval letter by review and approval authorities on the project proposal b) articles of association and feasibility study report c) nomination letter and proxy for legal representative and board members d) copies of all documents during step 1

acquiring approval certificate

business registration

banks customs house tax bureau others

Government, State-planned specialized cities, and special economic zones, when authorized by the Ministry of Foreign Trade and Economic Cooperation, or other bodies designated by relevant ministries, commissions, or bureaus of the State Council (hereafter referred to as the review and approval authorities).

For projects with an investment amount exceeding the approval authorization, those in areas restricted by the State for foreign investment, those whereby construction conditions, production and business conditions, or foreign exchange balancing (of revenues and expenses) are under State control, or those with products involving quota or permits control (regardless of the project size), the review and approval on project proposals and feasibility studies will be done by the State Planning Commission (or the State Economic and Trade Commission) and the Ministry of Foreign Trade and Economic Cooperation, together with other relevant departments of the Government. The contracts and articles of association will undergo review and approval by the Ministry of Foreign Trade and Economic Cooperation.

The review and approval authorities of the local governments of the coastal provinces, autonomous regions, municipalities directly under the Central Government, and State-planned specialized cities are authorized to review and approve projects with total foreign investment under US $30 million, as long as the projects fall within the areas of the State for foreign investment, have available construction conditions, production and business conditions, and foreign exchange balancing (of revenues and expenses) requiring no State control, and are manufacturing enterprises whose products do not involve quota or permits control.

The review and approval authorities of the inland provinces, autonomous regions, State-planned specialized cities, and relevant departments of the State Council are authorized to review and approve projects with total foreign investment of under US$10 million, as long as the projects fall within the areas of the State for foreign investment, have available construction conditions, production and business conditions, and foreign exchange balancing (of revenues and expenses) requiring no State control, and are manufacturing enterprises whose products do not involve quota or license control.

Projects involving the construction of airports, guest houses, hotels, commercial retail establishments, leasing, cargo shipment, financing or insurance, or the establishment of investment companies or joint stock companies undergo review and approval formalities with the Ministry of Foreign Trade and Economic Cooperation together with relevant government departments.

Approval certificates will be printed, coded, and issued by the Ministry of Foreign Trade and Economic Cooperation, no matter which review and approval authorities have approved an enterprise with foreign investment.

79. What are the application procedures for the establishment of a foreign-invested enterprise involving products under import and export license control?

According to stipulations by the State Council, the Ministry of Foreign Trade and Economic Cooperation issued more specific regulations on

19 June 1991 with regard to the issuance of an import and export license:

1. For any applications for or in reviewing and approving the establishment of enterprises with foreign investment or projects of compensatory trade, as long as import and export permits control is involved regarding the importing of raw materials or parts, or exporting products, including expansion of the business scope of enterprises, an increase or decrease of quantities of products covered by the license, or commodity export permits good for one time only, an official document shall be prepared by the economic and trade commissions or offices of concerned provinces, autonomous regions, municipalities directly under the State Council, and State-planned specialized cities, and submitted for review and approval by the Ministry of Foreign Trade and Economic Cooperation, for an official written approval issued in the name of the Ministry.

2. Permit-issuing authorities shall issue permits within the quantity as specified in the official document by the Ministry of Foreign Trade and Economic Cooperation, for products manufactured by the concerned enterprises themselves, when all stipulations contained in the official document are satisfied.

3. Enterprises with foreign investment are not allowed to purchase products for export without prior approval. In the case of a need to purchase such products in order to balance their foreign exchange revenues and expenses, procedures shall be followed according to relevant state regulations.

80. What are the documents to be submitted to review and approval authorities for application to establish a JV?

To apply for approval for the establishment of a JV enterprise, the Chinese partner is responsible for submitting to review and approval authorities the following official documents:

1. An application letter for the establishment of the JV enterprise.
2. The feasibility study report jointly compiled by all parties.
3. The JV contract and articles of association signed by duly authorized representatives of all parties.
4. A list of the Chairman, Vice Chairman, and members of the Board of Directors nominated by all parties.

5. Comments by the supervising government department in charge of the Chinese partner, as well as comments by the local governments of the province, autonomous region, or municipality directly under the State Council where the proposed JV enterprise is to be located.

These documents must be written in Chinese; documents 2, 3, and 4 may be concurrently written in a foreign language agreed to by all parties. The two versions are equally authentic.

81. What should be included in the application for the establishment of a wholly foreign-owned enterprise?

When a foreign business decides to establish a wholly owned enterprise, its representatives may officially apply to the Chinese Government by submitting for review and approval an application, with the articles of association of the enterprise attached, to a provincial-level government or the State-authorized local government in the locality of the investment project. When the project exceeds the approval authorization of the local government, the application shall be turned in to the Ministry of Foreign Trade and Economic Cooperation for review and approval. The application shall contain the following information:

1. Name, nationality, and legal address or residence of the investor.
2. Name, nationality, and position of the legal representative of the investor.
3. Name and address of the enterprise.
4. Total investment amount and registered capital.
5. Name and technological level of the products to be manufactured, size of production, and development plan.
6. Arrangements for the supply of raw materials and parts and the domestic procurement plan.
7. Land and built-up area needed and a list of materials and equipment to be imported.
8. Quantity of products to be sold in the domestic and international markets and market percentage shares.
9. Foreign exchange revenues and expenses.
10. Implementation program for the investment.
11. Number of staff, wages, labor insurance, and benefits, and
12. Other related issues.

82. What are the basic principles that review and approval authorities follow with regard to a contract and articles of association?

The basic principles for review and approval of a contract and articles of association are as follows:

1. Conformity with the PRC's laws, decrees, and regulations.
2. Conformity with the contents of the feasibility study of the project and with the approval letter.
3. Conformity with the principle of equal and mutual benefits.

83. What are the main issues that review and approval authorities examine with regard to a contract and articles of association?

The main issues to be reviewed in a contract and articles of association are as follows:

1. Legal validity, including whether the signatories are legal representatives or have a proxy by the legal representatives.
2. Omissions that should have been included and completeness of documents submitted as required.
3. Whether the terms involve government actions or bind a third party who is not a party to the contract.
4. Completion of the application and approval according to established procedures in the case of the project's falling within the areas restricted by the State for foreign investment, or calling for importing machinery and electric equipment restricted by the State, or whose products to be exported fall within export permits control.
5. Whether the scope of business is clear and specific, with strict and standard wording.
6. Terms of payment of loans between the parties.
7. Conformity of the terms on technological transfer with the State Administration Regulations on Contracts of Introducing Technologies and stipulations of the feasibility study report.
8. Procurement of equipment and raw materials, ratio of product sales in domestic and overseas markets, means of such sales, principles for pricing, and whether responsibilities are clear and specific.

9. Viability of the means of balancing foreign exchange revenues and the enterprise's expenses.
10. Salary and benefits for Chinese and foreign staff.
11. Formation and authorization of the Board of Directors, procedure for opening board meetings, and management and organizational setup.
12. Methods for resolving disputes and compensation in case of default.
13. Termination and liquidation of the enterprise and disposal of properties at liquidation.
14. Standardization and conformity of the contract and articles of association, as well as their appendixes, with the requirements of Chinese law.

84. What does the review and approval authorities' approval letter on contracts and articles of association contain?

According to requirements, the approval letter on contracts and articles of association shall not be oversimplified or abstract, and shall normally include the following information:

1. Name of the company and the parties to the contract.
2. Business scope and size of production of the enterprise.
3. Total investment amount, registered capital, percentage of loans by the parties and means of payment, and in the case of a cooperative JV enterprise, principles for profit distribution.
4. Term of business.
5. Confirmation of the list of equipment to be imported.
6. Inclusion of agreements on technological transfer, mandated management agreements, or contracted management agreements in the submitted documents for review and approval, either as attachments to the contract or as independent contracts themselves.

Although not necessary for review and approval, the contracts or agreements may refer to loans, purchase of equipment not involving technological transfer, leasing of plant houses, use of land, or sales of land.

The review and approval authorities make their decision based on the Chinese version of the documents. The signing parties are responsible for ensuring that the Chinese and foreign-language versions are identical.

85. What are the registration formalities an enterprise with foreign investment should go through after approval is granted by the Chinese Government?

An approval certificate is a legal document of the Chinese Government's approval of an enterprise with foreign investment. The enterprise may go through registration formalities with relevant government departments on the basis of the certificate.

During the stage of application for establishment, the enterprise has two steps to take in registering with the administration bodies for industry and commerce: (1) registration of the name of the enterprise upon approval by the review and approval authorities on the project proposal and (2) registration of the enterprise establishment upon approval by the review and approval authorities on the contract and articles of association.

Registration of the name of the enterprise is for the purpose of protecting the name from being duplicated or used by others.

Registration of the enterprise establishment is to be done within 30 days after approval of the contract and articles of association by the review and approval authorities, with the administrative bodies for industry and commerce in the locality of the enterprise. After checking, they issue the Business License of a Legal Corporation of the People's Republic of China. The date of issuance of the license is the date the enterprise is incorporated.

After obtaining the business license, the enterprise goes through registration formalities with such government bodies as taxation, exchange control, customs house, and the bank.

86. If there is a change in an enterprise with foreign investment in the course of implementing a contract (e.g., the address of the JV, the partner(s), the total investment amount, business scope, formation of the Board of Directors, nomination of the Board Chairman or Vice Chairman), is there a need to go through an alteration procedure and, if so, with which government agency?

Since such changes concern the contents of the agreement, contract, or articles of association already approved and the contents of the approval certificate already issued, Article 17 of the Implementing Regulations of the Law of the People's Republic of China on Chinese–Foreign Equity Joint Ventures reads: "Joint Venture Agreements, Contracts, and Articles of Association are to take effect after being approved by the examination and approval organs. The same applies in the event of amendments." For this purpose, the Ministry of Foreign Trade and Economic Cooperation reinstated on 5 October 1993 that alterations in major contents of the agreement, contract, or articles of association shall be approved by the same review and approval authorities. Upon approval, a new approval certificate shall be issued with the same serial number, and the old certificate shall be returned. Alteration registration formalities shall be completed with the same government administrative body for industry and commerce.

87. What is the application procedure if an enterprise with foreign investment needs additional investment?

When an approved enterprise with foreign investment needs additional investment (e.g., for production or operating purposes), the newly signed agreement for additional investment shall be submitted for approval by the same review and approval authorities while related formalities shall be completed. According to the requirement of the Notice of 17 December 1987 by the Ministry of Foreign Economic Relations and Trade, should the total of the additional investment and original investment exceed the authorization by the local review and approval authorities and when the additional part shall be within the same project, the newly signed agreement for additional investment shall be submitted, together with all other documents previously approved, to the Ministry of Foreign Trade and Economic Cooperation for review and approval.

88. Are branch organizations of an enterprise with foreign investment allowed to be established inside or outside China?

Enterprises with foreign investment may set up branch organizations inside or outside China according to their business needs. According to stipulations under the Implementing Regulations of the Law of the People's Republic of China on Chinese–Foreign Equity Joint Ventures, approval shall be obtained from the Ministry of Foreign Trade and Economic Cooperation for Chinese-foreign joint venture enterprises to establish branch (including sales) organizations outside China or in regions of Hong Kong or Macao. No transfer of investment in the joint ventures shall be allowed into such overseas branch organizations; and business revenues of the overseas branch organizations, when they originate in China, shall be subject to taxation in China.

In establishing branch organizations in Chinese cities other than the place of registration, enterprises with foreign investment shall apply for approval by the same review and approval authorities and proceed to relevant formalities, when approved, with local government foreign economic and trade organs and administration departments for industry and commerce in the locality of such branch organizations.

89. Can leased machines or equipment be used by a Sino–foreign JV enterprise or the Chinese or foreign investor(s) to this JV enterprise as part or whole of the registered capital of the joint venture?

Document 7 of the Ministry of Foreign Trade and Economic Cooperation of the People's Republic of China states that according to the stipulations of Article 25 of the Implementing Regulations of the Law of the People's Republic of China on Chinese–Foreign Equity Joint Ventures, "The participants in a joint-venture may use currency for capital contributions and may also use such items as buildings, factory premises, machinery, equipment or other materials, industrial property rights, proprietary technology, and rights to the use of sites, as valued, for capital contributions." However, investment made as registered capital, in kind or with industrial property rights, shall be from the possession of the investor: a lessee has only usage rights of the lease (including machines and equipment), not ownership. Therefore, no lease from a leasing firm shall be used by the JV enterprise or its Chinese or foreign investors as part or whole of the registered capital of the JV.

10.

The Organizational Structure and Management of an Enterprise With Foreign Investment

The management of an enterprise with foreign investment involves various divisions, such as personnel, finance, goods, production, supplies, and sales. Advanced means of management can be adopted in enterprises with foreign investment in accordance with common international practice and within the permitted scope according to relevant State laws and regulations.

90. What are the stipulations in Chinese laws or regulations in relation to the management structure of an enterprise with foreign investment?

Fairly detailed stipulations have been worked out by China on the management and organizational structure of Chinese–foreign equity JV enterprises, for reference also for the organization of Chinese–foreign cooperative joint ventures; no regulations are available for wholly foreign-owned enterprises in this respect. The management and organizational structure shall be designed in accordance with stipulations under Article 6 of the Law of the People's Republic of China on Chinese–Foreign Equity Joint Ventures and Chapter 5 of the Implementing Regulations of the Law of the People's Republic of China on Chinese–Foreign Equity Joint Ventures.

91. What is the procedure for setting up a JV management and organizational structure?

A management and organizational structure must be set up for equity JV enterprises. According to established procedures, the first step is to form the Board of Directors in accordance with the approved list of Board members. The Board, in conformity with the approved contract and articles of association, appoints the General Manager, Deputy General Manager(s), and other senior personnel. It also establishes the organizational structure and labor organizations, and adopts various management policies in accordance with the articles of association.

92. How is a Board of Directors established?

The Board of Directors is the highest authority of the JV enterprise. It has at least three members, who shall be distributed between the JV parties in accordance with their respective shares of the business. The Board members shall be nominated and substituted by the JV parties, and the term of office for a Board member is four years, renewable with continued authorization by the parties.

The Board shall have one Chairman and one or two Vice Chairmen. It decides on all matters of major importance to the JV, including the development program, production and business plan, budgeting, distribution of profits, payroll, and terminating the business, as well as the appointment or employment of the General Manager, Deputy General Manager(s), Chief Engineer, Chief Accountant, and Auditor, including duties and powers of and compensation for senior personnel.

Because an equity JV enterprise is a legal corporation, its legal representative is the Board Chairman. The Chairman is the top person in the organizational structure. The Chairman and Vice Chairmen shall be appointed by the JV parties after discussions and agreement or elected by the Board. When a Chinese party to the JV nominates the Chairman, other parties shall nominate the Vice Chairman or Chairmen.

The Board shall meet at least once a year, with the meeting convened and chaired by the Chairman. If the Chairman is unable to convene the meeting, he shall authorize the Vice Chairman or any other members of the Board to convene and chair the meeting on his behalf. A Board meeting can be held and a Board resolution made only when over two-thirds of the Board members participate in the meeting.

93. How is a JV's management structure set up?

The management structure of a JV enterprise is set up under the leadership of its Board of Directors, responsible for its daily management and operations. There shall be one General Manager and one (or more than one) Deputy General Manager in the structure. The General Manager is the final executor of resolutions made by the enterprise's management body, exercising duties and powers independently within the scope of authorization set out in the contract and articles of association and as authorized by the Board, to ensure normal operations of the joint venture. The Deputy General Manager(s) shall assist the General Manager in his duties.

Efficient, simple, and effective, the management structure shall have various functional departments (e.g., department of finance, production management, supply and sales, technology development, payroll). The structure of management, as well as any names involved, shall be decided by the Board of Directors.

In addition to the General Manager and Deputy General Manager(s), there shall be senior personnel in the management structure (e.g., Chief Engineer, Chief Accountant, Auditor).

94. Can a JV General Manager or Deputy General Manager be concurrently the General Manager or Deputy General Manager of another business organization?

Article 40 of the Implementing Regulations of the Law of the People's Republic of China on Chinese–Foreign Equity Joint Ventures stipulates: "The general manager and deputy general managers are to be retained by the board of directors of a joint venture. These positions may be held by Chinese citizens and may also be held by foreign citizens." The same article continues: "The general manager or deputy general managers must not concurrently act as general manager or deputy general managers of other economic organizations, and must not participate in commercial competition by other economic organizations with their own joint venture." On 5 October 1993, the PRC's Ministry of Foreign Trade and Economic Cooperation noted that expatriate General Managers of some Chinese–foreign equity joint ventures were holding the positions of General Manager and others of overseas enterprises, a violation of Chinese law, and must be stopped, since "any other economic organizations," as referred to under Article 40, means both domestic and foreign economic organizations.

95. Should a trade union be set up in an enterprise with foreign investment?

In accordance with Chapter 13 of the PRC's Implementing Regulations of the Law on Chinese–Foreign Equity Joint Ventures, employees of enterprises with foreign investment have the right to establish a grass-roots trade union and carry out trade union activities in accordance with the Law of the People's Republic of China on Trade Union, and the Constitution of Trade Union of China.

A trade union in an enterprise with foreign investment represents the employees and has the right to sign labor contracts with the enterprise on behalf of employees and to supervise the execution of those contracts.

Basic tasks of a trade union in an enterprise with foreign investment include:

- maintaining by law the democratic rights and material benefits of employees
- assisting the enterprise in the arrangement and reasonable use of welfare and bonus funds
- organizing employees in learning about the production, science and technology, techniques, and the business they are engaged in
- developing cultural and sports activities
- educating employees to abide by labor regulations and endeavor to complete the various economic tasks of the enterprise

Delegates of a trade union have the right to participate as nonvoting participants in a Board meeting in discussing such issues as the enterprise development program, production and business activities, employee incentive and disciplinary policies, the payroll system, benefits, labor protection, and insurance.

96. Can a grass-roots organization of Chinese political parties be established in an enterprise with foreign investment?

According to the Constitution of the People's Republic of China, all political parties have the right to carry out activities of all kinds in recruiting new members and setting up organizations in enterprises. The Communist

Party of China is the ruling party in China, with the largest number of party members. Therefore, it may set up an organization in any enterprise where there are three or more party members. The Party organization implements the Party's reforms and policies, plus policies for utilizing foreign investment. Also, it plays a supervisory role and helps the enterprise with foreign investment be successful because of the Party members. Regular Communist Party activities are held outside business hours. Communist Party organizations in enterprises with foreign investment, with support from the Board Chairman and General Manager, have played an active role in meeting the tasks and economic goals set for the enterprise.

97. What are the regulations on labor and personnel management in an enterprise with foreign investment?

Labor and personnel management in an enterprise with foreign investment shall be in accordance with the Regulations of the People's Republic of China on Labor Management in Chinese–Foreign Equity Joint Ventures. The Board of Directors has the right to determine the enterprise's labor program, submitting it to the government department in charge of the enterprise and the government's labor and personnel department. The enterprise also has the power to employ, dismiss, or discharge staff and to determine staff salaries, forms of payroll, incentives and benefits, disciplinary policies, and so forth. In short, enterprises with foreign investment enjoy full autonomy in personnel management, which serves as a great impetus to establishing a scientific system of administrating personnel and labor affairs and stimulating employee enthusiasm.

A strict personnel management system shall be established in enterprises with foreign investment, with policies on the use of personnel, employee training, staff performance appraisal, payroll, labor and welfare, and labor protection.

The labor contract system shall be fully implemented in enterprises with foreign investment; all staff, senior personnel and ordinary workers alike, sign a labor contract with the enterprise.

98. What are the regulations on financial management in an enterprise with foreign investment?

Financial management in an enterprise with foreign investment shall be done in accordance with relevant stipulations under such laws, decrees, and regulations as the General Financial Rules for Enterprises, Financial Systems for Subsector Enterprises, and the Accounting Regulations of the People's Republic of China for foreign-funded enterprises, while business characteristics and management requirements of the enterprise shall be incorporated. Financial management systems shall be established in enterprises with foreign investment that address the following issues:

- adoption of reasonable, scientific, and orderly management methods
- a financial management system with clearly defined powers and responsibilities of the functional departments in the area of financial management and effective controls
- procedures for preparing budgets and final accounts
- cost management and control systems
- systems for analyzing and reflecting the implementation of the enterprise's budgets and financial revenues and expenses programs
- systems for payment of all taxes and other proceeds according to State regulations, distribution of after-tax profits, and so forth

An accounting system shall be established in an equity JV enterprise. According to the Accounting Regulations of the People's Republic of China for Foreign-Funded Enterprises, an equity JV shall establish an independent accounting section for financial and accounting activities of the enterprise, doing its accounting in accordance with China's laws and regulations.

An equity JV is different from a State-owned enterprise in the accounting system and method of bookkeeping used: the internationally practiced accrual system and the debit credit bookkeeping method. All accounting records (vouchers, books, statements, etc.) shall be kept based on actual business, with formalities and documents complete, and bookkeeping accurate and done in time. Enterprises with foreign investment may refer to the standard financial and accounting systems adopted by the Ministry of Finance and work out their own system for finance and accounting, incorporating the actual situations of their enterprises, submitting such a system for file with the finance department and taxation authorities of the local government.

99. According to regulations, what currency should be used as the accounting unit in an enterprise with foreign investment?

According to the Implementing Regulations of the Law of the People's Republic of China on Chinese–Foreign Equity Joint Ventures, equity JV should use RMB as the standard money for bookkeeping; a convertible foreign currency may also be used as the standard money, with the agreement of all parties to the joint venture, but it shall be the same currency as the one used for business registration.

In addition to keeping books in the standard currency, accounts of cash, bank deposits, various documents, receipts or expenditures in other currencies, accounts receivable and payable, proceeds, and expenses shall also be recorded in the currency or currencies in which these receipts or expenses have actually occurred.

Enterprises with foreign investment that use a foreign currency in bookkeeping shall prepare a separate set of accounting statements in RMB converted from the foreign currency, in addition to accounting statements in the foreign currency.

Figures shall be taken for profit or loss accounts of the year in the case of gains or losses arising from fluctuations in exchange rates in bookkeeping; no adjustment shall be made for book balance in foreign currencies because of the exchange rate fluctuation in bookkeeping.

100. What fiscal year system should be applied in an enterprise with foreign investment, and what are the requirements for submitting accounting statements?

The calendar year system shall be applied for the fiscal year of equity JV enterprises, staring on 1 January and ending on 31 December of the Gregorian calendar.

An equity JV is to submit accounting statements on a quarterly and yearly basis to the government department in charge of the enterprise, local taxation authorities, and all parties to the JV, with all copies sent to the foreign investment administrative bodies of both the local government and the State. Annual accounting statements are valid only after they are verified by an accountant registered in China and with a verification certificate.

101. How are the three funds in a JV—the reserve, development, and staff incentive and welfare fund—to be drawn and used?

Enterprises with foreign investment shall draw on profits after paying income tax, according to the Income Tax Law of the People's Republic of China for Enterprises with Foreign Investment, for the reserve fund, the employee incentive and welfare fund, and the enterprise development fund, with the percentages to be determined by the Board of Directors, though normally within a range of 15% of the profits.

The *reserve fund* is for making up for losses of the enterprise and may be used to increase capital and expand production, after approval by the review and approval authorities; the *development fund* is for purchasing fixed assets, increasing working capital, and expanding production size; and the *staff incentive and welfare fund* is not to be used for any purposes other than the self-explanatory ones.

102. How are JV profits to be distributed?

According to the Income Tax Law of the People's Republic of China for Enterprises with Foreign Investment, the remaining profits of an equity JV enterprise, after the income tax and "three funds," are allowed for distribution to the parties to the JV in proportion to their respective shares of the registered capital, subject to the following: (1) the Board of Directors determines profits to be distributed for the year; (2) no profits for the year shall be distributed before losses of the previous year(s) are fully made up for; and (3) profits of the previous years not distributed can be added into profits of the year for distribution.

103. Is there sufficient autonomy in an enterprise with foreign investment for its manufacturing and other activities?

Within the confines of China's laws, decrees, and related regulations, as well as of the agreement, contract, and articles of association of the JV company, an enterprise with foreign investment has the right to make independent management and other operating decisions. The State and the government department in charge of the enterprise (the government body in charge of the Chinese partner to the joint venture or in charge of the business) are obligated to provide such JVs with guidance, assistance, and supervision, but without interference. The enterprise has the right to compile its own manufacturing and other operating plans, raise and use funds for purchase of means of production, and sell products.

104. Should the production and operating plan of an enterprise with foreign investment dovetail with the State's planning?

The production and operating plan of an enterprise shall be filed with the government department in charge of it, and it shall be coordinated with State plans, mainly through signing economic contracts. For example, for matters like the supply of water, electricity, and gas; the supply of raw materials and sales of products controlled by the State; and importing or exporting commodities under quota or permit control, contracts must be signed with relevant departments of the State. In this way, enterprises with foreign investment conduct their manufacturing and other activities in accordance with the State's central planning so that it can obtain necessary support and assistance from relevant government departments. This coordination will be beneficial to the development of the enterprise.

105. What are the State regulations regarding the procurement and sales activities of an enterprise with foreign investment?

Enterprises with foreign investment shall give priority to domestic Chinese markets in purchasing needed raw materials, fuel, and supplementary parts and may also directly purchase from overseas markets with their own foreign exchange, provided that the purchasing prices for these imported materials are not higher than those of commodities of the same type in the overseas markets at the time. Enterprises with foreign investment are strictly forbidden to import commodities not for self-use but for resale in domestic Chinese markets.

Enterprises with foreign investment are encouraged to sell their products outside China, so special preferential policies are in place for the establishment of exporting enterprises. Exporting products may be sold in the international market directly by the JV enterprise, by a related organization authorized by the JV, or through a foreign trade organization of China. The JV determines the price of its own products for export, but it shall also accept the coordination by the Council of Commerce for Exports and by the China Association of Enterprises with Foreign Investment, with the price of exporting products not unreasonably lower. According to regulations, enterprises with foreign investment are strictly forbidden to purchase products for export without approval.

Products manufactured by enterprises with foreign investment may also be sold in the domestic Chinese market, with the ratio of domestic and overseas sales to be determined by the investor and relevant government departments according to the characteristics of such products or in accordance with the percentage determined by the review and approval authorities. Under certain conditions, China may give some shares of the domestic market for products manufactured by enterprises with foreign investment, increasing the percentage for domestic sales, in order to introduce advanced foreign technologies more effectively. Although such enterprises have the right to determine the price of products to be sold domestically, they shall submit pricing documents for file with the government department in charge of the enterprise and with government pricing administration bodies, accepting in the meantime the supervision and coordination of the pricing administration bodies.

106. Is an enterprise with foreign investment subject to quota or license control in its import and export business?

The establishment of quota and license systems is an important measure taken to standardize the import and export activities of enterprises and foreign trade. Some quotas are determined by foreign governments as a restrictive measure to control Chinese commodities imported into their countries, which we refer to as *passive quotas*. Therefore, enterprises are to participate in tendering when their exporting products fall within the scope for quota bidding.

In accordance with stipulations under Article 63 of the Implementing Regulations of the Law of the People's Republic of China on Chinese–Foreign Equity Joint Ventures, equity JV enterprises shall work out their annual plans for importing materials (machinery and equipment, parts and accessories, raw materials, and fuels, etc.) and exporting their own products, if such materials or products to be imported or exported require import or export licenses according to State regulations. Then they shall submit such plans for review by local economic and trade departments and approval by the Ministry of Foreign Trade and Economic Cooperation. Review and approval will be done twice a year. Foreign investors may also directly apply for and obtain an import license by presenting approval documents from the review and approval authorities for machinery and equipment or any other materials to be imported as their investment.

11.

Resolving Disputes in the Course of a JV's Business Operations

107. What are the ways of resolving disputes?

In case of disputes arising from the agreement, contract, or articles of association, concerned parties to the equity JV shall apply principles and methods set out in the contract and articles of association to resolve differences. There are four major ways of resolving disputes: consultation, conciliation, arbitration, and lawsuit.

108. How is consultation done?

Concerned parties shall first resort to consultation among themselves in case of disputes. The Board of Directors shall undertake coordination and conduct primary conciliation, based on each party's comments and requests. In the spirit of mutual understanding, accommodation, benefits, and development, the disputing parties shall spare no efforts in seeking a way, acceptable to all parties, to resolve disputes within the range of the Board of Directors.

Direct discussions between the concerned parties are the best means of resolving disputes, with no party hurt and harmony maintained, to the benefit of the enterprise's long-term future.

109. How is conciliation done?

If there are large differences between the disputing parties and the issues are complex, consultation may not work. In this situation, the parties may bring the case for conciliation, usually by an arbitration organization or an authoritative third party accepted by all parties.

Years of experience show that conciliation by the original review and approval authorities or by the government department in charge of the enterprise, upon request by the disputing parties, typically brings about positive results. Since the review and approval authorities or the government department are clear about the actual situation of the enterprise, resolution of disputes has proved easier by this informal means of conciliation. When the disputes are presented to an arbitration organization for conciliation, a conciliator shall look into the facts, define the responsibilities of the parties concerned, distinguish rights and wrongs, and promote mutual understanding and accommodation, leading to a voluntary restoration of good relations in a fair and reasonable manner, with a signed agreement of conciliation. On the basis of this agreement, the conciliator shall work out a conciliation letter and close the case, announcing success of the conciliation and resolution of disputes.

The Beijing Conciliation Center is the only conciliation organization in China involving foreign interests. Disputing parties can apply for conciliation by the Center only when a written agreement of conciliation has been signed. The Center has signed with Germany the Beijing-Hamburg Rules for Conciliation, resorting to "united conciliation," which can be done in Beijing or Hamburg, or another location agreed on by the disputing parties and the conciliator. In addition, application can be made for conciliation by the Arbitration Committee of the China Council for the Promotion of International Trade or the China Maritime Arbitration Committee.

Conciliation is not a compulsory stage for arbitration; it is only a means of mediation. Conciliation shall cease at any time when any of the parties so requests, the conciliation has taken too much time, conciliation no longer seems possible, or any of the parties is unwilling to accept conciliation. In such cases, conciliation shall immediately give way to arbitration, according to established procedures.

110. How is arbitration done?

Arbitration is a process of investigation, by a neutral organization (mainly an arbitration organization) agreed on by the parties concerned, that leads to judgment and adjudication. As a quasi-legal procedure, arbitration is both strict and standard. Many other countries have accepted the legal status of arbitration in resolving disputes. An arbitration organization involving foreign interests was established in China as early as the 1950s, with arbitration rules adopted; it developed a reputation for fair and reasonable conciliation and arbitration in resolving disputes. China is now second in the world in conciliation and arbitration.

Before applying for arbitration, decisions shall be made on the choice of an arbitration organization, an arbitration procedure, rules of arbitration, applicable laws, and working languages, and the relevant regulations of the arbitration organization selected shall be followed.

Arbitration Process

Arbitration must be done strictly in accordance with the established procedure, which mainly consists of the following steps:

1. Submission of application to the arbitration organization.
2. Submission of documents, including statements of the appealing party's opinions as well as written material and audio or visual testimony.
3. Appointment of an arbitrator from a list of arbitrators, who is trusted and experienced, or authorization of the Chairman of the arbitration organization to appoint an arbitrator.
4. Advance payment of arbitration fees.
5. Open or closed trial by the arbitration organization according to its rules of arbitration.
6. Statements by the appealing party and argument by the accused party in accordance with the rules.
7. Close of the hearing and announcement of final adjudication, with neither party permitted to lodge an appeal with any other arbitration organization for a different adjudication or to bring the case to court. The parties concerned are to execute the adjudication as announced.

Arbitration Execution

In general, it is comparatively easier to request an enforced execution of an adjudication of an arbitration organization by the court of the country where the organization is located. If a law court of the home country is to execute an adjudication made by a foreign arbitration organization, the execution might confront difficulties as the interests of the concerned party of the home country, or even the interests of the home country, might get involved. Some countries have requested the application of "mutually beneficial" or "equal" principles in execution of a foreign adjudication, or have imposed restrictions—for instance, by stipulating that execution of a foreign adjudication shall not be in violation of the "public order" of the country.

Arbitration for an enterprise with foreign investment shall be done in China, as this is where the enterprise is located. Generally unless there are special reasons or conditions, arbitration shall not be done by a foreign arbitration organization. In case of absolute necessity, caution shall be taken if the decision is made to resort to arbitration by a foreign organization, with a prior, thorough understanding of the implications, to avoid difficulties in the execution of the adjudication in the future.

In addition, China in 1992 joined the Washington Convention, or Convention on Resolving Investment Disputes Between the Country and Foreign Nationals, under which, in case of disputes between the investor of one country and the government of another country that is introducing foreign investment, application can be made for arbitration to be done by the International Center for Resolving Investment Disputes. Since foreign investment in China now comes from over 120 countries and regions, this convention has provided a means for resolving disputes.

China has also joined the New York Treaty of 1958, or Treaty on Recognition and Execution of Foreign Arbitration Adjudication, which means that an adjudication made by an arbitration organization in China is to be recognized and executed in over 80 member countries to the treaty. In practice, however, the party concerned is advised to seek the assistance of an experienced lawyer from the place of execution to handle related matters of application for such recognition and execution.

In case of adjudication by a foreign arbitration organization to be recognized and executed by a Chinese court, so will it be done, as long as the adjudication is fair and not contrary to the laws of China, according to international treaties China has entered into or joined, or in the principle of mutual benefit.

Adoption to the means of arbitration has many advantages: arbitration is more timely; the adjudication is final and so is executed immediately with no need to obtain approval from supervising or other bodies; the arbitrator is appointed or selected by the parties concerned; the trial can be open or not; an arbitration procedure is flexible; and the cost of arbitration is lower than the cost of a lawsuit.

China has approved the incorporation of over 200,000 enterprises with foreign investment. Almost all disputes are resolved by means of arbitration, and almost all such cases are tried in China.

111. How is a lawsuit applied?

A lawsuit in this case means a suit lodged by one disputing party with a law court. As long as there is no written agreement on arbitration, any disputing party has the right to lodge a suit with a law court according to judicial procedures.

Although any disputing party has the right to lodge a suit with a law court, this method of resolving disputes takes a long time, easily leads to a breakup of relationships, and results in added difficulties for the future cooperation between the parties or for the management of the enterprise. Therefore, for ordinary disputes, most people have resorted to arbitration, not lawsuits.

12.

Terminating an Enterprise With Foreign Investment

112. Under what circumstances can an enterprise with foreign investment be terminated?

Enterprises with foreign investment can be terminated when their term of business (including an extended term) ends or when a stipulated condition for termination occurs. Termination here usually means the end of the contract or articles of association; the enterprise still exists, whether it has its shares transferred, or is put up for sale, or is liquidated. Along with the end of the contract and articles of association, the original enterprise with foreign investment is canceled, ownership transferred, a new mode comes in place, and a new set of laws or a new type of an economic contract signed by parties concerned will properly transfer and handle the rights in production, finance, and personnel or the original enterprise.

The concerned parties shall strictly follow Chinese law regarding procedures for termination, liquidation, and disbandment. In the spirit of "good alliance with good parting," the parties shall work with each other to ensure a good finish. In the course of liquidation of the enterprise, the parties are to maintain the safety of the properties of the enterprise, prevent any loss of such properties, and maintain the legitimate rights of the interests of the investors, creditors, debtors, and other parties to the enterprise.

113. Under what conditions can an enterprise with foreign investment be terminated?

An enterprise with foreign investment shall be terminated if any of the following occurs:

1. The agreed term of business has come to an end, or stipulated conditions for termination have occurred.
2. The enterprise cannot continue its business operations due to poor management and operation and serious losses, and the investors decide to disband it.
3. Any investor or party does not perform its obligations as stipulated in the enterprise's agreement, contract, or articles of association, resulting in the inability of the enterprise to continue operation.
4. Inability of continued operation is caused by serious losses due to force majeure factors, such as a natural disaster or war.
5. The enterprise becomes bankrupt.
6. The enterprise is canceled because its activities violate China's laws or regulations or cause harm to social and public interests.
7. Other incidents stipulated in the contract and articles of association for disbandment have occurred.

114. How are termination and liquidation of an enterprise with foreign investment conducted?

When conditions occur for the termination of the enterprise, the Board of Directors shall submit an application to the review and approval authorities for verification. The date of verification by these authorities shall be the date of termination of the enterprise. No matter what has caused such termination, the enterprise shall, within 15 days after the date of termination, make a public announcement in newspapers, radios, or other media and inform all creditors and debtors that the enterprise has gone into the termination and liquidation stage. In the meantime, the enterprise shall propose procedures and principles for liquidation, as well as form the liquidation committee according to China's laws and regulations. The liquidation committee shall consist of the legal representative of the enterprise, the representative of creditors, and the representative of the government department in charge of the enterprise, and it shall invite the participation of accountants and lawyers registered in China. The enterprise shall also submit its liquidation plan and other related documents to the government department in charge of the business for verification and supervision.

115. How is the aftermath taken care of?

At termination, the liquidation shall be done in accordance with Chinese laws and regulations, or the ownership of the properties of the enterprise shall be determined according to the agreement reached in the contract or articles of association.

Before the end of liquidation, no investor shall for any reason transfer or remit to take outside China the funds of the enterprise, nor shall any investor dispose of properties of the enterprise without authorization.

After liquidation, the part of the enterprise's net assets or remaining assets exceeding the registered capital shall be regarded as profits gained in China and therefore are subject to income tax according to Chinese laws.

After liquidation, formalities shall be completed with the government administration office for industry and commerce for cancellation of registration, and the business license of the enterprise shall be returned.

When the enterprise is disbanded, no accounting books or documents or any other related materials shall be destroyed, transferred, or lost. They shall be kept by the Chinese party for a period of not less than 10 years.

13.

Administration of Foreign Investment by the Chinese Government

116. What are the basic principles of the administration of foreign investment?

Under the socialist market economy system, the State administers enterprises with foreign investment according to the law of market economy. As a legal entity, a foreign-invested enterprise, once examined and approved by relevant government departments and registered with the industrial and commercial administration, operates autonomously and assumes sole responsibility for its profits and losses. Between the government and foreign-invested enterprises, no relationship of administrative subordination exists. The government directs and supervises the production management of foreign-invested enterprises in accordance with the laws and stipulations and policies.

117. What administrative system does the State take in the administration of foreign investment?

The State practices the system of administration at different levels regarding foreign-invested enterprises. The State Council and its various functional departments, in line with relevant laws and the State's general principles of opening up, deliberate and formulate national policies of utilizing foreign capital and give guidance to local governments and their departments in relation to their utilization of foreign capital. Relevant examination and approval authorities are responsible for examining and approving major projects with quotas and some projects under State restriction in utilizing foreign capital. Under the direction of the State Council and its functional departments, various provinces, autonomous regions, municipalities directly under the Central Government, and cities under separate planning take charge of the examination and approval and administration of the utilization of foreign capital in their own areas. In accordance with their own characteristics, various places adopt different managing patterns of different levels, and the cities, districts, and counties under their jurisdiction assume the responsibility for examining and approving the utilization of foreign capital and its administration in their own places.

118. What are the major State bodies responsible for administering foreign investment?

With a view to strengthening the administrative work of foreign investment, the State Council in May 1994 set up the National Leading Group in charge of the work of foreign investment. This group organizes relevant departments to study the major problems in utilizing foreign capital, coordinates policies concerning foreign capital utilization, and directs the work of utilizing foreign capital in China.

Under the leadership of a Vice Premier responsible for utilizing foreign capital, the major state bodies responsible for administering foreign investment are the following:

State Planning Commission
State Economy and Trade Commission
Office of Special Economic Zones, under the State Council
Ministry of Foreign Trade and Economic Cooperation
Ministry of Finance
People's Bank of China
Ministry of Personnel
Ministry of Labor
State General Administration of Tax
State Administration Bureau for Industry and Commerce
State Administration of Foreign Exchange Control
State Land Administration
Bureau of Legislative Affairs, under the State Council
Bank of China
General Administration of Customs
State Import and Export Commodity Inspection Bureau

119. What are the main parts of the government's administration of foreign investment?

The main parts of administering foreign investment are as follows:

1. Administering the examination and approval of foreign-invested projects. According to relevant laws, the establishment of a foreign-invested enterprise shall be examined and approved by relevant departments and its registration examined and approved by the industrial and commercial authorities. No unapproved foreign-invested projects shall be granted legal status. To hasten the procedure of examining and approving foreign-invested projects, the State has lowered the limits of power of examination and approval. Except for a few major projects and projects under special management, most projects can be examined and approved by local authorities.

2. Supervising according to laws the production and operating activities of foreign-invested enterprises. According to law, various government departments supervise the implementation of contracts and production and operating activities of foreign-invested enterprises. Supervision is also enforced so that these enterprises subscribe to the timely capital contribution, operate by law, and protect the lawful rights and interests of staff and workers.

3. Providing services for the construction and production and operating activities of foreign-invested enterprises already established and helping them to solve problems stemming from construction and production and management. In the initial stage of development of a socialist market economy in China, the provision of services to foreign-invested enterprises rendered by relevant government departments, the China Association for Enterprises with Foreign Investment, and the subassociations throughout the country is indispensable for guaranteeing the healthy development of foreign-invested enterprises.

14.

Taxation

120. How is foreign tax revenue collected by the State tax authorities involving foreign-invested enterprises administered?

Currently in China, tax collection involving foreign investment and that involving domestic investment is basically identical, mainly including:

- *Tax registration.* An enterprise shall, by tax law, register with the local tax authorities with relevant documents within 30 days after it obtains business license.
- *Account books and vouchers.* An enterprise shall set up its accounting vouchers and books in order to calculate its taxable revenue and its income.
- *Tax declaration.* An enterprise shall, within the time limit of filing stipulated by laws and rules and regulations, file its tax returns, financial accounting statements, and other documents.
- *Tax payment collection.* The tax-gathering methods imposed on enterprises by tax authorities are worked out in the light of their conditions and in accordance with their size, management level, and financial base.
- *Invoice administration.* This includes the administration of general invoices and special invoices.
- *Tax examination.* This includes the implementation of the State's tax laws and decrees by enterprises, their observance of the financial and accounting systems and laws and regulations pertaining to finance and economy, and their production and operating activities and economic accounting.
- *Legal liabilities.*
- *Handling of tax disputes.*

121. What taxes does the Chinese government collect from foreign-invested enterprises?

In accordance with the stipulations of the Chinese government, the following tax categories are applicable to foreign-invested enterprises:

- Value-added tax
- Consumption tax
- Business tax
- Income tax for foreign-invested enterprises and wholly foreign-owned enterprises
- Increment tax on land value
- Resources tax
- Stamp duty
- Tax on slaughtered animals
- Urban real estate tax
- Driver's license tax on vehicles and boats
- Contract Tax

Customs duty is levied on goods that enter and exit China, and an income tax is imposed on individuals.

122. What are the income tax rates for foreign-invested enterprises? How are they computed?

According to the stipulations of the Income Tax Law of the People's Republic of China for Enterprises with Foreign Investment and Foreign Enterprises, the rate on the taxable income of such enterprises shall be 30%, and a local income tax shall be computed on the taxable income at the rate of 3%.

The taxable income is computed in accordance with the amount remaining from the gross income in a tax year of an establishment or a place set up in China by a foreign-invested enterprise to engage in production or business operations after the deductible costs, expenses, and losses.

123. What are the regulations concerning reduction of or exemption from income tax?

To guide foreign investment in China in accordance with the country's strategic distribution of opening up from the coastal areas and gradually moving to the inland areas and the industrial policies and key points of encouraging foreign investment, the income tax on foreign-invested enterprises is levied through the means of dividing into different regions and layers and with emphasis, and preferential treatments are adopted accordingly:

1. *Income tax imposed by deducting the tax rate in a number of limited regions and industrial projects.* In order to conform to the country's strategic distribution of opening up, facilitate opening up first in the coastal areas, and promote the speedy development of key projects, reduced tax rates of 15% and 24%, respectively, are given to some regions and the key invested projects encouraged by the State. The 15% deductible tax rate mainly covers:

- foreign-invested enterprises set up in the special economic zones
- productive foreign-invested enterprises set up in the economic and technological development zones and bonded areas
- foreign-invested enterprises confirmed as new- and high-technology enterprises set up in the national high- and new-technology industrial development zones
- Chinese-foreign joint ventures engaged in the construction of ports and harbors
- foreign banks and Chinese-foreign joint banks with invested capital or allocated operating funds by foreign investors of over US$10 million and with a business period of 10 years and more
- the technology-intensive and knowledge-intensive projects approved by the State General Administration of Tax—projects with a foreign investment of over US$30 million and a long time period for recovery of investment and projects in energy, transportation, and port construction

Those enjoying a 24% deductible tax rate refer to the foreign-invested productive enterprises set up in the coastal open areas and open cities and provincial (autonomous regional) capitals along the coasts, rivers and borders, and enterprises in the tourist and holiday resort areas.

2. *Reduction of or exemption from income tax for a fixed period for limited trades and projects.* To encourage foreign investment and give priority to certain regions and industries, reduction of or exemption from income tax for a fixed period for foreign-invested enterprises is offered selectively.

Enterprises operating for a period of 10 years or more, exempted from income tax in the first profit-making year and allowed a 50% reduction of income tax in the following two years, fall into two groups: one referring to foreign-invested enterprises set up in the special economic zones engaged in the service trades with an excess of US$5 million of foreign investment, the other referring to foreign banks, Chinese-foreign joint banks, and other financial institutions set up in the special economic zones and other regions approved by the State Council with an excess of US$10 million of invested capital or allocated operating funds by foreign investors.

Foreign-invested productive enterprises operating for a period of 10 years or more shall be exempted from income tax in the first two profit-making years and allowed a 50% reduction of income tax in the following three years.

Those exempted from income tax in the first five profit-making years and allowed a 50% reduction of income tax for the following five years include Chinese-foreign joint venture enterprises engaged in the construction of ports and harbors and operating for a period of 15 years or more; foreign-invested enterprises set up in the Hainan Special Economic Zone and engaged in such infrastructure projects as airport, seaport, harbor, railway, highway, power station, coal mine, and water conservancy or in agricultural development and management operating for a period of 15 years or more; and foreign-invested enterprises set up in the Shanghai Pudong New Area engaged in airport, seaport, railway, highway, power station, and other energy and transport construction projects.

Enterprises with foreign investment producing export products may be allowed a 50% reduction of the income tax following the expiration of the period of exemption and reductions specified in the tax law if the value of export products of that year exceeds 70% of the output value of the same year. Foreign-invested enterprises engaged in agriculture, forestry, or animal husbandry or set up in remote, economically underdeveloped regions may be allowed a 15% to 30% reduction of the income tax for another 10 years following the expiration of the specified period of exemption and reduction.

3. *Tax refunded for reinvestment.* In order to encourage capital investment, foreign investors who reinvest in China their profits obtained from foreign-invested enterprises shall be refunded the income tax in either of two ways. They may be refunded 40% of the income tax already paid on the reinvested portion that was, by increasing registered capital, directly reinvested in the profit-allocating enterprises, or directly using the profits as capital for investment in another newly established foreign-invested enterprise. Or they may be refunded all the income tax already paid on the

reinvested portion if they reinvest in setting up or expanding enterprises producing export products or with advanced technology, or directly invest in the infrastructure and agricultural development projects in the Hainan Special Economic Zone with the profits obtained from the enterprises set up within the zone. There are limited conditions for the refund of income tax for reinvestment: The reinvestment must be part or all of the profits obtained from the foreign-invested enterprises after paying the income tax; the reinvestment must be used directly to increase the registered capital of their own enterprises or as capital for investment in opening another foreign-invested enterprise; refund of income tax must be handled at the tax authorities in the original taxpaying place within one year from the day when the reinvestment capital is actually put in; or the reinvested enterprises must operate for a period of not less than five years.

4. *Reduction of or exemption from income tax on the investment returns under limited scope and conditions.* Many tax preferences are specified in China's tax law concerning foreign investors' indirect investment by providing funds and technology. Mainly they are that foreign investors are exempted from income tax on the profits (dividends and bonuses) obtained from the enterprises they invested in; they are exempted from paying income tax on the interest on loans provided by international financial institutions to the Chinese government and national banks and on interest on governmental loans; and a 10% reduction in the income tax is allowed on the royalties obtained by foreign investors in providing proprietary technology for China to develop production in agriculture and animal husbandry, develop and save energy, develop transportation, prevent or remedy environmental pollution, and develop major technical field. Exemption from income tax may be rendered for those with advanced techniques and favorable conditions.

5. *Reduction of or exemption from local income tax.* The exemption from or reduction of local income tax on trades and projects encouraged by the State for foreign investment shall be decided by the people's governments or provinces, autonomous regions, and municipalities directly under the Central Government in accordance with the local conditions.

124. Under what conditions is the value-added tax levied? What are the tax rates? How is the tax amount computed?

Any unit or individual (hereafter referred to as the taxpayer) who sells goods or provides processing, fixing, and repair services as well as imports goods shall pay value-added tax according to the regulations.

The value-added tax rates are as follows:

1. A taxpayer shall pay a value-added tax at the rate of 13% in the case of sales or import of any of the following goods:
   (a) food grain and edible oil
   (b) running water, warm air, cool air, hot water, gas, liquefied petroleum gas, methane, and civil coal products
   (c) books, newspapers, and magazines
   (d) fodder, chemical fertilizer, pesticides, farm tools, and agricultural films
   (e) other goods specified by the State Council.
   Except for the above-mentioned goods, other goods sold or imported shall be levied a value-added tax at the rate of 17%.
2. The goods exported by a taxpayer pay no value-added tax except for those goods specified separately by the State Council.
3. A 17% value-added tax is imposed on processing, fixing, and repairing services provided by taxpayers. The formula for calculating payable tax is:

$$\text{Payable tax} = \text{Current sales tax amount} - \text{current income tax amount}$$

$$\text{Sales tax} = \text{Sales volume} \times \text{tax rate}$$

The formula for calculating payable tax on imported goods is:

$$\text{Payable tax} = (\text{customs price} + \text{customs duties} + \text{consumption tax}) \times \text{tax rate}$$

125. Under what conditions is a business tax levied? What is the tax rate? How is the tax amount payable computed?

Any unit or individual who provides within the PRC labor services (including transportation, construction, banking and insurance, postal and telecommunications, cultural and sports, entertainment and service trades), transfers intangible assets, or sells real estate shall pay business tax according to stipulations.

The tax rates of business tax are:

Taxable Items	Incidence of taxation	Rates
Communications and transportation	Land, water and air transportation, pipeline transport and load-and-unload transport	3%
Construction	Construction, installation, repair, decoration, and other engineering operations	3%
Banking and insurance		5%
Posts and telecommunications		3%
Culture and sports		3%
Entertainment	Music hall, ballroom, karaoke song and dance hall, music teahouse, billiards, golf, bowling and amusement	5%-20%
Services	Agency, hotel, food and drinks, tourism, warehouse, leasing, advertising and other services	5%
Transfer of intangible assets	Transfer of land use right, patent right, nonproprietary right, trademark right, copyright, and goodwill	5%
Sale of real estate	Sale of buildings and other land appurtenances	5%

The formula for calculating the amount payable is:

Payable tax = Turnover $\times$ tax rate

Turnover means all the costs and other charges a taxpayer receives from clients in providing taxable labor service, transferring intangible assets, or selling real estate; with the following exceptions:

- If a transport enterprise undertakes to ship passengers or cargo out of the PRC and outside the borders has other transport enterprise(s) carry them, the turnover is the balance of the through freight minus the fares for the carriers.
- If a tourist enterprise organizes a tourist group for a tour outside the PRC and the group is taken over by other tourist enterprise(s)

outside the borders, the turnover is the balance of the through rates minus the fares for the take-over tourist enterprise(s).

- If an overall construction contractor subcontracts the project to others, the turnover is the balance of the full amount of the contract minus the cost paid to the subcontractors.
- Enlending. The turnover is the balance of the loan interest minus the lending interest.
- Foreign exchange, negotiable securities, and futures trading business. The turnover is the balance of the selling price minus the purchasing price.

126. On what consumer goods is a consumption tax levied? What are the tax rates? How is the tax amount payable computed?

Any unit or individual that undertakes production, consignment manufacturing, and importation of the following consumer goods shall pay the consumption tax:

Taxable Items	Incidence of Taxation	Unit	Rates
1. Tobacco a. class A cigarettes	including various kinds of imported cigarettes		45%
b. class B cigarettes			40%
c. cigars			40%
d. cut tobacco			30%
2. Wine and alcohol			
a. grain white, spirit			25%
b. tuber crop white spirit			15%
c. yellow rice wine		ton	RMB 240 yuan
d. beer		ton	RMB 220 yuan
e. other wines			10%
f. alcohol			5%
3. Cosmetics			30%
4. Skin and hair care articles			17%
5. Valuable jewels, pearls, and gems	including various kinds of gold, silver, jewels, pearls, ornaments, and gems		10%

6. Firecrackers and fireworks		15%
7. Gasoline	liter	RMB 0.2 yuan
8. Diesel oil	liter	RMB 0.1 yuan
9. Automobile tire		10%
10. Motorcycle		10%
11. Sedan car		
a. cylinder capacity (exhaustion, the same below) of over 2200 liters		8%
cylinder capacity of 1000–2200 liters		5%
cylinder capacity under 1000 liters		3%
b. cross-country vehicle (4WD): cylinder capacity of over 2400 liters		5%
cylinder capacity under 2400 liters		3%
c. minibus (van) with 22 seats or less: cylinder capacity of over 2000 liters		5%
cylinder capacity under 2000 liters		3%

127. Under what conditions is the resource tax levied? What is the tax rate?

Any unit or individual in the PRC who undertakes to exploit crude oil, natural gas, coal, other nonmetal raw ores, ferrous metal raw ores, or nonferrous metal raw ores or produce salt shall pay a resource tax in accordance with the stipulations.

A fixed rate is applied to the resource tax, as follows:

Crude oil: RMB 8–30 yuan
Natural gas: RMB 2–15 yuan per 1,000 cubic meters
Coal: RMB 0.3–5 yuan
Other nonmetal raw ores: RMB 0.5–20 yuan per ton
Ferrous metal raw ores: RMB 2–30 yuan per ton
Nonferrous metal raw ores: RMB 0.4–30 yuan per ton
Salt: solid salt, 10–60 yuan per ton; liquid salt, RMB 2–10 yuan

128. Under what conditions is the increment tax on land value levied? What is the tax rate?

Any unit or individual in the PRC who undertakes to transfer land use rights and the buildings and their appurtenances (hereafter referred to as transferring real estate) and receives revenue shall pay the increment tax on land value in line with the stipulations.

The formula for calculating the increment tax is:

Increment tax = Revenue for selling real estate − payment paid for obtaining land use right − cost for land developing − cost of the buildings on ground and relevant charges − sales tax

The increment tax on land value is computed at four progressive rates levied on income in excess of specified amounts:

1. If the increment amount is not more than 50% of the amount of the deductible items, the tax rate is 30%.
2. If the increment amount is more than 50% but not more than 100% of the amount of the deductible items, the tax rate is 40%.
3. If the increment amount is more than 100% but not more than 200% of the amount of deductible items, the tax rate is 50%.
4. If the increment amount is more than 200% of the amount of the deductible items, the tax rate is 60%.

129. Under what conditions is the individual income tax levied? What are the tax rates?

All individuals with a residence or without a residence but residing for one year or more in the PRC shall pay the individual income tax on their income gained within or outside China in accordance with the law.

An individual without a residence and not residing in the PRC or an individual without a residence but residing in China for less than one year shall pay the individual income tax on the income gained within China according to the law.

The Chinese government allows a taxpayer to deduct the income tax amount paid outside the territory from the taxable amount on the income gained from outside China, but the deduction shall not exceed the taxable amount on the income gained by the taxpayer outside China, computed according to stipulations of the Chinese government.

For income from wages and salaries, the taxable amount is the balance after the deduction of RMB 800 yuan for expenses.

For income from wages and salaries of foreign personnel and overseas Chinese and compatriots from Hong Kong, Macao, and Taiwan working in foreign-invested enterprises and foreign enterprises in China, a monthly deduction of RMB 4,000 yuan shall be allowed for expenses; the remainder is the taxable amount.

The income tax rates on individuals' wages and salaries are computed by a nine-label progressive tax rate, from a minimum of 5% to a maximum of 45%.

Level	Monthly Taxable Amount	Tax rate (%)
1	Less than RMB 500 yuan	5
2	The portion from RMB 500 to 2,000 yuan	10
3	The portion from RMB 2,000 to 5,000 yuan	15
4	The portion from RMB 5,000 to 20,000 yuan	20
5	The portion from RMB 20,000 to 40,000 yuan	25
6	The portion from RMB 40,000 to 60,000 yuan	30
7	The portion from RMB 60,000 to 80,000 yuan	35
8	The portion from RMB 80,000 to 100,000 yuan	40
9	The portion exceeding RMB 100,000 yuan	45

15.

Foreign Exchange

130. What control of foreign exchange does China's Administration of Foreign Exchange Control exercise on foreign-invested enterprises?

China has adopted fairly loose and flexible foreign exchange control policies toward foreign-invested enterprises, with supervision and management carried out according to the stipulations specified in the Provisional Regulations of the People's Republic of China on Foreign Exchange Control and the Rules for the Implementation of Foreign Exchange Control Regulations Relating to Overseas Chinese Enterprises, Foreign Enterprises and Chinese-Foreign Joint Ventures. The main points are as follows:

1. *Foreign exchange registration.* After obtaining a business license, a foreign-invested enterprise shall go through the formalities of foreign exchange registration at the local foreign exchange control departments, which, after examination and confirmation, will issue a Foreign-Invested Enterprise Foreign Exchange Registration Certificate to the enterprise.

2. *Management of foreign exchange accounts and foreign exchange revenue and expenditure.* The implementation of the Foreign Exchange Registration Certificate is aimed at facilitating foreign exchange revenue and expenditure of enterprises, which can take them directly to banks of deposit. For this purpose, enterprises are required to repatriate their foreign exchange into China and have the exchange deposited in their foreign exchange accounts. All foreign exchange expenditures can be handled directly at the banks of deposit based on the certificate.

3. *Balance of foreign exchange and foreign exchange readjustment.* Beginning 1 April 1994, China canceled all clearing forms of foreign currency valuation within the borders. But in support of the balance of foreign ex-

change of foreign-invested enterprises whose products are sold mainly to the home market, while instituting such reform measures as practicing the foreign exchange settlement and sale system and setting up the National Foreign Exchange Swap Center as an interim measure, the foreign exchange swap market with foreign-invested enterprises as the main body is retained so as to help foreign-invested enterprises make up the deficiency for exchange surplus and balance the foreign exchange revenue and expenditure.

4. *Administering foreign exchange loans.* Foreign-invested enterprises can loan money from abroad but shall complete the foreign debt registration procedures at the foreign exchange control departments within a set time period, obtain the Foreign Debt Registration Certificate, and, while repaying the capital and interest, produce the certificate for approval of remitting. The foreign loans of foreign-invested enterprises that are tendered a guarantee by Chinese enterprises within China shall be included in the aggregate control and quota administration.

131. What is the content of the reform of the foreign exchange control system effected by the Chinese Government in 1994? What special provisions are directed toward foreign-invested enterprises?

In order to build a socialist market-oriented economy system and establish a floating exchange rate system with the market as the basis and gradually enable the RMB to become a convertible currency on the international market, the Chinese Government decided to undertake major reforms in the foreign exchange control system in 1994:

1. Beginning 1 January 1994, merging the two exchange rates (price quotation and market-adjustment price) and imposing a single, managed floating exchange rate with market supply and demand.
2. Implementing the bank exchange settlement and sale system, canceling the turnover and retained portion of foreign exchange.
3. Establishing an interbank exchange deal market for improving the exchange rate mechanism.
4. Forbidding the valuation, settlement, and circulation of foreign currencies within China.
5. Canceling the mandatory plans for foreign exchange revenue and expenditure and the State's using economic and legal means to realize macro control on foreign exchange and international balance of payment.

With the foreign exchange control of foreign-invested enterprises, the existing method remains unchanged. That is, foreign-invested enterprises can still retain their spot exchange accounts in China's authorized banks or foreign banks in China for dealing in foreign exchange. The foreign exchange for remittance for production, operation, and repaying capital and interest in excess of the balance in the spot exchange accounts of foreign-invested enterprises can be purchased at authorized banks subject to the examination and approval by departments of the State Administration of Exchange Control. In the case of foreign exchange surplus and deficiency retained in the foreign exchange swap center, foreign-invested enterprises can swap exchange at the center in pursuance of the State relevant stipulations.

132. Can foreign investors with investment in China freely remit abroad the profits, the capital sum recovered on the expiration of investment, service receipts, and revenue from technology transfer?

Foreign investors with investment in China can freely remit abroad the profits, the capital sum recovered on the expiration of investment, service receipts, and revenue from technology transfer so long as it does not exceed the balance held on foreign exchange deposit accounts. The portion in excess of this amount can be remitted abroad only after the enterprises purchase the foreign exchange from the bank or obtain foreign exchange at the foreign exchange swap center in accordance with relevant stipulations of the State exchange control department.

133. What is the current situation concerning foreign exchange revenue and expenditure of foreign-invested enterprises?

As a whole, foreign-invested enterprises in China have maintained a balance between their foreign exchange receipts and payments with a surplus—their income is greater than their outlay—and every year part of the foreign exchange is adjusted at the foreign exchange swap center to other enterprises. After the 1994 reform of the foreign exchange system, foreign-invested tourist hotels stopped accepting foreign exchange or foreign exchange certificates, but in view of the transactions handled by foreign-invested enterprises at the foreign exchange swap centers, the amount that goes out is still bigger than what comes in.

134. What will happen if a foreign-invested enterprise incurs a deficit, with its foreign exchange expenditure being larger than revenue? Can it convert the RMB it receives into foreign exchange?

If when applying for its establishment, a foreign-invested enterprise is allowed a deficit in foreign exchange receipts and payments with the approval of the foreign exchange control department, it may, on the basis of the documents of approval, exchange its revenue of RMB for foreign exchange according to the stipulations at an authorized bank.

Foreign-invested enterprises also may apply to the foreign exchange control department for transactions at the foreign exchange swap center to exchange their RMB for foreign exchange.

135. In which Chinese cities have foreign exchange swap markets been set up? How does a foreign-invested enterprise enter such markets?

Foreign exchange swap centers have been set up in almost all the municipalities directly under the Central Government, with provincial capitals and cities under separate planning in China. Twenty of them have formed computer networks: Shanghai, Beijing, Tianjin, Xiamen, Hangzhou, Shenzhen, Chengdu, Guangzhou, Fuzhou, Chongqing, Changsha, Wuhan, Hefei, Dalian, Zhengzhou, Haikou, Nanjing, Shijiazhuang, Xi'an, and Qingdao.

If a foreign-invested enterprise wants to enter into the foreign exchange swap center, it may obtain a registration certificate at the foreign exchange control department with its business license and be subject to annual examination; with the registration certificate and year-end examination certification, it may directly enter into the center for exchange swap.

16.

Custom

136. How does Customs administer foreign-invested enterprises?

There are two aspects to Customs's supervision and administration of foreign-invested enterprises. One is to implement export-import laws and regulations and relevant foreign trade policies formulated by the State; enforce supervision and administration over the import and export of goods, articles, and means of transportation; and collect taxes according to the law. The other is to carry out the State's tax policy concerning foreign-invested enterprises and provide convenient services so as to promote their development. The Customs supervision and administration is based on the Customs Law of the People's Republic of China and the Regulations of the General Administration of Customs of the People's Republic of China Concerning the Supervision and Control over the Levying and Exemption of Duties on Imports and Exports of Chinese-Foreign Joint Ventures mapped out in accordance with relevant laws and regulations of the country. These laws do the following:

- Handle the registration of such enterprises. Any Chinese-foreign joint venture enterprises that need to go through customs procedures shall register in advance, assign their declarations, and obtain a declaration certificate
- Handle the import and export declaration
- Handle the imposition and exemption of customs duties for their import and exports
- Carry out Customs follow-up administration, namely, supervision and administration after the import of goods and the cancellation after verification
- Supervise the bonded warehouse and bonded factory system and assume supervision and administration of imported raw materi-

als, fuels, bulk cargoes, components and parts, auxiliary equipment, auxiliary materials, and packing materials needed by foreign-invested enterprises for exporting their products
• Work out favorable supervisory and administrative measures in the interest of such enterprises

137. What stipulations does Customs have concerning foreign-invested enterprises?

In 1992, the General Administration of Customs issued the Regulations of the General Administration of Customs of the People's Republic of China Concerning the Supervision and Control over the Levying and Exemption of Duties on Imports and Exports by Chinese-Foreign Joint Ventures. According to the regulations, foreign-invested enterprises shall fulfill all obligations as stipulated in State laws and regulations, as well as in the regulations, truthfully declare their imports and exports to Customs, accept its supervision, and enjoy relevant favorable terms.

According to the regulations, Customs shall exempt the import duty and value-added tax on the following goods imported by Chinese-foreign joint venture enterprises and foreign enterprises:

• Machinery equipment, components and parts, and other materials that are contributed in accordance with the contract as part of the foreign venture's investment
• Machinery equipment, components and parts, and other materials imported with funds within the limit of the total investment
• With additional capital, machinery and equipment and other materials for which there can be no guarantee of domestic production
• Machinery and equipment, spare parts, and materials for direct use in the Chinese-foreign cooperative exploitation of offshore petroleum; components and parts and materials needed to manufacture machinery and equipment for use in these operations and utilizing foreign capital for imports of capital construction for energy development, railways, public roads or harbors, and projects in industry, agriculture, forestry, scientific research, education, and public health; machinery and equipment in accordance with the contracting and materials needed to build factories (sites) and to install and reinforce machinery and equipment
• Raw materials and components and parts for direct use in the export of products by foreign-invested enterprises in fulfilling export contracts

Goods imported by Chinese-foreign cooperative enterprises engaged in commerce, the food and beverage industry, photography and other service industries, maintenance and repair centers, vocational training for staff and workers, motor transportation of passengers and cargo, and coastal fishing industries as well as other lines of business, except those under separate stipulations by the State, shall pay import customs duties and value-added tax according to the regulations.

138. What are the State's stipulations for administering imports and exports by foreign-invested enterprises?

According to relevant law, a foreign-invested enterprise, from the day of its establishment, determines what to import and export, but this is limited to the import of materials for its own use and export of its own products. No enterprise is allowed to resell imported materials for a profit or to purchase products for export that it did not produce.

The import of materials and export of products by foreign-invested enterprises usually can go through the import and export procedures at Customs according to contract. As for the few categories of import and export commodities limited by the State (including foreign countries' limited commodities), enterprises shall apply for import and export quotas and an import and export license. No such license is needed for the import of materials needed to fulfill the product export contract, but it is subject to Customs for supervision and administration. As for commodities under export quotas, export quotas shall be obtained first before the materials are imported.

On 1 April 1994, China began bidding for export quotas for commodities, so export quotas can be obtained through fair competition. As foreign trade structural reform continues, the kinds of commodities that require quotas and licenses will become fewer, and the procedures for imports and exports will be further simplified.

139. What stipulations has China worked out concerning bonded areas?

In order to facilitate foreign-invested enterprises' production and hasten the development of some key areas, China established its first bonded area, the Waigaoqiao Bonded Area in the Special District of Pudong in Shanghai, in 1990. Since then, 14 more bonded areas have been approved and set up in major cities throughout the country, including

Tianjin, Futian of Shenzhen, Shatoujiao of Shenzhen, Dalian, Guangzhou, Qingdao, Zhangjiagang, Ningbo, Fuzhou, Zhuhai, Hainan, Shantou, and Xiamen.

The primary goal of bonded areas is to promote trade and export processing services and conduct such trade service activities as processing, packing, storing, and commodity exhibition so as to promote the development of China's export economy. In terms of preferential tax treatment, enterprises within the bonded area shall be dealt with in accordance with the tax rates prevailing in the areas where the bonded area is located.

The following preferential policies are applied to bonded areas:

1. Foreign business institutions set up within bonded areas are allowed to import the raw materials and spare parts for production purposes and to export the products of the enterprises with foreign investment located in the bonded areas.

2. Machinery, equipment, building materials, vehicles, transport means, and office supplies imported for the construction of infrastructure in bonded areas; raw materials, components, and packing materials imported for the manufacture of export products; transit goods in storage; and export products processed in bonded areas are exempt from an import and export license and are eligible for exemption of the import and export duty.

140. How does Customs exercise supervision over bonded warehouses?

According to stipulations of the General Administration of Customs, foreign-invested enterprises, in conformity with the conditions for customs supervision, are eligible for approval to set up bonded warehouses and bonded factories. Customs, if necessary, may assign its officers to foreign-invested enterprises to exercise supervision and handle customs formalities.

Foreign-invested enterprises shall establish special account books on the import, storage, use, and transfer to other factories for processing of the materials and parts in bond, as well as on the storage, export, and sales on the domestic market of the processed products, and regularly report to Customs for verification.

Unless otherwise permitted by the Customs, the above-mentioned goods can never be arbitrarily sold, transferred, mortgaged, or switched to another usage.

If the above-mentioned imported materials and parts and the processed products are sold on the domestic market, it is necessary to have approval from the authorized foreign trade and economic cooperation department and pay Customs duties and value-added tax for the imported materials and parts. If the materials and parts come under the license administration, the license shall be produced for examination.

17.

Financial Accounting

141. What does financial and accounting management do regarding foreign-invested enterprises?

In accordance with the General Rules of Business Finance, the Standards of Enterprise Accounting, the trade accounting system and requirements of relevant stipulations, financial and accounting management concerning foreign-invested enterprises does the following:

- Financial and accounting setup and finance supervision
- Capital fund system
- Management of circulating assets
- Depreciation of fixed assets
- Valuation and amortization of intangible assets
- Control of costs
- Business revenue and profits distribution
- Foreign currency business accounting
- Clearing requirements
- Financial reports and financial evaluation
- Accounting calculations

142. What are the requirements of the financial and tax bodies for the establishment of the financial and accounting systems of foreign-invested enterprises and supervision of their finances?

A foreign-invested enterprise shall set up in China a financial and accounting system and assign qualified financial accounting personnel. This is the basis for carrying out the financial and accounting work. Foreign-invested enterprises must accept the supervision of financial and tax bodies over their financial and accounting work. In case of legal violations, the financial and tax bodies may impose a fine, and the administrative departments for industry and commerce may order the suspension of the business and may even revoke their business license.

A foreign-invested enterprise shall, within 30 days after it completes the industrial and commercial registration, proffer duplicates of the certificate of approval for its establishment, business license, contract, and articles of association to the correct financial and tax department. If the enterprise moves, merges, separates, or undergoes any other similar change, it shall also proffer the duplicates of documents containing the changes to the correct financial and tax department within a specified period of time so that the tax department may exercise financial control and supervision.

143. What does the capital fund system do?

The capital fund, or registered capital, system is the legal norm formulated by the State regarding the raising and management of the capital fund of an enterprise as well as the responsibility, power, and interests of the owners, aimed at protecting the rights and interests of the owners and creditors so as to facilitate the enterprise to assume sole responsibility for its own profits and losses. The main components of the capital fund system are the composition, raising, and management of the capital fund. The composition of the capital fund of a foreign-invested enterprise can be divided into the capital fund from the Chinese partner and that from the foreign investor. The forms of capital fund raising may vary. It could be the monetary capital investment from both the Chinese and foreign sides; the investment of buildings, factory, and machinery equipment; or even the investment of intangible assets like land use rights, industrial property rights, and proprietary technology. The conditions for raising a capital fund are that the amount of contribution subscribed by the Chinese and foreign sides to the joint venture enterprise must be their own cash, objects in kind, or intangible assets that are void of any security interest. The investment of intangible assets absorbed by a foreign enterprise shall not exceed 20% of the registered capital. The capital fund of an enterprise can be raised at one time or in installments. If it is raised at one time, the raising shall be completed within six months of the issuance of the business license; if it is done in installments, the maximum period shall not be longer than three years. An investor who breaks a contract during the contributing process shall be responsible. The capital fund raised by an enterprise shall be verified by a Chinese CPA and issued a capital verification report.

The main areas of administration of capital funds are the capital fund lien securing claim and the investors' rights and obligations for the contributed investment. The capital fund lien securing claim requires that enterprises, after raising the capital fund, not disinvest and reduce the registered capital during the production and operating period except the lawful transfer of the capital subscribed on any part of the investors according to the law. The investors' rights and obligations for the contributed investment mean that the investors share the profits and risks and losses of the enterprise according to the ratio of their contributed investment or the stipulations of the contract and articles of association. The investors bear limited responsibility by sharing losses within the limit of the registered capital.

144. How are circulating assets administered?

The circulating assets of a foreign-invested enterprise include monetary capital, goods in stocks, deferred expenses, and other circulating assets. The administration of monetary capital stipulates that such an enterprise in China may do the following:

- Open an RMB savings account and a foreign exchange account with any Chinese bank that handles foreign exchange business.
- Assign full-time financial accounting personnel to deal with receipts and payments, settlements, and oversight of the monetary capital.
- Accounts receivable shall be collected in a timely manner in accordance with the contract or agreement.
- An enterprise engaged in credit and leasing businesses, according to the year-end balance of account receivables, may accrue bad debts totaling no more than 3% of the bad debt provision.
- The internal control system shall be improved. Various items of cash payments shall be strictly controlled. Accounts shall agree with physical inventory, with each other, and with reports.

The administration of goods in stocks calls for an enterprise to do inventory carefully. If inventory losses or damage occur to goods in stock, the cause shall be identified, and the person(s) incurring the losses shall be compensated accordingly.

145. How are fixed assets to be depreciated?

The fixed assets of a foreign-invested enterprise can be divided into three basic categories: (1) houses and other buildings; (2) trains, ships, machinery, and other production equipment; and (3) electronic equipment and means of transport other than trains and ships, as well as articles, tools, and furniture relating to production and management. The service life periods for these three categories of fixed assets are 20, 10, and 5 years, respectively. Foreign-invested enterprises shall confirm their fixed assets in accord with the specified conditions and accrue the depreciation of the fixed assets in accordance with the service life periods and depreciation methods. If an enterprise needs to use a depreciation method other than those stipulated or for special reasons shorten the service life period for depreciation, it may so apply. Implementation can be carried out after it is approved by the department in charge.

146. How are intangible assets to be valued and amortized?

Intangible assets refer to the assets used by an enterprise for a long time with no real form, such as a patent right, a trademark right, or a land use right. An enterprise must classify and arrive at a valuation of its intangible assets in accordance with regulations. The valuation of intangible assets is fairly complicated, but the general principle is that intangible assets are valued according to the actual cost when they are obtained. If the investor presents the capital fund or cooperative conditions as intangible assets of the enterprise, then they are valued according to the assessment or the agreed amount on the contract or agreement. After their entry into account, the intangible assets of an enterprise are amortized under the straight-line method in a fixed period of time from the day they gain profit.

147. How is cost computed?

The manufacturing cost method is adopted in administering costs. The cost of products is computed by distributing and pooling the expenses that have the closest and most direct relationship to production operation only; any other expenses are directly entered in current profits and losses. According to the manufacturing method, direct materials, direct wages, and manufacturing expenses are distributed and entered in the cost of products; administration expenses, financial expenses, and market expenses are directly deducted from the current profits and losses.

148. How is operating revenue computed, and how are profits distributed?

Operating revenue refers to the receipts gained by an enterprise that, through its normal economic activities, has manufactured and delivered the products or completed the labor service. Operating revenue can be divided into two categories: basic business income and other operating income.

The gross profits of an enterprise encompass operating profit, net investment income, and net amount of nonoperating income and expenses; operating profit is the largest, obtained by deducting operating costs and business tax from the operating revenue.

The profits realized by an enterprise are to be distributed according to China's tax law, which directs that profit-gaining enterprises shall, according to the amount of profits realized, compute and pay income tax at the specified tax rate. After-tax profits are to be distributed by the enterprise according to the law. First, they are used to offset the forfeited financial and material losses, disburse the delayed payment or fine of tax receipts, and make up for past annual losses; then the stock fund, enterprise development fund, and bonus and welfare fund of the staff and workers can be withdrawn; the remaining profits are to be distributed to investors.

149. How is the accounting of foreign currency operations computed?

The foreign currency operations of a foreign-invested enterprise refer to the business of receipts and payments, current settlements, and valuation using the currency other than the bookkeeping base currency. If foreign currency operation occurs in an enterprise using RMB as the bookkeeping base currency, it shall keep accounts by converting the amount of foreign currency into the bookkeeping base currency in addition to registering the amount of foreign currency. The conversion rate can be either the market rate when the operation occurs or that published by the People's Bank in the early current period.

150. What are the requirements for liquidating a foreign-invested enterprise?

If a foreign-invested enterprise declares its dissolution, bankruptcy, or termination for special reasons, its property, financial claims and debts shall be liquidated. When the liquidation is complete, the liquidation committee shall prepare the balance sheet and profit and loss statement from the beginning to the end of the liquidation. The liquidation statements and reports shall be audited by Chinese CPAs and an audit report issued. After terminating its industrial and commercial and tax registration at the industrial and commercial administration and tax authorities, the enterprise shall close and seal all account books and turn them over to relevant departments to keep.

151. How are financial statements and financial evaluation carried out?

Financial statements, including financial reports and financial condition statements, are summarizing documents reflecting the financial standing and business performance of a foreign-invested enterprise. The main financial reports are the balance sheet, profit sheet, and statement of changes in financial position. An enterprise shall prepare its financial statement on schedule and submit it to relevant departments. The annual financial statement, together with the audit report from Chinese CPAs, shall be submitted to the competent tax authorities and relevant departments.

The financial evaluation targets of a foreign-invested enterprise can be divided into three categories: debt-paying ability, operating capacity, and capacity to earn profit. These evaluation targets reflect the financial standing and business performance of an enterprise and can meet the needs of investors, creditors, managers, and government departments.

152. What are the requirements for accounting calculation?

Foreign-invested enterprises shall carry out their accounting calculation work in accordance with the Standards of Enterprise Accounting and stipulations of accounting systems of different trades.

18.

Labor Management

153. What stipulations does the Chinese government have concerning labor management in foreign-invested enterprises?

In order to strengthen labor management, correct infringements of labor laws and regulations, and protect the legal rights and interests of the staff and workers of foreign-invested enterprises, in 1994 China's Ministry of Labor, the Ministry of Public Security, and the All-China Federation of Trade Unions jointly issued the Notice on Strengthening Labor Management in Foreign-Invested Enterprises and Private Enterprises and Effectively Protecting the Legal Rights and Interests of Staff and Workers. The following requirements apply to labor management in foreign-invested enterprises:

1. Foreign-invested enterprises shall recruit and employ staff and workers in accordance with the stipulations of the State's labor law and regulations and policies. Without authorization, no enterprise is allowed to recruit peasant-workers, nor is it allowed to recruit women workers to forbidden posts and child laborers. The enterprise shall sign a labor contract separately with each of the employed staff and workers in conformity with the principles of equality, voluntary participation, and consensus through consultation. After its signing, the labor contract shall be verified by the local labor management department. Enterprises that refuse to implement the State's stipulations in recruiting and employing staff and workers shall be ordered by the labor supervisory department to return the recruited staff and workers, and a fine will be imposed according to the law.

2. No foreign-invested enterprise is allowed to collect currency or anything in kind as a "guarantee" deposit to be employed by the enter-

prise, nor is it allowed to retain or mortgage any employees' credentials, such as residents' identity card, temporary residence permits, or other status identification documents. As for those arbitrarily retaining and mortgaging any of the certificates, the public security department and labor supervisory department shall order the enterprise to return them to the owners immediately.

3. The wage level of the staff and workers working in a foreign-invested enterprise shall not be lower than that set by the State and local governments. In line with its production and operation and the rise of a country's price index, foreign-invested enterprises shall adjust the wages of the staff and workers from time to time. They shall pay wages to the staff and workers in currency on schedule and in full; no arrears or withholding is allowed. If the wage level of the staff and workers is lower than the minimum level set by the State and local governments or the wages of the staff and workers are withheld, the labor supervisory department shall order the enterprise to make up the amount and may impose a fine on it according to the law.

4. Foreign-invested enterprises shall strictly implement the working hours and holiday schedules defined by the State. The staff and workers work 8 hours a day, or 40 hours a week on average. An enterprise may extend the working hours because of production and operating needs after seeking the approval of the trade unions and consulting with the staff and workers. But the extension shall not be longer than 3 hours a day or longer than 40 hours a month. The enterprise shall pay the staff and workers who are working extra shifts and hours remuneration that is higher than that for the normal working hours set by the State. If an enterprise forces staff and workers to work overtime in violation of the State law, they may refuse to do so, and the enterprise is not allowed to garnish their wages or dismiss them for this reason.

5. Foreign-invested enterprises shall strictly implement the State's laws and regulations and policies concerning social security and welfare of the staff and workers, and, according to the stipulations, pay for them the funds for their pension, unemployment, medical care, industrial accident and child-bearing and other social insurance, and provide necessary social welfare facilities.

6. Foreign-invested enterprises shall strictly carry out the State's laws and regulations on labor protection and on safety and health, provide staff and workers with working conditions that meet safety and health requirements, and safeguard their safety and health. Technical staff and workers can assume on-job duties only after being qualified through training. If they suffer on-the-job injury or an occupational disease, the en-

terprise shall take responsibility for their medical treatment. If the staff or worker is partly disabled after medical treatment, the enterprise shall make appropriate job arrangements; it is not allowed to revoke the labor contract. The enterprise shall make compensation to a completely disabled worker according to relevant stipulations and guarantee his or her daily life expenditures.

Enterprises must strictly implement the State's labor protection laws and regulations for female staff and workers and do a good job in ensuring their four-period protection.*

7. In accordance with the Trade Union Law, foreign-invested enterprises shall support staff and workers in organizing and participating in trade unions and enable these unions to carry out their activities. The trade union has the right on behalf of the staff and workers to request the enterprise to raise wages and improve benefits and working conditions. Enterprises shall set up a system of consultation and negotiations held between trade union representatives or representatives of staff and workers and the enterprise for signing a collective agreement (collective contract). The trade union organization shall supervise the enterprise's observance of the labor laws and regulations. If any violation of law is found, the trade union organization shall raise the issue in a timely manner and supervise the correction by the enterprise. If the enterprise does not correct the problem, the case shall be reported to the labor management department, and measures will be taken to have the enterprise make the correction.

8. Foreign-invested enterprises are strictly forbidden to carry out corporal punishment of staff and workers, beat them up, conduct body searches or other insults, or restrict their personal freedom by locking the work sites or their dormitory. If any violation of these stipulations is disclosed, the enterprise shall be subject to the labor supervisory department's investigation and prosecution. If the case turns out to run counter to public security administration, the public security department shall enforce punishment in line with the stipulations of the Regulations of Punishment of the People's Republic of China Concerning Public Security Administration. If it constitutes a crime, the judicial department determines criminal responsibility.

9. Strengthen government departments' supervision and inspection of foreign-invested enterprises on their observance of labor laws and regulations. Inspectors shall carefully inspect the production and living en-

*"Four-period protection" refers to the health of female staff and workers' during periods of menstruation, pregnancy, maternity, and breast-feeding.

vironments of the enterprise and have the right to inquire about the persons concerned. If law violations are found, the inspectors may order the enterprise to correct them within a stipulated time. The enterprise is obliged to coordinate and is not allowed to obstruct the inspection work. If any enterprise obstructs or rejects the State administrative body's execution of public functions according to the law, the public security department shall mete out an administrative penalty in accordance with the Regulations of Punishment of the People's Republic of China Concerning Public Security Administration.

10. Labor disputes between the enterprise and the staff and workers shall be resolved through mediation and arbitration in line with the Regulations of the People's Republic of China on Handling Labor Disputes in Enterprises. The labor disputes arbitration committee shall hear the claim from the staff and workers and handle it as quickly as possible in line with relevant laws and regulations, so that every labor dispute can be solved in a timely manner.

11. Strengthen the education of labor law on the enterprise operators and the staff and workers. It is necessary to use all means to publicize the labor laws and regulations, disseminate knowledge of labor laws and regulations, and enhance the legal sense of the enterprise and staff and workers and their self-protection awareness, creating a favorable environment in the socialist labor legal system to deepen reforms.

154. Do foreign-invested enterprises have the right to recruit and dismiss staff and workers? What stipulations does the Chinese government have in this connection?

Foreign-invested enterprises can recruit staff and workers and choose the best employees through examinations.

In accordance with the Provisions of the People's Republic of China for Labor Management in Joint Ventures Using Chinese and Foreign Investment, employment of the staff and workers of a joint venture, whether recommended by the local department in charge of the venture or the local labor department, must be decided by the joint venture on its own; no designation is allowed. In its recruitment of workers, a joint venture shall apply for the quota of recruited number of workers from the local labor management department and set the standards for recruitment. The labor department defines the areas, departments, and scope of recruitment for the venture to choose the best to employ.

In 1986, the Ministry of Labor and Personnel promulgated the Provisions on the Autonomy in the Employment of Personnel and in Fixing Wages and Insurance and Welfare Funds in Joint Ventures Using Chinese and Foreign Investment. It is stipulated that in line with production and management needs, enterprises can make their own decisions on their organizational structure and personnel employment. Assisted by the local labor and personnel departments, they can recruit staff and workers and choose the best through examinations. If the locality cannot provide the needed personnel, they can recruit them in other parts of the country with the coordination of the labor department. Persons who prove unqualified after a probationary period and redundant persons may be dismissed by enterprises.

After recruiting the staff and workers, the two sides shall sign a labor contract and abide by it. According to the stipulations of China's Labor Law, if any laborer is found to be under one of the following conditions, the employing unit may revoke the labor contract:

1. Proved unqualified for the recruitment requirements during the probationary period
2. Seriously violating labor discipline or the rules and regulations
3. Gross neglect of duty and involvement in corruption, causing serious damage to the interests of the employing unit
4. Be prosecuted for his (her) criminal liability.

155. What is the wage level of staff and workers of foreign-invested enterprises in China? Does the Chinese government set the ceiling and bottom limits for the wages?

Compared with other countries, the wages of Chinese staff and workers are relatively low. But the wage gap is fairly big considering the difference of professions and cultural quality, the difference of work posts and labor intensity, and the difference of regions (generally wages in the coastal regions are higher than those in the central and western regions). Therefore, it is very difficult to set a precise wage level.

According to the stipulations of China's Labor Law, a foreign-invested enterprise may, in line with its characteristics of production and business and economic benefits, determine its own wage allocation method and wage level. The State sets the minimum wage. The minimum wage standard is set by the people's governments of various provinces, autonomous regions, and municipalities directly under the Central Government. The wages paid by the employing unit to the laborers shall not be lower than the local minimum wage standard.

19.

Bank Loans and Guarantees

156. What Chinese banks are qualified to provide loans to foreign-invested enterprises?

Enterprises with foreign investment can arrange for a loan from any of the following Chinese banks: Bank of China; Chinese specialized banks such as industrial and commercial banks, agricultural banks, or banks of construction; foreign banks (inside or outside China); or banks in Hong Kong and Macao. They can also arrange for a loan from any of the international trust and investment corporations that have made investments in them. The foreign exchange funds contracted from these foreign banks and international trust and investment corporations should be reported to the State Administration of Foreign Exchange Control or its branches in China's provinces, municipalities, or autonomous regions.

157. What forms of loans will the Bank of China grant to foreign-invested enterprises?

According to the purpose for which loans are to be granted, the major loan forms that the Bank of China grants to foreign-invested enterprises are classified into three categories: working capital loan, loans for the settlement of accounts, and fixed assets loans. Apart from loans in RMB, the Bank of China grants loans in US dollars, British sterling, Deutsche marks, Japanese yen, Hong Kong dollars, and other convertible currencies it may agree to grant.

158. What are the requirements for the loans that the Bank of China grants to foreign-invested enterprises?

Following are the requirements for loans granted by the Bank of China to loan-applying foreign-invested enterprises:

- Those having registered with the State Administration for Industry and Commerce, acquired the Business Licenses it issued, and opened an account with Bank of China
- Those having put in the registered capital on schedule and in full and having it evaluated in accordance with the legal procedures concerned
- Those having been enlisted into the fixed investment plan of the government planning department
- Those having debt-service ability and ability to provide a reliable debt-service guarantee

159. How is the interest on loans granted by the Bank of China to be set?

The interest on loans granted by the Bank of China varies by loan currency, usage, and terms. For RMB loans, the interest rate is the consolidated interest rate set and made public by the People's Bank of China. For foreign currency loans, the interest rate is set in the light of international market conditions plus a certain margin. For loans of a special source, the interest rate is set according to the cost incurred. In a word, the interest rates of foreign currency loans are set mainly in accordance with the amount and term of the loan, the risks involved, as well as the credit of the enterprise concerned.

160. What stipulations has the Bank of China laid down on loan terms?

The Bank of China provides a long- and medium-term fixed assets loan and a short-term working capital loan and loan for the settlement of accounts as well. The loan periods can be 3 months, 6 months, 1 year, 3 years, 5 years, 7 years, or 10 years.

161. What financial institutions are eligible to provide a banker's guarantee to foreign-invested enterprises for a foreign loan from abroad?

According to the decrees in effect, neither domestic Chinese financial institutions nor enterprises are eligible to provide any guarantee to foreign-invested enterprises for a foreign currency loan from abroad except those financial institutions that have been approved by the State Administration of Exchange Control to conduct foreign exchange business and activities.

162. What are the Bank of China's requirements to provide a banker's guarantee to foreign-invested enterprises for a foreign currency loan from abroad?

Essentially a guarantee means that the guarantor commits himself to shoulder the responsibility for the repayment of the loans he has guaranteed. In terms of risk, a guarantee is exactly the same as a loan, though slightly different from it in practice. In order to avoid or diminish risk, the Bank of China, when providing a guarantee to a foreign-invested enterprise, shall examine whether it meets the requirements, demonstrates the ability to guarantee the project, and calls for a counter-guarantee from the enterprise itself or from its investors, Chinese or foreign.

20.

Land Use

163. What are the legal provisions concerning land use by foreign-invested enterprises?

The main policies, laws, and regulations concerning land use by foreign-invested enterprises are the Law of the People's Republic of China on Land Administration, the Law of the People's Republic of China on Chinese–Foreign Equity Joint Ventures, the Implementing Regulations of the Law of the People's Republic of China on Joint Ventures Using Chinese and Foreign Investment, and the Provisional Regulations on Leasing Tracts of Land to Foreign Investors for Development and Management. "Land use by foreign-invested enterprises" means the use of land necessary for the construction, operation, and production of their projects as well as the development and management of tracts of land by such enterprises. The characteristics in this regard can be summed up as (1) the use of land with compensation and within a limited period of time by foreign-invested enterprises and (2) by signing a land use contract, defining the rights and obligations of both the land user and the land owner.

164. How does a foreign-invested enterprise obtain land use rights in China?

China implements the socialist public ownership of land: ownership by the whole people (i.e., state ownership) and collective ownership by working people. Urban land belongs to the state; all rural and urban land belongs to the collectives except the land owned by the state as stipulated by laws.

In China, there are four ways for foreign-invested enterprises to obtain state-owned land use rights:

1. *Granting of state-owned land use rights.* According to the Provisional Regulations on Granting and Transferring of Use Rights of Urban State-Owned Land of the People's Republic of China, the state, as the landowner, may, by means of public bidding, auction, or agreement, extend land use rights for a certain number of years to foreign-invested enterprises that pay for it by a lump-sum fee, sign a contract obtaining the land use rights with the state land management departments, go through registration formalities, and acquire a land use certificate. Land use rights obtained in this way can be transferred, leased, or mortgaged.

2. *Allotting of land use rights.* Foreign-invested enterprises shall, when obtaining land use rights in this way, sign a land use contract with the municipality- or county-level land management department, go through land registration formalities, and acquire a land use certificate, thus obtaining land use rights. Enterprises obtaining land use rights by allotment shall pay the government either a lump-sum site-use fee and an annual land use fee or, by consolidating the two fees, an annual site-use fee. If the land use rights obtained by allotting are transferred, leased, or mortgaged, the foreign-invested enterprise shall, in accordance with relevant regulations, go through the granting formalities retroactively and make up for the land granting fee due. At this time, land use rights allotted to foreign-invested enterprises are limited to the use of land for projects as encouraged and supported by state industrial policies. For land users for other purposes, granting is of the usual practice.

3. *Coinvestment and cooperation.* This means that Chinese enterprises may, by using their workshops, installations, and land use rights as stock or conditions, establish joint ventures or cooperative joint ventures with foreign business. Enterprises set up in this way must, before starting operation, go through the land use procedures with the land management departments. In addition, if the land use rights are obtained by allotting, they must go through the granting formalities retroactively and make up for the land granting fee due.

4. *Leasing buildings and sites.* By this land use method, foreign-invested enterprises may lease buildings or sites directly from state-run enterprises, urban collective-run enterprises, township enterprises, or other urban collective economic organizations and pay them either annual or monthly rent as set out in the leasing contract between them. The buildings are leased in conjunction with their land use rights. If the land for leasing is obtained by granting, the leasing is legal; if the land for leasing is obtained by allotting, the leasing is illegal unless the foreign-invested enterprises go retroactively through the granting formalities and make up for the granting fee due.

In addition, foreign-invested enterprises can obtain collective-owned land use rights in either of the following two ways:

1. Collective-owned land must be requisitioned by the government for state-owned land before it is granted to foreign-invested enterprises since, collective-owned land in China is not allowed to be granted or leased directly to foreign-invested enterprises.
2. When rural collective economic organizations or village or township enterprises use their own collective-owned land as stock or conditions to set up joint ventures or cooperative joint ventures with foreign business, the projects to be jointly undertaken must be approved by the county-level people's government. In examining and approving the land use rights of this sort, the government may consult and follow the relevant regulations on land use by village or township enterprises. Used in this way, the ownership of the collective-owned land can never be transferred.

165. What are China's regulations on leasing tracts of land to foreign investors for development and management?

According to the Provisional Regulations on Leasing Tracts of Land to Foreign Investors for Development and Management, development and management of tracts of land by foreign investors denotes that, having obtained the state-owned land use rights and strictly following the plans for development of tracts of land, foreign investors will clear the land; construct such public facilities as water supply, sewage, electricity and heat, roads, and communications; make the land usable for industry and other construction projects; then transfer the land use rights and operate the public facilities, or construct universal factory premises, auxiliary production and service facilities, and transfer or lease the buildings on the ground.

Development of tracts of land is, as a rule, of a considerable scale and length. Priority is given to development and construction of production-oriented projects and invitation of foreign investment, but the granting of land-use rights is a prerequisite for such development. In addition, development of tracts of land should have both clear aims and intentions for the construction projects on the developed land. People's governments at the municipal and county levels should draw up proposals (or preliminary feasibility study reports) on items and projects for the tracts of land to be developed with foreign investment, submit them to relevant government bodies for examination and approval, and establish enterprises for developing tracts of land, which should work out plans for the development of tracts of land or feasibility study reports and submit them to a higher level for examination and approval.

166. What regulations has China laid down on the authorization of approval of land use by foreign-invested enterprises?

According to the Provisional Regulations Governing Development and Operation of Tracts of Land with Foreign Investment promulgated by the State Council of the People's Republic of China, the authorization of approval of governments at different levels on land use by foreign-invested enterprises is as follows:

1. Acquisitioning (allotting) or granting a piece of farmland larger than 66 hectares and of land larger than 132 hectares, submitted to the State Council for examination and approval
2. Requisitioning (allotting) or granting a piece of farmland between 0.2 and 66 hectares and of land between 0.6 and 132 hectares, submitted to the provincial people's government for examination and approval
3. Requisitioning (allotting) or granting a piece of farmland under 0.2 hectare and of land under 0.6 hectare, submitted to the county-level people's government for examination and approval

21.

Environmental Protection

167. What regulations has the Chinese Government adopted to strengthen the protection of China's environment?

In accordance with relevant Chinese laws and regulations concerning utilization of direct foreign investment, in particular the provisions under the Notice on Strengthening the Administration of Environmental Protection in Projects with Foreign Investment, foreign businesses are to abide by relevant laws, decrees, and regulations on environmental protection when investing in projects, to protect the nation from environmental pollution and ecological detriment and to accept the supervision and administration of administrative bodies in charge of environmental protection. Such projects with foreign investment shall be in compliance with technical codes and relevant requirements of the State on environmental protection. Approval will not be granted to enterprises with foreign investment that bring about or may bring about environmental pollution.

According to the Decision of the State Council on the Focal Points of the Present Industrial Policies, China does the following:

- Exercises strict control over imported raw materials, products, technologies, and equipment that result in serious environmental pollution that is hard to treat, in order to prevent foreign polluting sources from entering China
- Forbids the introduction of projects that degrade natural resources or human health or seriously pollute the environment with no effective counteractive measures or emit pollutants that exceed State standards
- Restricts the introduction of projects that may result in serious,

hard-to-treat environmental pollution, such as dismantling and re-conditioning of old vehicles or retreading of old tires
- Stipulates that advanced technologies and relevant advanced fa-cilities for environmental protection shall be concurrently intro-duced for projects involving pollution problems for which China does not have relevant treatment facilities

Foreign businesses are encouraged to introduce highly efficient pesticide technologies with low toxic content and environmental pollution treat-ment technologies and to establish projects with advanced technologies such as commodity paper pulp, leather processing; dyeing, treatment, and processing of linens; highly efficient raw chemical drugs; and phar-maceutical intermediates.

168. How has the administration of the examination and approval of construction projects on environmental protection been strengthened?

According to relevant Chinese laws and regulations, projects with foreign investment that affect the environment must be in compliance with China's regulations regarding environmental protection of investment projects, following examination and approval procedures, to avoid dam-age to China's environment arising from random construction.

1. Prior to project approval, a written report on environmental im-pact shall be submitted to the administration bodies in charge of examination and approval. The report shall include the selected project site and layout, scope, products scheme, technological process, equipment, emissions, extent of possible environmental pollution, and measures for treatment of possible pollution.

   The examination and approval of the environmental impact re-port submitted by Sino–foreign equity joint ventures and Sino–foreign cooperative joint ventures shall be done according to es-tablished authorities and procedures for examination and ap-proval; in the case of wholly foreign-owned construction projects, such written reports shall be examined and approved by the gov-ernment bodies in charge of environmental protection, which are of the same administrative level as the examination and approval authorities for the establishment of the projects.
2. Government economic relations and trade departments or other examination and approval bodies authorized by the government

shall not process the application for establishment of enterprises with foreign investment without an environmental impact report approved by relevant bodies in charge of environmental protection.

The environmental protection facilities of a foreign-invested construction project shall be in compliance with the environmental impact report and its approval comments, and shall be designed in accordance with the Design Codes on Environmental Protection for Construction Projects, following the system under which the design, construction, and application and operation of facilities for protection from pollution and other public detriment shall be done at the same time as the principal part of the project.

After completion of construction, the project's emissions shall satisfy relevant State and local codes and the requirements for control of total volume of pollutants of the region where such control is exercised. Prior to the official start of production or use, the project shall, in accordance with established procedures and requirements, apply to the original examination and approval bodies in charge of environmental protection for their inspection and acceptance of environmental protection facilities. A facility that fails shall not start production or use.

169. What are the requirements for administration of environmental protection after enterprises with foreign investment have gone into the production stage?

1. *The responsibility system on environmental protection.* Leaders of enterprises with foreign investment shall establish their tasks and targets regarding environmental protection during their term of office and shall be responsible for environmental protection and treatment of pollution in their enterprises.

2. *The license system for emitting pollutants.* This system includes application for emission of pollutants, determination of total volume of pollutants to be emitted and allocation of decreased total amount of pollutants, issuance of a license for emissions, and supervision and checking on the performance of the enterprise in this respect.

3. *Charges for emission of pollutants.* Enterprises with foreign investment will be charged for emissions that exceed relevant codes, for use of pollution treatment.

4. *Treatment of pollution sources within a given period.* The State or local governments shall determine a time limit within which enterprises with foreign investment, approved in the past and bringing about relatively more serious pollution, must treat the pollution.

5. *The evaluation system on environmental protection of enterprises.* Together with product quality, material consumption, and economic benefits, environmental protection is included in the list for evaluation of enterprises with foreign investment, thus tying together environmental protection and development interests of enterprises to avoid separating the production and operation of enterprises from environmental protection.

22.

Administration for Industry and Commerce

170. What are the legal regulations on the supervision and administration functions of registration bodies?

In accordance with the provisions of the Implementing Law of the People's Republic of China on Regulations of the Joint Ventures Using Chinese and Foreign Investment, the Regulations of the People's Republic of China for Administrating the Registration of Corporate Legal Persons, and other related laws and decrees of the State, government bodies in charge of registration have the following responsibilities:

- Supervise and check the execution of joint venture contracts and articles of association
- Order a business to close or revoke its business license should an enterprise with foreign investment not or refuse to place its accounting books within China or if any joint venture parties fail to pay its subscribed capital within the specified time
- Supervise enterprises as they register opening, alteration, or cancellation
- Check on business activities of enterprises for conformity to registered items and with the articles of association and contract or agreement
- Supervise enterprises in their completion of formalities for annual examination according to relevant regulations
- Supervise enterprises and their legal representatives in abiding by relevant State laws, regulations, and policies

171. How does a registration body conduct an annual examination on enterprises with foreign investment?

Government bodies in charge of registration conduct annual examinations of enterprises with foreign investment. Enterprises with foreign investment shall submit an annual examination report, and their balance sheet or assets and liability statements within the time period set by the registration body, which shall examine the major items as registered by the legal persons.

The annual examination exercised by registration bodies on enterprises with foreign investment consists mainly of the following:

- The payment of subscribed capital by joint venture parties
- Conformity of manufacturing or business operations to the contents of the contract and the business scope as checked by registration bodies
- Activities of counterfeiting, alteration, leasing, lending, transfer, or sales of the business license
- Activities within the terms of the joint venture of withdrawing the registered capital, transfer of properties, or dodging liabilities
- Engagement in any illegal business operations

172. How do registration bodies enforce penalties for violations?

According to the Provisions of the People's Republic of China on the Contributions Made by the Parties to Joint Ventures Using Chinese and Foreign Investment, in the case of the joint venture contracts requiring one-time payment of subscribed capital, such payment shall be made by the parties within six months after issuance of the business license. In the case of the joint venture contract requiring payment of subscribed capital in installments, the first payment shall be made by the parties in an amount of not less than 15% of the respective subscriptions by the parties and within three months after issuance of the business license. Any violation of these provisions shall constitute an automatic loss of effectiveness of the joint venture's Certificate of Approval, and the joint venture enterprise shall go through formalities with relevant registration bodies for cancellation of registration and shall return the business license. Should the enterprise fail to do so, registration bodies shall revoke the business license and make a public announcement.

The registration bodies shall take action when any of the joint venture parties fails to make full payment of subscribed capital within the time period specified in the joint venture contract. This can mean failure to effect payment by installments within specified time limits; failure by all parties to effect payment after the first installment; failure to honor a commitment in payment of subscriptions unilaterally by one party; or failure to fulfill a commitment to make payment in equipment. When after payment of the first installment the parties' payment of subscriptions in any other installments is three months later than contract stipulations call for, the registration bodies, together with the examination and approval bodies, issue to the enterprise a Notice Pressing for Payment. This Notice requests the parties concerned to make payment within the time limit set out in the Notice; the examination and approval bodies have the right to revoke the business license if the parties concerned fail to make payment as called for by the Notice and may make a public announcement to that effect. In the case of unilateral default in payment of subscriptions within the time set out in the joint venture contract, the registration bodies shall alter or cancel the registration according to the will of the party or parties not in default. Also it shall have the right to revoke the business license and make a public announcement to that effect should the party in default fail to identify another cooperation partner(s) or go through the cancellation formalities with the registration body.

In order to strengthen the supervision and administration of enterprises with foreign investment and to protect their legitimate business operations, penalties shall be imposed on enterprises with foreign investment that engage in activities in violation of registration regulations. In imposing penalties on such enterprises, all levels of authorized registration bodies shall strictly follow provisions of relevant state laws, regulations, and policies in its investigations and disciplinary actions for activities violating registration regulations within the regions of their governance and file with the highest registration authority of the state.

173. What are the regulations on disciplining local registration bodies that engage in illegal activities?

Based on the authorizing-authorized status and relationship, local registration bodies shall be responsible to the highest registration authority of the State in their business portfolios and shall maintain the highest unanimity with the State authority both in implementing State laws, regulations, and policies and in following work procedures for registration bodies.

In the case of local registration bodies that engage in administrative activities in serious violation of State laws, regulations, or policies, the

State authority in charge of the registration shall correct, warn, make public criticism, or even withdraw from the local body its power in inspecting and registering enterprises with foreign investment. In the case of the said local bodies' negligence of public criticism and failure to correct wrongs done, the highest registration authority of the State shall take the severest measure and withdraw the authority delegated to such local bodies. The local bodies shall not be reauthorized until after one-year or longer probationary period conducted by the highest authority of the State, and when leaders and staff of the disciplined local body are believed to have strengthened their understanding with improved performance in their work after retraining and examination.

23.

China Association of Enterprises with Foreign Investment

174. What is the China Association of Enterprises with Foreign Investment? What functions does it have in the government's administration of enterprises with foreign investment?

The China Association of Enterprises with Foreign Investment was established in November 1987 when the total number of enterprises with foreign investment came to over ten thousand. As an organization of these enterprises that serves as a bridge to and link with the Chinese government, the market, and the broad enterprise members, the Association is a safeguard of the lawful rights and interests of the enterprise members and the social order, and an assistant to the Chinese government as well as an adviser to the enterprises. The Association has played an important role in such respects as bettering the enterprises, promoting their mutual understanding, serving, notarizing, coordinating, guiding, and supervising economic matters of all kinds arising in the course of their production and operations, thus greatly improving their work.

To date, the Association has had over 60,000 enterprise members, and subassociations of enterprises with foreign investment have been set up in almost all of China's provinces, autonomous regions, and municipalities.

175. What are the purposes and main tasks of the China Association of Enterprises with Foreign Investment?

The Association's purposes are to:

- Implement the policies, laws, and regulations formulated by the Chinese government relating to the opening policy and invitation of foreign investment
- Provide services to both the enterprise members and foreign investors and protect their lawful rights and interests
- Promote mutual understanding, friendship, and cooperation between Chinese and foreign partners among the enterprises so as to urge the members to play a positive role in China's modernization and the cause of international economic cooperation

The Association's main tasks are to:

- Publicize the policies, laws, and regulations formulated by the Chinese government in relation to the open policy and invitation of foreign investment and introduce China's investment environment to foreign investors
- Provide enterprises with foreign investment and foreign investors with services such as information and consultancy
- Protect the lawful rights and interests of the enterprise members, report the problems encountered and requests made by enterprises with foreign investment to the government and departments concerned, and help them resolve any difficulties
- Mediate economic disputes arising among the enterprise members
- Conduct training courses, study groups, symposiums, and investigations necessary for the production and operation of the members' enterprises
- Exchange information between Chinese and foreign partners in such areas as contract performance, cooperation, business operations, and independence in management in accordance with the laws, strengthening business administration, raising economic results, and improving labor protection
- Organize exhibitions for enterprises with foreign investment and promote sales of their products, both at home and abroad
- Exchange friendly visits with relevant overseas economic organizations and promote international economic cooperation
- Conduct scientific research and edit and publish books and peri-

odicals on theory and policy in relation to the absorption of foreign investment

176. How many departments are there under the Association?

There are seven offices and departments under the Association: the Liaison Department, Training Department, Survey and Study Department, Product Coordination Department, Department of Investment Consultancy, Exhibition Department, and General Office. Also set up are such legal entities as the China Association of Enterprises with Foreign Investment Service Co., Zhonglian International Business and Investment Consultants Co., and Junda Lawyer's Office. The periodical *Foreign Investment in China*, published by the Association, first appeared at the end of 1992.

24.

China's Development Strategies Regarding Foreign Capital

Utilization of foreign capital in economic construction is an important part of China's reforms and opening policies, as well as an important factor in China's economic and technical cooperation with foreign countries and development of foreign economic relations. The second and third strategic targets in China's own brand of socialism in realization of China's economic development are to expand its opening to the outside world and utilize foreign capital in a greater quantity and better quality. To reach such goals, China seeks to develop strategies in utilizing foreign capital that mesh with China's situation. The international environment offers opportunities and challenges.

177. What are the major international opportunities that China faces?

1. The relatively peaceful and stable world political situation provides a fine environment for the economic development of all countries and favorable conditions for China's economic development and utilization of foreign capital.

2. Asia has become a focal point for international capital because of its advantages in economic growth, opening policies, and social stability. Especially since the 1980s, more and more direct investment is flowing into the developing countries and those in Asia in particular—in 1991, 60% of the US$43 billion worth of the total direct investment in the developing countries.

3. After 15 years of reforms and opening, China has undergone obvious changes in its social and economic situation, with sustained fast economic growth and great achievements made in building infrastructure facilities, as well as an increasingly prosperous domestic market, notable improvement of purchasing power, increasingly favorable foreign policies and legislation, and political and social stability. In addition, China is a great attraction for foreign capital, with a huge potential market, a relatively strong industrial base, a high scientific level with a large force in scientific research, and a great number of skilled workers and outstanding management personnel.

4. Modern science and technology as well as the resulting worldwide adjustment of industrial structure have provided a good climate for developing countries to build their expertise in traditional industries and led to a new technological revolution that enables developing countries to pool their personnel, materials, and financial resources in the selection of one or more new and high-tech industries as breakthrough points to bring about the development of other industries.

These conditions provided by the international environment are generating fine opportunities and possibilities for China's utilization of foreign capital.

178. What are the major challenges that China faces?

1. Since the 1990s, in order to stimulate economic growth, Western industrialized and developed countries have been taking measures to adjust their own domestic economic structure, to speed up the transformation process of science and technology into production power, and to stimulate and encourage domestic capital input in high-tech industries. Among such Western countries, the United States, for instance, needs large amounts of capital to ease the difficulties posed by large financial and foreign trade deficits; there is a huge demand for capital in Germany for its eastern regions, making it difficult for Germany to make large overseas investment; and the oil-producing countries from the Gulf are so preoccupied with declining of oil prices and postwar reconstruction that they are unable to inject more "oil dollars" into the international capital market. These factors have negatively influenced the supply of capital in the international capital market as well as the international capital investment in developing countries.

2. There is an increased need for capital in some countries. Russia and Eastern Europe require a lot of capital for economic recovery. Unless

there is a fundamental change in the situations, those countries will gradually become large consumers in the international capital market. From the standpoint of needs for international capital by developing countries, since the 1980s countries in Latin America and Asia, including China, have resorted to still greater opening, policy adjustment, and increased opportunities for foreign capital in order to promote the development of their domestic economy, while some debtor countries, in response to the debt-servicing programs of international organizations and creditor countries, are engaging in attracting international capital to boost their domestic economy. This situation leads to a great demand for international capital and some competition among developing countries for relatively limited supply of international capital.

179. What are China's guiding principles in utilizing foreign capital?

China's general guiding principles in utilizing foreign capital are to expand openness to the outside world; to utilize foreign capital, resources, technologies, and managerial expertise; and to speed up its modernization process.

Further openness to the outside world calls for regional expansion, the expansion of areas in which to utilize foreign capital, and the opening of the international market to promote diversity in foreign trade and development of an outward-oriented economy.

In preparing development strategies for utilization of foreign capital, China should take into consideration the international environment and its own developing domestic economy. Following the gradual expansion of the size of foreign capital utilized by China are the accumulation of foreign capital, a fairly high level of absolute amount of foreign debts, and an annual increase in the amounts of payable principal and interests. Following the increase in direct foreign investment has been an annual increase in dividends remitted outside China and the debt-servicing amounts payable by enterprises with foreign investment. Therefore, a large amount of foreign exchange is needed. To ensure servicing of foreign debts and balancing of international revenues and expenditures, China will have to be realistic and seek an effective use of foreign capital in full consideration of the special Chinese characteristics so as to improve the economic benefits in utilizing foreign capital.

180. What are the trends in China's opening and utilization of foreign capital?

First, further efforts will be made in China in opening to the outside world the special economic zones, Shanghai Pudong New Zone, and border, riverside, and inland central cities, to upgrade the level of openness; better management of the special economic zones, open coastal cities, and open coastal economic zones; expansion of opened border regions to speed up the process of opening inland cities and autonomous regions; opening of Changjiang (Yangtze) River-side cities, following the opening of Shanghai Pudong New Zone, in order to build Shanghai as quickly as possible into an international economic, financial, and trade center to bring about an economic upsurge of Changjiang (Yangtze) River Delta as well as of the whole region along the Changjiang (Yangtze) River reaches; and expediting the opening and development of the provinces of Guangdong, Fujian, and Hainan and the Bohai Sea gulf regions, with a 20-year target of building Guangdong and other regions with similar conditions into modernized regions.

With its vast land area and huge population, it is more than necessary for China to establish a nationwide economic system with a fairly complete range of categories and broad development, so as to establish a solid foundation for China's economy and gain a favorable international position. However, with limitations on natural resources, geographic conditions, and existing economic and technological bases, it is not necessary or possible to establish an economic system with a complete range of categories for all regions; rather, with centralized planning and guidance by the State, unique industrial strengths shall be built in different regions according to unique situations, with a rational division of work among the regions and full use of their strengths. Nor should a small but complete economic system be encouraged in the utilization of foreign capital to avoid repetition of construction. Coastal regions are to give full display of their strengths to attract foreign capital for the development of capital- or technology-intensive industries and of development of foreign economy and to improve the competitiveness of their products in the world market, while some labor-intensive projects and projects in resource development should be gradually relocated to inland China. Inland regions are to develop industries that draw on their unique strengths based on their own characteristics in resource supplies. Such promotion and development in a tiered pattern with focal areas for development constitute China's strategy for utilization of foreign capital.

Second, China is to continue to attract foreign investment, continue to improve its investment environment by providing more convenient conditions and secure legal guarantees for business operations of foreign business, and actively attract foreign investment in accordance with industrial policies, to guide foreign investment mainly in infrastructure facilities, basic industries, enterprises with technological renovations, and capital- or technology-intensive industries and moderately to areas of financing, commerce, tourism, and real estate. Foreign businesses are encouraged to establish export-oriented enterprises; conditions will be created to grant national treatment to enterprises with foreign investment, and administration of enterprises with foreign investment shall be improved. Foreign loans of various kinds will be used in a more active, effective, and appropriate manner. Attention is to be paid to maintaining an appropriate size of foreign loans and a rational foreign debt structure in order to maintain a sound credit reputation, so that the increase of foreign loans will be made at the same speed as that of the development of the national economy, the demands for investment, and international balancing of revenues and expenses.

181. What are China's strategic objectives in utilization of foreign capital?

China's adoption of appropriate development strategies for foreign capital utilization includes a reasonable determination of the size, structure, and orientation of the foreign capital to be used, a crucial issue with a bearing on the overall opening and economic construction.

The Communist Party of China proposed establishing definite guiding principles for the utilization of foreign capital in greater quantity and better quality at its 14th Central Committee and its Third Plenary Session. According to the strategic arrangement of the modernization of China's national economy to be realized in three steps, the Eighth National People's Congress set an annual growth rate for China's national economy during the 1990s at 8% to 9%; this is the basis for planning foreign capital utilization.

Centering around rationalizing structure and improving overall economic benefits, China's strategic objectives in foreign capital utilization are to maintain the growth rate of foreign capital utilization in pace with national economic development, debt-servicing capabilities, domestic supplementing capabilities, and capacity for absorbing foreign capital.

Too much caution in utilizing foreign capital would mean a loss of international opportunities and a slowing of economic development; negligence of conditions and overuse of foreign capital would lead to a debt crisis, forestalling economic development. Therefore, foreign capital shall be utilized in an active and safe manner, holding to the size and growth speed that fit with the national power.

In order to achieve strategic objectives in foreign capital utilization, a substantial improvement shall be made in such utilization, focusing on the structure, quality, and economic benefits instead of quantity and speed, as in the past; on guidance and administration instead of project examinations and approval; on directing foreign capital in capital- and technology-intensive projects instead of only labor-intensive projects; and on establishing high-appreciation-value projects instead of ordinary processing projects. The quantity of foreign capital to be used shall be incorporated into actual results of such usage, so that equal attention is paid to the structure, quality, results, and speed.

182. What are China's specific strategic measures in foreign capital utilization?

1. Perfecting the investment environment to attract foreign capital and further attracting foreign capital to continue improving the investment environment.

2. Through active and effective industrial policies, directing foreign capital to flow into areas in urgent need of development as called for by the national economy.

3. Based on actual situations in economic development of different regions, giving full display to regional economic strengths to form a reasonable pattern of work division.

4. Promoting active cooperation between China's large enterprise groups and foreign transnational corporations, for the benefit of the change of operational mechanisms and technological renewal and progress in China's enterprise groups.

5. Giving full consideration to the characteristics of China for the length of border and number of neighboring countries, for coastal and border provinces and cities to participate in economic relations and cooperation with neighboring regions.

6. Making full use of China's strengths in the great number of new- and high-technology scientific and research results by the strong contingent of scientific and technological workers in China, by introducing foreign capital for joint development, in order to bring about the industrialization and commercialization of new and high technologies.

7. Insisting on the principle under which the users and beneficiaries of loans are to repay such loans, and implementing the policy of foreign loans to be borrowed by the State and repaid by the user, or of foreign loans to be borrowed and repaid by the user, while in the case of State-level key industries for development and of projects with outstanding social benefits, part of the loans may be repaid by the State.

183. What is China's industrial orientation for utilizing foreign capital?

It is necessary to use industrial policies to guide the limited foreign investment into the industrial sectors of the national economy that urgently need development.

After more than 10 years of reforms and development, great changes have taken place in China's economic setup, including infrastructure facilities, basic industries, the structure of exporting products, and domestic consumption needs, and production power has been greatly upgraded. The previous industrial policies have been outdated and replaced, and the means of economic operations are at the transition stage of system changes, with market mechanisms yet to play a full role in the distribution of resources.

Industrial policies will have to be thoroughly implemented in loaning international capital, to insist on using foreign capital for the purposes of development and manufacturing (i.e., the investment in fixed assets) and in the introduction of technologies, equipment, and materials, so that direct contributions can be made to the development of the national economy and a solid foundation laid for future debt servicing. This is the key to improving the economic results of utilizing foreign loans and also the basic guarantee for a healthy circulation of foreign capital utilization. It should be prohibited to use foreign loans to cover domestic financial deficits or to import consumer goods or to convert into RMB for use. The key orientation for foreign capital utilization should be infrastructure facilities, basic industries, agriculture, and environment protection—in particular, the infrastructure projects that are confining the development of the national economy, such as energy, communications, and raw materials. These industries have a direct bearing on overall national economic development and are China's weak points, now and into the future. Growth in these industries will be beneficial to China's overall economic development. However, such projects usually do not yield good economic profits and have no capability for making foreign exchange earnings. Therefore, great attention shall be paid to exporting and hard-currency-making industries in order to improve China's debt-servicing capabilities. From the standpoint of regional orientation, foreign loans during the 1980s were mainly used in the coastal regions; more loans should be arranged for inland provinces and regions. And preferential loan facilities from international organizations and government loans should be used more in midwestern regions of China.

Efforts will be made to combine the latest State industrial policies of the 1990s with the characteristics of foreign investment to guide the orientation of foreign investment for the latter to help improve weaknesses in China's economic development and promote the upgrading of the industrial structure. For this purpose, preferential policies will be implemented in favor of certain key industries, offering major assistance to infrastructure facilities and certain basic industries and other capital- or technology-intensive industries. Sufficient favors will be granted by the State in areas of capital input, the time period for the deduction of and exemption from taxes, domestic market shares, and land usage fees. In the meantime, appropriate preferential treatment will be given to investment in projects of ordinary manufacturing industries and renovation of existing enterprises that help to expand domestic production capacity and the export market. The national-status treatment with no special preferential policies will be granted to other projects, while market competition mechanisms will be given full display.

Areas in which China actively encourages foreign investment include the following:

1. Comprehensive development of agriculture and projects of new agricultural technologies, such as reclaiming of wasteland, uncultivated mountains, underdeveloped slopes and shoals, re-formation of fields with medium or low yields, development of new products, introduction of fine forestry seeds, breeding of fine poultry and livestock, development of forage proteins, and new varieties of highly effective and safe pesticides and high-concentration chemical fertilizers.

2. Infrastructure facilities and basic industries, including projects urgently calling for development in China such as energy (coal, electric power, petroleum), communications (railway, highway, seaport, airport), and key raw materials (iron and steel, nonferrous metals, chemical industry, building materials).

3. Backbone industries that China plans for speedier development in the future, such as machinery and electronics, petrochemicals, automobile manufacturing, and construction.

4. New equipment and materials projects that bring in advanced technologies urgently needed in China, improve product performance, conserve energy or raw materials, and enhance technological and economic benefits of enterprises, or whose products are nonexistent in China but suitable for market needs.

5. Projects that suit the needs of international markets to increase exports and yield foreign currency, upgrade product levels, and expand product sales, in particular those exporting and hard-currency-making projects with high appreciation values.

6. New technology or equipment projects with comprehensive use of resources or reclaimed resources, such as comprehensive development and utilization of fuels with low calorific values or of associated resources, and comprehensive development and utilization of industrial waste materials.

China will no longer encourage or restrict foreign investment in technologies already developed in China, or projects possessing a production capacity sufficient for the market needs, or engaged in pure assembly against imported parts with products to be sold 100% in the domestic market. More specifically such projects as not encouraged or restricted include cotton yarn, photocopiers, washing machines, refrigerators, and tape recorders. Projects with great market profits, few obstacles in the introduction of technologies, and a high probability of forming a market monopoly will be restricted by means of shareholding, such as certain pilot projects of services and trade with foreign capital introduced. Projects will be prohibited when they involve State security, are detrimental to national economic and social development or public interests, pollute the environment, or harm the environment.

184. What are the principles that China follows in improving its investment environment?

In investing in China, foreign businesses need not only the correct material conditions for their business operations, but also an environment that offers the social services necessary for business development.

After over 10 years of effort in reforms and opening, China has made notable improvements in its investment environment, though some problems remain.

A good investment environment is the result of a comprehensive interaction of various factors, not something that can be attained through a single measure. To improve the level of projects with foreign investment and attract more foreign investment, much work must be undertaken. On the one hand, investment in the construction of the "hard" part of the environment should be strengthened: improving infrastructure facilities, while reinforcing the construction of social service facilities. When it is difficult to attain a satisfactory status within a short time through investment in the "hard" part of the environment, full display should be given to strengths of the socialist system in perfecting the "soft" part of the investment, to make up for the weak "hard" with a better "soft" part. For this reason, efforts should be made to continue to improve laws and regulations in relation to foreign capital utilization, provide more convenience and sufficient legal protection for foreign investment, strengthen the administration of foreign capital utilization, improve the foreign investment administrative bodies, improve work efficiency and service quality, and do away with bureaucracy, in order to create good investment conditions in China.

In order to achieve its strategic objectives of foreign capital utilization, China will shift its attention from compiling preferential treatment for foreign investment to creating an investment environment that stresses fair competition, building up a foreign capital utilization administration system from the macro point of view that fits with the socialist market economy, and installing a management system in foreign capital utilization and of enterprises with foreign investment from the micro point of view, which operates in line with common international practice and yet is harmonious with the Chinese context.

APPENDIX ONE

Foreign Investment Laws and Regulations

1. The Law of the People's Republic of China on Chinese–Foreign Equity Joint Ventures

Adopted on 1 July 1979 at the Second Session of the Fifth National People's Congress, and amended pursuant to the Decision on Amendment of the Law of the People's Republic of China on Chinese–Foreign Equity Joint Ventures passed on 4 April 1990 at the Third Session of the Seventh National People's Congress.

Article 1　The People's Republic of China, in order to expand international economic cooperation and technological exchange, permits foreign companies, enterprises, and other economic organizations or individuals (hereinafter referred to as the foreign party) to jointly establish and operate equity joint ventures within the territory of the People's Republic of China with Chinese companies, enterprises, or other economic organizations (hereinafter referred to as the Chinese party) based on the principle of equality and mutual benefit, and upon the approval of the Chinese Government.

Article 2　The Chinese Government shall protect in accordance with law the investments of the foreign party, the profits due to it, and its other lawful rights and interests in an equity joint venture under the Agreement, Contract, and Articles of Association approved by the Chinese Government.

All the activities of an equity joint venture shall comply with the provisions of the laws, decrees, and relevant rules and regulations of the People's Republic of China.

The state will not nationalize or expropriate equity joint ventures; under special circumstances, based on the requirements of social and public interests, equity joint ventures may be expropriated in accordance with legal procedures, and corresponding compensation shall be provided.

Article 3   The Agreement, Contract, and Articles of Association of an equity joint venture signed by the parties to the venture shall be submitted to the state department in charge of foreign economic relations and trade (hereinafter referred to as the Examination and Approval Authority) for examination and approval. The Examination and Approval Authority shall decide within three months to approve or disapprove. After an equity joint venture has been approved, it shall register with the state department in charge of Administration of Industry and Commerce, obtain its Business License, and commence business operations.

Article 4   The form of an equity joint venture shall be a limited liability company.

The proportion of the foreign party's contribution to the registered capital of an equity joint venture shall in general not be less than 25%.

The parties to the venture shall share profits and bear risks and losses in proportion to their respective contributions to the registered capital.

The transfer of a party's contribution to the registered capital must be agreed upon by each party to the venture.

Article 5   The parties to an equity joint venture may make their investments in cash, in kind, in industrial property rights, etc.

The technology and equipment contributed by a foreign party as its investment must be advanced technology and equipment which is truly suited to the needs of China. In case of losses caused by deception through intentional provision of outdated technology and equipment, compensation shall be paid for such losses.

The investment of a Chinese party may include providing the right to use a site during the term of operation of the equity joint venture. If the right to use a site is not a part of the investment by a Chinese party, the venture shall pay the Chinese Government a fee for its use.

The various investments mentioned above shall be specified in the Contract and Articles of Association of the equity joint venture, and the value of each contribution (except for the site) shall be appraised and determined through discussions between the parties to the venture.

Article 6   An equity joint venture shall establish a board of directors
with a size and composition stipulated in the Contract and the Articles of
Association after consultation between the parties to the venture; and each
party to the venture shall appoint and replace its own director(s). The
chairman and the vice chairman of the board shall be determined through
consultation between the parties to the venture or elected by the board.
Where a director appointed by the Chinese party or the foreign party
serves as chairman, a director appointed by the other party shall serve as
vice chairman. The board of directors shall decide important issues concerning the equity joint venture based on the principle of equality and mutual benefit.

The function and powers of the board of directors shall be to discuss
and decide, pursuant to the provisions of the Articles of Association of the
equity joint venture, all important issues concerning the venture, namely:
the development plan of the enterprise, production and business programs, the budget, distribution of profits, plans concerning labor and
wages, the termination of business, and the appointment or hiring of the
general manager, the deputy general manager(s), the chief engineer, the
chief accountant, and the auditor, as well as their functions and powers
and their remuneration, etc.

The positions of general manager and deputy general manager(s) (or
the factory manager and deputy factory manager(s)) shall be assumed by
nominees of the respective parties to the venture.

The employment and dismissal of the staff and workers of an equity
joint venture shall be stipulated according to law in the Agreement or
Contract between the parties to the venture.

Article 7   From the gross profit earned by an equity joint venture,
after payment of the venture's income tax in accordance with the provisions of the tax laws of the People's Republic of China, deductions shall
be made for the reserved fund, the bonus and welfare fund for staff and
workers, and the enterprise development fund as stipulated in the Articles of Association of the venture and the net profit shall be distributed to
the parties to the venture in proportion to their respective contributions to
the registered capital.

Any equity joint venture may enjoy preferential treatment in the
form of tax reductions and exemptions in accordance with provisions of
state laws and administrative regulations relating to taxation.

When a foreign party uses its share of the net profit as reinvestment
within the territory of China, it may apply for a refund of part of the income tax already paid.

Article 8   An equity joint venture shall, on the basis of its Business License, open a foreign-exchange account with a bank or another financial institution which is permitted by the state foreign-exchange control authority to engage in foreign-exchange business.

Matters concerning the foreign exchange of an equity joint venture shall be handled in conformity with the foreign-exchange control regulations of the People's Republic of China.

An equity joint venture may, in the course of its business activities, raise funds directly from foreign banks.

The various items of insurance of an equity joint venture shall be obtained from China's insurance companies.

Article 9   The plans for production and business operations of an equity joint venture shall be filed for the record with the department in charge and implemented through economic contracts.

For the raw and processed materials, fuel, auxiliary equipment, etc. needed by an equity joint venture, priority shall be given to purchasing in China, but such purchases may also be made directly on the international market with foreign exchange raised by the equity joint venture itself.

An equity joint venture shall be encouraged to sell its products outside the territory of China. Export products may be sold on foreign markets by an equity joint venture directly or by entrusted institutions related to it, and they may also be sold through China's foreign-trade institutions. The products of an equity joint venture may also be sold on the Chinese market.

When necessary, an equity joint venture may set up branch institutions outside China.

Article 10   The net profit received by a foreign party after fulfillment of its obligations at law and under the provisions of agreements and contracts, the funds received by it upon the expiration or termination of an equity joint venture as well as other funds may be remitted abroad in accordance with foreign-exchange control regulations in the currency stipulated in the joint venture contract.

The foreign party shall be encouraged to deposit in the Bank of China the foreign exchange which may be remitted abroad.

Article 11   The wage income and other legitimate income of foreign staff and workers of an equity joint venture may be remitted abroad in accordance with foreign-exchange control regulations after payment of individual income tax under the tax laws of the People's Republic of China.

Article 12   The term of operation of equity joint ventures may be agreed upon differently according to different lines of business and different circumstances. The term of operation of equity joint ventures engaged in some lines of business shall be fixed, while the term of operation of equity joint ventures engaged in other lines of business may or may not be fixed. Where the parties to an equity joint venture with a fixed term of operation agree to extend the term of operation, they shall submit an application to the Examination and Approval Authority not later than six months prior to the expiration of the operation term. The Examination and Approval Authority shall decide, within one month of receipt of the application, to approve or disapprove.

Article 13   If serious losses are incurred by an equity joint venture, or one party fails to fulfill its obligations under the Contract and the Articles of Association, or an event of *force majeure* occurs, etc., the contract may be terminated after consultation and agreement between the parties to the venture, subject to approval by the Examination and Approval Authority and to registration with the state department in charge of Administration of Industry and Commerce. In case of losses caused by breach of contract, economic responsibility shall be borne by the breaching party.

Article 14   When a dispute arises between the parties to a venture and the board of directors is unable to resolve it through consultation, the dispute shall be settled through conciliation or arbitration conducted by an arbitral institution of China, or through arbitration by another arbitral institution agreed upon by the parties to the venture.

Article 15   This law shall come into force on the date of its promulgation. The power to amend this law is vested in the National's People's Congress.

2. Implementing Regulations of the Law of the People's Republic of China on Joint Ventures Using Chinese and Foreign Investment

Promulgated by the State Council on 20 September 1983

Chapter I General Provisions

Article 1   These Regulations are specially formulated in order to facilitate the smooth implementation of the Law of the People's Republic of

China on Joint Ventures Using Chinese and Foreign Investment (hereinafter referred to as the Law on Joint Ventures Using Chinese and Foreign Investment).

Article 2 Joint ventures using Chinese and foreign investment (hereinafter referred to as joint ventures) established in China in accordance with the Law on Joint Ventures Using Chinese and Foreign Investment are Chinese legal persons and are subject to the jurisdiction and receive the protection of Chinese law.

Article 3 Joint ventures established in China shall be able to promote the development of China's economy and the raising of scientific and technical levels, benefiting socialist modernization and construction. The main industries in which it is permitted to establish joint ventures are:

1. Energy development, building materials, chemicals, and metallurgy
2. Machine manufacturing, instruments and meters, and offshore-petroleum exploitation equipment manufacturing
3. Electronics, computers, and communications equipment manufacturing
4. Light industry, textiles, foodstuffs, medicine and medical apparatus, and packaging
5. Agriculture, animal husbandry, and aquaculture
6. Tourism and services

Article 4 Joint ventures for which establishment is applied shall put stress on economic results and shall meet one or several of the following requirements:

1. They shall adopt advanced technical equipment and scientific management methods, enabling them to increase the variety of products, raise the quality and quantity of products, and conserve energy and materials.
2. They shall be of benefit to the technical reform of enterprises, enabling them to achieve apparent results quickly and large returns with small investment.
3. They shall be able to expand the export of products, increasing foreign-exchange income.
4. They shall be able to train technical personnel and managerial personnel.

Article 5   Joint ventures for which establishment is applied are not to be approved if one of the following circumstances is involved:

1. Detriment to China's sovereignty
2. Violation of Chinese law
3. Nonconformity with the requirements of the development of China's national economy
4. Causing of environmental pollution
5. The Agreement, Contract, or Articles of Association signed are obviously unfair, harming the rights and interests of one party to the joint venture.

Article 6   Unless otherwise stipulated, the government department in charge of the Chinese participant in a joint venture is to be the department in charge of the joint venture (hereinafter referred to as the department in charge of the enterprise). When a joint venture has two or more Chinese participants and these are under different departments or regions, the relevant departments or regions shall have discussions and determine one department in charge of the enterprise.

The department in charge of the enterprise is responsible for guidance of, assistance to, and supervision over the joint venture.

Article 7   Joint ventures have the right to conduct operations and management autonomously within the scope of the stipulations of Chinese laws and regulations and of joint venture Agreements, Contracts, and Articles of Association. The various relevant departments shall provide support and assistance.

Chapter II Establishment and Registration

Article 8   The establishment of joint ventures in China must be examined and approved by the Ministry of Foreign Economic Relations and Trade of the People's Republic of China (hereafter referred to as the Ministry of Foreign Economic Relations and Trade). After approval, the Ministry of Foreign Economic Relations and Trade is to issue a Certificate of Approval.

In any cases where the following conditions exist, the Ministry of Foreign Economic Relations and Trade must entrust the people's government of the relevant province, autonomous region, or directly administered municipality or the relevant ministry or bureau of the State Council (hereafter referred to as the entrusted organs) with examination and approval:

1. The total amount of investment is within the sum stipulated by the State Council and the source of capital of the Chinese participants has already been ascertained;
2. The additional allocation of raw materials by the state is not required and the national balance in such areas as fuel, power, transportation, and foreign trade export quotas is not affected.

The entrusted organ, after approving the establishment of a joint venture, shall report to the Ministry of Foreign Economic Relations and Trade for the record, and the Certificate of Approval is to be issued by the Ministry of Foreign Economic Relations and Trade.

(The Ministry of Foreign Economic Relations and Trade and the entrusted organs are hereafter collectively referred to as the examination and approval organs.)

Article 9   The establishment of joint ventures is to be handled in accordance with the following procedures:

1. The Chinese participant in a joint venture is to submit to its department in charge a project proposal on the intended establishment of a joint venture with (a) foreign participant(s) and a preliminary feasibility study report. Only after the said proposal and preliminary feasibility study report have been examined and agreed to by the department in charge and passed on to the examination and approval organ and approved, can the joint venture parties conduct various work centered on a feasibility study, and, on this basis, discuss and sign the joint venture Agreement, Contract, and Articles of Association.
2. When applying for the establishment of a joint venture, the Chinese participant in the joint venture is to be responsible for the delivery of the following official documents to the examination and approval organ:
   a. Application for the establishment of a joint venture;
   b. The feasibility study report jointly prepared by the joint venture parties;
   c. The joint venture Agreement, Contract, and Articles of Association signed by authorized representatives of the joint venture parties;
   d. The list of persons appointed by the joint venture parties as chairman, vice-chairman, and directors of the joint venture;
   e. Signed opinions of the department in charge of the Chinese participant in the joint venture and the people's government of

the province, autonomous region, or directly administered municipality where the joint venture is located with regard to the establishment of the joint venture in question.

The above documents must be written in the Chinese language. The documents in b, c, and d above may be written concurrently in a foreign language decided on by the joint venture parties. The documents written in both languages are to have equal validity.

Article 10   The examination and approval organ shall, within three months from the date of receipt of all the documents stipulated in item 2 of Article 9 of these Regulations, decide whether to approve or disapprove them. If the examination and approval organ discovers that there are improper points in the above documents, it shall demand amendment within a limited time, failing which it is not to grant approval.

Article 11   Applicants shall, within one month after receipt of the Certificate of Approval, undertake registration procedures with the Administrative Bureau for Industry and Commerce of the province, autonomous region, or directly administered municipality where the joint venture is located (hereafter referred to as the registration and administration organ) on the strength of the Certificate of Approval, in accordance with the stipulations of the Regulations of the People's Republic of China on the Registration and Administration of Joint Ventures Using Chinese and Foreign Investment. The date of issue of the Business License of a joint venture is the date of establishment of the said joint venture.

Article 12   Any foreign investor interested in establishing a joint venture in China but having no specific cooperating partner on the Chinese side may submit a preliminary plan for the joint venture project and entrust the China International Trust and Investment Corporation or the trust and investment organ of the relevant province, autonomous region, or directly administered municipality and relevant government departments or people's organizations with the introduction of a cooperating partner.

Article 13   The joint venture Agreement mentioned in this chapter refers to a document concluded by the joint venture parties upon agreement on certain main points and principles regarding the establishment of a joint venture.

The joint venture Contract refers to a document concluded by the joint venture parties upon agreement on the relationship between the parties concerning their rights and obligations for the establishment of a joint venture. The Articles of Association of the joint venture refer to a document that, in accordance with the principles stipulated in the joint venture Contract and upon full agreement by the joint venture parties, stipulates such items as the purpose, organizational principles, and operational and managerial methods of the joint venture.

If there is conflict between the joint venture Agreement and the joint venture Contract, the joint venture Contract shall prevail.

Upon agreement by the joint venture parties, they may also conclude only a joint venture Contract and Articles of Association and not conclude a joint venture Agreement.

Article 14 Joint Venture Contracts shall include the following main contents:

1. The names, countries of registration, and legal address of the joint venture parties, and the names, positions and nationalities of their legal representatives;
2. The name of the joint venture, its legal address, purpose, scope, and scale of business;
3. The total amount of investment and the registered capital of the joint venture, the amounts of capital contribution by the joint venture parties, the ratio of capital contributions, the forms of capital contribution, the time limit for paying in capital contributions, and stipulations on shortfalls in paying in and assignment of amounts of capital contribution;
4. The ratio of distribution of profits to and the bearing of losses by the joint venture parties;
5. The composition of the board of directors of the joint venture, the distribution of the numbers of directors, and the responsibilities, limits of authority, and method of employment of the general manager, deputy general managers, and other high-level management personnel;
6. The main production equipment and production technology to be adopted and their sources;
7. The means of purchase of raw materials and of sale of products, and the ratio of products to be sold inside and outside China;
8. Arrangements for receipts and disbursements of foreign-exchange funds;
9. Principles for the handling of finance, accounting, and auditing;

10. Stipulations regarding such matters as labor management, wages, welfare, and labor insurance;
11. The term of the joint venture, its dissolution, and liquidation procedures;
12. Responsibilities for violation of the Contract;
13. Means and procedures for the resolution of disputes between the joint venture parties;
14. The language adopted for the Contract text and the conditions for effectiveness of the Contract.

Appendixes to joint venture contracts are to have equal validity with the joint venture Contract.

Article 15   The conclusion, validity, interpretation and implementation of joint venture Contracts and the resolution of disputes thereunder shall all be governed by Chinese law.

Article 16   Articles of Association of joint ventures shall include the following contents:

1. The name of the joint venture and its legal address;
2. The purpose, business scope, and term of the joint venture;
3. The names, countries of registration and legal addresses of the joint venture parties, and the names, positions, and nationalities of their legal representatives;
4. The total amount of investment and the registered capital of the joint venture, the amounts of capital contribution by the joint venture parties, the ratio of capital contributions, stipulations on the assignment of amounts of capital contribution, the ratio of distribution of profits to and bearing of losses by the joint venture parties;
5. The composition, authority, and rules of procedure of the board of directors, the terms of office of the directors, and the responsibilities of the chairman and vice-chairman of the board of directors;
6. The setting up of management organs, administrative rules, the responsibilities, and methods of appointment and dismissal of the general manager, deputy general managers, and other high-level managerial personnel;
7. Principles of the financial, accounting, and auditing systems;
8. Dissolution and liquidation;
9. Procedures for amendment of the Articles of Association.

Article 17   Joint venture Agreements, Contracts, and Articles of Association are to take effect after being approved by the examination and approval organs. The same applies in the event of amendments.

Article 18   The examination and approval organs and the registration and administration organs are responsible for supervising and inspecting the implementation of joint venture Contracts and Articles of Association.

Chapter III Form of Organization and Registered Capital

Article 19   Joint ventures are limited liability companies. The liability of joint venture parties to a joint venture is limited to the amounts of capital contribution subscribed by each.

Article 20   The total amount of investment of a joint venture (including loans) refers to the total of the construction funds and the production circulating funds needed to be injected in accordance with the scale of production stipulated in the joint venture Contract and Articles of Association.

Article 21   The registered capital of a joint venture refers to the total amount of capital registered at the registration and administration organ for the establishment of the joint venture, and shall be the total of the amounts of capital contribution subscribed by the joint venture parties.

The registered capital of joint ventures shall generally be expressed in Renminbi. It may also be expressed in a foreign currency agreed upon by the joint venture parties.

Article 22   Joint ventures must not reduce their registered capital during their terms.

Article 23   When one joint venture party is to assign all or part of its amount of capital contribution to a third party, it must obtain the consent of the other joint venture party and approval from the examination and approval organ.

When one joint venture party is to assign all or part of its amount of capital contribution, the other joint venture party has a preemptive right to purchase.

The conditions under which one joint venture party assigns its amount of capital contribution to a third party must not be more preferential than the conditions for assignment to the other joint venture party.

Assignments in violation of the above stipulations are invalid.

Article 24 The increase, assignment, or disposition by other means of the registered capital of joint ventures shall be passed by a meeting of the board of directors and reported to the original examination and approval organ for approval. Alterations to the registered particulars are to be undertaken at the original registration and administration organ.

Chapter IV Forms of Capital Contribution

Article 25 The participants in a joint venture may use currency for capital contributions and may also use such items as buildings, factory premises, machinery, equipment or other materials, industrial property rights, proprietary technology, and rights to the use of sites, as valued, for capital contributions. In cases where buildings, factories, machinery, equipment or other materials, industrial property rights, or proprietary technology are used as capital contributions, their valuation is to be discussed and determined by the joint venture parties in accordance with the principles of fairness and reasonableness, or a third party agreed upon by the joint venture parties is to be retained to make an assessment.

Article 26 Foreign currency contributed by foreign participants in a joint venture as capital contribution is to be converted into Renminbi in accordance with the posted exchange rate announced by the State Administration of Foreign Exchange Control of the People's Republic of China (hereafter referred to as the State Administration of Foreign Exchange Control) on the day of its payment or is to be cross-converted into the agreed foreign currency.

If it is required to convert the Renminbi cash contributed by Chinese participants in a joint venture as a capital contribution into foreign currency, it is to be converted in accordance with the posted exchange rate announced by the State Administration of Foreign Exchange Control on the day of its payment.

Article 27 The machinery, equipment, or other materials contributed by foreign participants in a joint venture as capital contributions must meet all of the following conditions:

1. They must be indispensable to the joint venture's production;
2. They must be items that China cannot produce, or, although China can produce them, the prices are overly high or the items are un-

able to guarantee the meeting of requirements with respect to technical function and time of supply; and

3. The valuation must not be higher than the current international market price for similar machinery, equipment, or other materials.

Article 28 The industrial property rights or proprietary technology contributed by foreign participants in a joint venture as capital contributions must meet one of the following conditions:

1. They must enable the production of new products that China urgently needs or products suitable for export;
2. They must enable the making of marked improvements in the function and quality of existing products and the raising of productivity; and
3. They must enable marked conservation of raw materials, fuel, or power.

Article 29 Foreign participants in a joint venture who contribute industrial property rights or proprietary technology as capital contributions shall present relevant documentation on the said industrial property rights or proprietary technology, including such relevant documents as photocopies of the patent certificates or trademark registration certificates, documents indicating the state of validity, technical characteristics, practical value, the basis for calculating the valuation, and the valuation agreement signed with the Chinese participants in the joint venture, with these documents to serve as appendixes to the joint venture contract.

Article 30 Machinery, equipment or other materials, industrial property rights, or proprietary technology contributed by foreign participants in a joint venture as capital contributions shall be examined and agreed to by the department in charge of the Chinese participants in the joint venture and submitted to the examination and approval organ for approval.

Article 31 Joint venture parties shall pay in the amounts of their respective capital contributions in full in accordance with the time limit stipulated in the Contract. In cases of overdue payment or incomplete payment, interest for the delay or compensation for losses shall be paid in accordance with the stipulations of the Contract.

Article 32 After the joint venture parties have paid in the amounts of their capital contributions, these shall be verified by a Chinese registered accountant, who is to issue a report of verification of capital, on the basis of which the joint venture is afterward to issue Certificates of Capital Contribution. Certificates of Capital Contribution are to state the following items: the name of the joint venture; the day, month, and year of the establishment of the joint venture; the names of the joint venturing entities or individuals; the amounts of their capital contributions and the day, month, and year of the capital contributions; and the day, month, and year of issuance of the Certificates of Capital Contribution.

Chapter V Board of Directors and Management Organs

Article 33   The board of directors is the highest organ of authority of a joint venture. It decides all major questions of the questions of the joint venture.

Article 34   The board of directors must have no fewer than three members. The distribution of the numbers of directors is to be determined by discussion between the joint venture parties by reference to the ratio of capital contributions.

The directors are to be appointed by the joint venture parties. The chairman of the board of directors is to be appointed by the Chinese participant in the joint venture, and the vice-chairman of the board of directors is to be appointed by the foreign participant in the joint venture.

The term of office for directors is four years; they may have their terms consecutively renewed through reappointment by the joint venture parties.

Article 35   A board of directors meeting is to be convened at least once each year. The chairman of the board of directors is to be responsible for calling and presiding over the meeting. When the chairman of the board of directors is unable to call the meeting, he is to entrust the vice chairman of the board of directors or another director to call and preside over the board of directors meeting. The chairman of the board of directors may convene an interim board of directors meeting upon proposal by more than one-third of the directors.

A board of directors meeting shall only be held if over two-thirds of the directors are in attendance. When a director is unable to attend, he may issue a proxy entrusting another to represent him in attendance and vote for him.

Board of directors meetings shall generally be held at the location of the joint venture's legal address.

Article 36 Resolutions on the following items may be made only after being unanimously passed by the directors in attendance at a board meeting:

1. Amendment of the joint venture Articles of Association;
2. Termination and dissolution of the joint venture;
3. Increase or assignment of the registered capital of the joint venture; and
4. Merger of the joint venture with another economic organization.

Resolutions on other items may be made according to the rules of procedure stated in the joint venture Articles of Association.

Article 37 The chairman of the board of directors is the legal representative of a joint venture. When the chairman of the board of directors is unable to perform his responsibilities, he shall authorize the vice chairman of the board of directors or another director to represent the joint venture.

Article 38 Joint ventures are the establishment organs to be responsible for the daily operational and managerial work of the joint venture. Management organs are to have a general manager and several deputy general managers. The deputy managers assist the general manager in his work.

Article 39 The general manager carries out the various resolutions of board of directors meetings and organizes and leads the daily operational and managerial work of a joint venture. The general manager, within the scope of authorization of the board of directors, is to represent the joint venture in external affairs and, internally, to appoint and dismiss subordinate personnel and exercise other responsibilities as authorized by the board of directors.

Article 40 The general manager and deputy general managers are to be retained by the board of directors of a joint venture. These positions may be held by Chinese citizens and may also be held by foreign citizens.

The chairman of the board of directors, the vice chairman of the board of directors, and the directors may be retained by the board of directors to act concurrently in the capacity of general manager, deputy general managers, or other high-level managerial positions of a joint venture.

In handling major questions, the general manager shall discuss them with the deputy general managers.

The general manager or the deputy general managers must not concurrently act as general manager or deputy general managers of other economic organizations and must not participate in commercial competition by other economic organizations with their own joint venture.

Article 41   In the case of engagement in malpractice for private gain or serious dereliction of duty on the part of the general manager, deputy general managers, or other high-level managerial personnel, they may be dismissed at any time by resolution of the board of directors.

Article 42   When joint ventures need to establish branch organs (including sales organs) abroad or in Xianggang (Hong Kong) and Aomen (Macao), they must report the matter to the Ministry of Foreign Economic Relations and Trade for approval.

Chapter VI Importation of Technology

Article 43   The importation of technology mentioned in this chapter refers to a joint venture's acquisition of needed technology by means of technology transfer from a third party or a participant in the joint venture.

Article 44   Technology imported by joint ventures shall be appropriate and advanced, enabling the resulting products to display marked social and economic results domestically or to have competitive capacity on the international market.

Article 45   In concluding Technology Transfer Agreements, the right of joint ventures to conduct operations and management independently must be maintained, and the technology exporter is to be required to provide relevant materials by reference to the stipulations of Article 29 of these Regulations.

Article 46   Technology Transfer Agreements concluded by joint ventures shall be examined and agreed to by the department in charge of the enterprise and reported to the examination and approval organ for approval.

Technology Transfer Agreements must meet the following stipulations:

1. The fees for the use of technology shall be fair and reasonable. Royalties shall generally be adopted as the form of payment.

When royalties are adopted as the form of payment of fees for the use of technology, the royalty rate must not be higher than the common international level. Royalty rates shall be calculated on the basis of the net sales amount of the products produced with the technology in question or other reasonable means agreed upon by the parties;

2. Unless otherwise agreed upon by both parties, the technology exporter must not restrict the regions, quantities, and prices of the technology importer's export of the resulting products;
3. The term of Technology Transfer Agreements is generally not to exceed ten years;
4. After the expiration of Technology Transfer Agreements, the technology importer is to have the right to continue to use the technology in question;
5. The terms for mutual exchange of improvements in the technology shall be reciprocal for the parties concluding Technology Transfer Agreements;
6. The technology importer is to have the right to purchase needed equipment, parts, and raw materials from sources it considers suitable; and
7. No unreasonable restrictive clauses prohibited by Chinese law and regulations must be included.

Chapter VII Right to the Use of Sites and the Fees Therefor

Article 47 In using sites, joint ventures must practice the principle of thrift in the use of land. Joint ventures shall submit applications for their required sites to the municipal (county) level department in charge of land in the location of the joint venture and, after approval, obtain the right to use of a site by signing a contract. The contract shall state such items as the area, location, and use to be made of the site, the contract term and fee for the right to use of the site (hereafter referred to as the site-use fees), the rights and obligations of the parties, and penalty provisions for violation of the contract.

Article 48 If a Chinese participant in a joint venture already possesses the right to the use of the site required by the joint venture, the Chinese participant may use it as a capital contribution to the joint venture. The amount of its valuation shall be equivalent to the use fee to be paid for obtaining the right to the site use of a similar site.

Article 49   The standards for site-use fees shall be stipulated by the people's government for the province, autonomous region, or directly administered municipality where a site is located according to such factors as the use to be made of the site in question, geographic and environmental conditions, expenses for requisitioning the site, demolishing structures and resettlement arrangements, and the joint venture's requirements with regard to infrastructure, and the standards filed for the record with the Ministry of Foreign Economic Relations and Trade and the state department in charge of land.

Article 50   A joint venture engaged in agriculture or animal husbandry, with the agreement of the people's government of the province, autonomous region, or directly administered municipality where it is located, may pay site-use fees to the department in charge of land in its locality based on a percentage of the joint venture's business income.

In the case of projects of a development nature in economically undeveloped regions, special preferences may be granted in respect of site-use fees with the agreement of the local people's government.

Article 51   Site-use fees are not to be adjusted within five years from the start of use of a site. Afterward, when adjustments are needed in line with changes in economic development, the circumstances of supply and demand, and changes in geographical and environmental conditions, the interval between adjustments shall not be less than three years.

Site-use fees used as capital contribution by Chinese participants in a joint venture must not be adjusted during the term of the contract in question.

Article 52   The site-use fees for the right to the use of sites obtained by joint ventures in accordance with Article 47 of these Regulations shall be paid annually over the period of use of the site stipulated in the contract starting from the beginning of the period. If the period of use of the site in the first calendar year exceeds six months, the fee is to be calculated on the basis of a half-year; if it is less than six months, there is to be exemption from fees. During the contract period, if there are adjustments in the site-use fees, joint ventures shall pay fees in accordance with the new fee standards starting from the year of adjustment.

Article 53   Joint ventures only have the right of use of sites they are permitted to use and do not have ownership rights. There must be no assignment of their right to the use of sites.

Chapter VIII Planning, Purchases, and Sales

Article 54   The basic construction plan of a joint venture (including such items as construction force, various building materials, water, power, and gas) shall be prepared according to the approved feasibility study report and entered into the basic construction plan of the department in charge of the enterprise. The department in charge of the enterprise shall give it priority in making arrangements and guarantee its implementation.

Article 55   The basic construction funds of joint ventures are to be under the unified control of the bank where the joint venture opens an account.

Article 56   The production and operating plan formulated by a joint venture in accordance with the scope of operations and scale of production stipulated in the Contract are to be implemented upon approval of the board of directors and reported to the department in charge of the enterprise for the record.

Departments in charge of enterprises and planning control departments at various levels are not to issue mandatory production and operating plans to joint ventures.

Article 57   In their purchases of such items as required machinery, equipment, raw materials, fuel, parts, means of transport, and articles for office use (hereafter referred to as materials), joint ventures have the right to decide on their own whether to purchase in China or abroad. However, under equal conditions, they shall give priority to purchasing in China.

Article 58   The supply channels for joint ventures' purchase of materials in China are as follows:

1. Materials under planned distribution are to be entered into the supply plan of the department in charge of the enterprise and the supply guaranteed in accordance with contracts by the materials and commercial departments or production enterprises;
2. Materials handled by the materials and commercial departments are to be purchased from the relevant materials business unit;
3. Materials freely circulating on the market are to be purchased from production enterprises or their sales organs or commission agencies; and
4. Export materials handled by foreign trade corporations are to be purchased from the relevant foreign trade corporation.

Article 59   The articles for office and personal use that joint ventures need to purchase in China are to be purchased in accordance with the amounts needed and are not subject to restriction.

Article 60   The Chinese government encourages joint ventures to sell their products on the international market.

Article 61   Products produced by joint ventures that China urgently needs or that China needs to import may be sold mainly on the Chinese domestic market.

Article 62   Joint ventures have the right to export their products themselves and may also entrust the sales organs of the foreign participant in a joint venture or Chinese foreign trade corporations with commission sales or distribution.

Article 63   With respect to any machinery, equipment, parts, raw materials, and fuel needed for the enterprise's production that joint ventures import within the scope of operations stipulated by the joint venture Contract and that fall within those items for which the state stipulates that import licenses must be obtained, joint ventures are to prepare plans each year and apply to obtain the licenses every six months. For machines, equipment, and other materials that foreign participants in a joint venture contribute as capital contributions, import licenses may be handled directly and the items imported on the strength of the approval documents of the examination and approval organ. With respect to materials to be imported that go beyond the stipulated scope of the joint venture Contract and for which the state stipulates that import licenses must be obtained, applications shall be made separately.

Joint ventures may handle the export of the products they produce autonomously. With respect to those that fall within those items for which the state stipulates that export licenses must be obtained, joint ventures are to apply to obtain the licenses every six months in accordance with the enterprise's export plan for the year.

Article 64   Joint ventures may handle the sale of their products in China in the following ways:

1. Materials under planned distribution are to be entered by the department in charge of the enterprise into the distribution plans of the materials control departments, to be sold to designated customers in accordance with the plans;

2. Materials handled by the materials and commercial departments are to be ordered by the materials and commercial departments from joint ventures;

3. With respect to the portions of materials in the above two categories outside of the planned purchases and materials not falling under the above two categories, joint ventures have the right to sell them themselves or to entrust relevant units to sell them on commission; and

4. Export products of joint ventures that are materials which Chinese foreign trade corporations want to import may be sold by joint ventures to Chinese foreign trade corporations for foreign exchange.

Article 65 Pricing for materials and needed services purchased in China by joint ventures is to be implemented in accordance with the following stipulations:

1. The six raw materials gold, silver, platinum, petroleum, coal, and timber that are used directly in the production of export products are to be priced in accordance with the international market prices provided by the State Administration of Foreign Exchange Control or the foreign trade departments, and paid for in foreign currency or Renminbi;

2. For purchases of export commodities or import commodities handled by Chinese foreign trade corporations, the supplier and buyer are to discuss and fix the price by reference to international market prices, with payment made in foreign currency; and

3. As regards the prices for purchases of coal for fuel and oil for vehicles which are needed for use in the production of products to be sold domestically in China, and materials other than those listed in items 1 and 2 of this Article, and the fees charged for such items as water, electricity, gas, heat, transport of goods, labor services, engineering design, consultation services and advertising provided to joint ventures, the treatment shall be equal to that for state enterprises with payment in Renminbi.

Article 66 With respect to products of joint ventures sold domestically in China, except for those items for which the price-control departments approve the fixing of prices by reference to international market prices, the state-stipulated prices shall be implemented, with prices determined in accordance with quality, and Renminbi shall be used for payment. Joint ventures shall report the product sales prices they formulate to the department in charge of the enterprise and the price-control departments for the record.

Prices of export products of joint ventures are to be formulated by joint ventures themselves and reported to the department in charge of the enterprise and the price-control departments for the record.

Article 67   In economic contracts between joint ventures and other Chinese economic organizations, the parties are to undertake economic responsibilities and resolve contractual disputes in accordance with the relevant legal stipulations and contracts concluded between the parties.

Article 68   Joint ventures must fill out statistical forms on production, supply, and sales in accordance with relevant stipulations and report them to the department in charge of the enterprise, the statistics departments, and other relevant departments for the record.

Chapter IX Taxes

Article 69   Joint ventures shall pay various taxes in accordance with the stipulations of the relevant laws of the People's Republic of China.

Article 70   Staff and workers of joint ventures shall pay individual income tax according to the Individual Income Tax Law of the People's Republic of China.

Article 71   Joint ventures are to be exempt from customs duty and industrial and commercial consolidated tax on the import of the following materials:

1. Machinery, equipment, parts and other materials ("other materials" as used here and hereafter refers to materials required for a joint venture's construction of the factory (site) and for installation and reinforcement of machinery) which serve as capital contributions of a foreign participant in a joint venture in accordance with the stipulations of the Contract;
2. Machinery, equipment, parts, and other materials imported with funds which are within the total amount of investment of a joint venture;
3. Machinery, equipment, parts, and other materials of which the production and supply cannot be guaranteed in China which, with the approval of the examination and approval organ, are imported by a joint venture with additional capital; and
4. Raw materials, auxiliary materials, components, parts, and pack-

aging materials imported by a joint venture from abroad for the production of export products.

Taxes shall be paid or made up according to regulations when the above-mentioned duty-free materials are approved for sale domestically in China or diverted for use in products for sale domestically in China.

Article 72　Except for items of which the state restricts export, export products produced by joint ventures may, with the approval of the Ministry of Finance of the People's Republic of China, be exempt from consolidated industrial and commercial tax.

Joint ventures that have difficulty in the beginning period of operations paying taxes on products produced for domestic sale may apply for reduction or exemption of industrial and commercial consolidated tax for a fixed period.

Chapter X Foreign Exchange Control

Article 73　All foreign exchange matters of a joint venture are to be handled in accordance with the stipulation of the Provisional Regulations on Foreign Exchange Control of the People's Republic of China and relevant control measures.

Article 74　Joint ventures are, on the strength of the Business License issued by the State Administration for Industry and Commerce of the People's Republic of China, to open foreign exchange deposit accounts and Renminbi deposit accounts with the Bank of China, or other designated banks, with the bank where the account is opened to supervise receipts and disbursements.

All foreign exchange income of a joint venture must be deposited in the foreign exchange deposit account in the bank where an account has been opened; all foreign exchange disbursements are to be made from the foreign exchange deposit account. The interest rates on deposits are to be implemented in accordance with the interest rates announced by the Bank of China.

Article 75　Joint ventures shall in general maintain a balance between their foreign exchange receipts and disbursements. In cases where, according to the approved feasibility study report and Contract of the joint venture, the joint venture's products are mainly sold domestically and foreign exchange cannot be balanced, the matter is to be resolved by adjustment from the retained foreign exchange of the people's government of the relevant province, autonomous region, or directly administered municipality or State Council department in charge. If the matter cannot be resolved in this way, it shall be resolved by entering the matter into the plan after examination and approval by the Ministry of Foreign Economic Relations and Trade together with the State Planning Commission of the People's Republic of China.

Article 76   Joint ventures shall obtain the approval of the State Administration of Foreign Exchange Control or its branches to open foreign exchange deposit accounts in banks abroad or in Xianggang (Hong Kong) and Aomen (Macao), and shall report to the State Administration of Foreign Exchange Control or its branches the receipts and disbursements circumstances and provide account statements.

Article 77   Branch organs established by joint ventures abroad or in Xianggang (Hong Kong) and Aomen (Macao) shall open accounts with the Bank of China whenever there is a Bank of China in the locality. They shall deliver their annual statements of assets and liabilities and annual profit statements to the State Administration of Foreign Exchange Control or its branches through the joint venture.

Article 78   Joint ventures may, according to the requirements of their business, apply to the Bank of China for foreign exchange loans and Renminbi loans in accordance with the Provisional Regulations for Providing Loans to Joint Ventures Using Chinese and Foreign Investment by the Bank of China. Interest rates on loans to joint ventures are to be implemented in accordance with the interest rates announced by the Bank of China. Joint ventures may also borrow foreign exchange funds from banks abroad or in Xianggang (Hong Kong) or Aomen (Macao) but must file the matter with the State Administration of Foreign Exchange Control or one of its branches for the record.

Article 79   Foreign staff and workers and Xianggang (Hong Kong) and Aomen (Macao) staff and workers of joint ventures, after paying tax according to law, and after taking out money for expenses in China, may apply to the Bank of China to remit out all the remaining portion of their wages and other legitimate income.

Chapter XI Finance and Accounting

Article 80   The financial and accounting systems of joint ventures are to be formulated according to the stipulations of the relevant laws and financial and accounting systems of China in combination with the circumstances of the joint venture, and are to be reported to the finance departments and tax offices of the locality for the record.

Article 81   Joint ventures are to have an accountant to assist the general manager in his responsibility for presiding over the financial and accounting work of the enterprise. When necessary, there may be a deputy accountant.

Article 82   Joint ventures are to have an auditor (small enterprises may elect not to have one) to be responsible for examining and checking financial receipts and disbursements and accounts of the joint venture, and for submitting reports to the board of directors and the general manager.

Article 83   The calendar year is to be adopted as the fiscal year of joint ventures, a fiscal year being from 1 January to 31 December in the Gregorian calendar.

Article 84   In their accounting, joint ventures are to adopt the internationally used accrual system and debit and credit method for the keeping of accounts. All vouchers, accounts books, and statements prepared by the enterprise itself must be written in the Chinese language. They may be written concurrently in a foreign language decided upon by the joint venture parties.

Article 85   Joint ventures in principle are to adopt Renminbi as the standard currency for the keeping of accounts. Upon the decision of the joint venture parties, a given foreign currency may be adopted as the standard currency.

Article 86   In joint venture accounts, in addition to keeping records in the standard currency used in the keeping of accounts, cash, bank deposits, amounts in other currencies, and such items as creditors rights, debts, receipts, and expenses which are in different currencies from the standard currency used in the keeping of accounts shall also be recorded in the accounts in the currencies actually used in the receipts or disbursements.

Joint ventures using a foreign currency in the keeping of accounts, in addition to preparing accounting statements in the foreign currency, shall separately prepare accounting statements converted into Renminbi.

The actual amounts of exchange losses and gain caused by differences in exchange rates are to be recorded in the accounts as that year's losses and gains. Adjustments are not to be made for changes in exchange rates used for the keeping of accounting or for remaining amounts on the books of various relevant foreign currency accounts.

Article 87   The principles of profit distribution after the payment of income tax by joint ventures in accordance with the Income Tax Law of the People's Republic of China Concerning Joint Ventures Using Chinese and Foreign Investment are as follows:

1. Withdrawals are to be made for the reserve fund, staff and workers incentive and welfare fund and enterprise expansion fund of the joint venture, the ratios of withdrawal to be decided by the board of directors;
2. The reserve fund, in addition to being used to make up the losses of the joint venture, may also, with the approval of the examination and approval organ, be used to increase the capital of the enterprise for the expansion of production; and
3. The profits available for distribution after withdrawals for the three funds in accordance with the stipulations of item 1 of this Article shall, if the board of directors decides to distribute them, be distributed in accordance with the ratio of capital contributions of the joint venture parties.

Article 88   Profits must not be distributed until the losses of previous years have been made up. Undistributed profits from previous years may be distributed together with the profits of the current year.

Article 89   Joint ventures shall deliver quarterly annual accounting statements to the joint venture parties, the tax office in the locality, the department in charge of the enterprise, and the financial department at the same level.

A copy of the annual accounting statements shall be delivered to the original examination and approval organ.

Article 90   The following joint venture documents, certificates and statements are only to be valid after being verified by a Chinese registered accountant and a certificate has issued:

1. The Certificates of Capital Contribution of the joint venture parties (whether materials, rights to the use of sites, industrial property rights, or proprietary technology are used as capital contributions,

the list of estimated property values signed and agreed to by the joint venture parties and the agreement documents thereon shall be included);

2. Annual accounting statements of joint ventures; and
3. Accounting statements on liquidation of joint ventures.

Chapter XII Staff and Workers

Article 91 Matters relating to the staff and workers of joint ventures such as their recruitment, employment, dismissal, resignation, wages, welfare benefits, labor insurance, labor protection, labor discipline, etc. are to be handled in accordance with the Regulations of the People's Republic of China on Labor Management in Joint Ventures Using Chinese and Foreign Investment.

Article 92 Joint ventures shall strengthen professional and technical training of staff and workers and establish strict examination systems enabling staff and workers to meet the requirements of a modern enterprise for production and managerial skills.

Article 93 The wages and incentive systems of joint ventures must comply with the principles of each accordingly to his work and more pay for more work.

Article 94 The wage treatment of such high-level managerial personnel as the general manager and deputy general managers, chief and deputy engineers, chief and deputy accountants and auditors is to be decided upon by the board of directors.

Chapter XIII Trade Unions

Article 95 Staff and workers of joint ventures have the right to establish grass-roots labor unions and develop labor union activities in accordance with the Trade Union Law of the People's Republic of China (hereafter referred to as the Trade Union Law of China) and the Articles of Association of Chinese Trade Unions.

Article 96 The trade union of a joint venture is the representative of the interests of the staff and workers. It has the right to represent the staff and workers in signing labor contracts with the joint venture and to supervise the implementation of such contracts.

Article 97   The basic tasks of trade unions in joint ventures are to protect the democratic rights and material interests of the staff and workers according to law, to assist the joint venture with the arrangement and reasonable use of welfare and incentive funds, to organize the staff and workers in the study of political, professional, scientific and technical, and professional knowledge, and develop literary, artistic and athletic activities, and to educate the staff and workers to observe labor discipline and to exert their efforts to fulfill the various economic tasks of the enterprise.

Article 98   Trade union representatives have the right to attend as nonvoting delegates, making known the opinions and demands of the staff and workers, at meetings of the board of directors at which such major matters as development plans and production and operational activities of the joint venture are under discussion.

Trade union representatives have the right to attend as nonvoting delegates at meetings of the board of directors at which such questions as those relating to staff and worker rewards and penalties, wage systems, welfare benefits, labor protection, and labor insurance are considered and decided. The board of directors shall heed the opinions of the trade union and obtain the trade union's cooperation.

Article 99   Joint ventures shall actively support the work of the trade union in the enterprise. Joint ventures shall, in accordance with the stipulations of the Trade Union Law of China, provide necessary housing and facilities to the trade union organization for use for office work and meetings, and in conducting collective welfare, cultural, and athletic activities. Joint ventures are each month to allot 2% of the total amount of the real wages of the enterprise's staff and workers for payment into the trade union fund, for the enterprise trade union's use in accordance with the relevant control measures for trade union funds formulated by the All-China Federation of Trade Unions.

Chapter XIV Term, Dissolution, and Liquidation

Article 100   The term of a joint venture is to be discussed and decided by the joint venture parties according to the specific circumstances of different industries and projects. Joint venture terms for average projects in principle are from 10 to 30 years. Joint venture terms for projects with large investments, long construction periods, and low rates of return on capital may be more than 30 years.

Article 101   The term of joint ventures is to be stipulated by the joint venture parties in the joint venture Agreement, Contract, and Articles of Association. The joint venture term is counted from the day when the joint venture Business License is issued.

If the joint venture parties agree to extend the joint venture term, an application for extension of the joint venture term signed by authorized representatives of the joint venture parties shall be delivered to the examination and approval organ six months before the date of expiration of the joint venture term. The examination and approval organ shall give a reply within one month of receiving the application.

After approval of the extension of a joint venture's term, the joint venture shall undertake alteration of registration procedures in accordance with the Regulations of the People's Republic of China on the Registration and Administration of Joint Ventures Using Chinese and Foreign Investment.

Article 102

A joint venture is to be dissolved in the following situations:

1. Expiration of its term;
2. The incidence of severe losses to the enterprise, making it unable to continue operations;
3. The failure of one of the joint venture parties to perform the obligations stipulated in the joint venture Agreement, Contract, or Articles of Association, making the enterprise unable to continue operations;
4. The suffering of severe losses because of such incidents of *force majeure* as natural disasters and wars;
5. Inability of the joint venture to attain its business goals and, at the same time, lack of a future for development; and
6. The occurrence of other reasons for dissolution stipulated in the joint venture Contract or Articles of Association.

When the circumstances in items 2, 3, 4, 5, and 6 of this Article arise, the board of directors shall submit an application for dissolution to the examination and approval organ for approval.

Under the circumstances in item 3 of this Article, the party that has failed to perform the obligations stipulated in the joint venture Agreement, Contract or Articles of Association shall be liable to compensate the joint venture for the losses caused thereby.

Article 103   When joint ventures announce dissolution, the board of directors shall submit the procedures and principles for liquidation and the members of the liquidation committee to the department in charge of the enterprise for examination and supervision of the liquidation.

Article 104   The members of the liquidation committee generally shall be appointed from among the directors of the joint venture. When the directors cannot serve or are unsuitable to serve as members of the liquidation committee, the joint venture may invite Chinese registered accountants or lawyers to serve. When the examination and approval organ considers it necessary, it may send people to supervise.

The liquidation expenses and remuneration of members of the liquidation committee are to be paid from the existing property of the joint venture and are to be given priority.

Article 105   The tasks of the liquidation committee are to conduct a complete check of the joint venture's property and its creditors' rights and debts, to prepare a statement of assets and liabilities and a list of property, to submit a valuation of the property and the basis of calculation, to formulate a liquidation plan, and to submit these to a meeting of the board of directors and implement them after adoption.

During the period of liquidation, the liquidation committee is to represent the joint venture in question in suing and being sued.

Article 106   Joint ventures bear liability for their debts in respect of all of their assets. The property remaining after the clearance of debts of joint ventures is to be distributed in accordance with the ratio of capital contributions of the joint venture parties, with the exception of cases in which the joint venture Agreement, Contract, or Articles of Association have other stipulations.

When the net amount of assets or remaining property of a dissolving joint venture exceeds the registered capital, the portion of added value is regarded as profit, and income tax shall be paid according to law. Income tax shall be paid according to law on the remittance abroad by a foreign participant in a joint venture of the portion of the net amount of assets or remaining property distributed to it that exceeds its capital contribution.

Article 107   On completion of the liquidation work of a joint venture, the liquidation committee is to submit a report on the completion of liquidation to a meeting of the board of directors, after adoption by which it is to be reported to the original examination and approval organ. Cancellation of registration procedures are to be undertaken at the original registration control organ and the Business License handed in for cancellation.

Article 108   After dissolution of a joint venture, its various accounts books and documents shall be held by the Chinese participant in the joint venture.

Chapter XV Resolution of Disputes

Article 109   If disputes arise over the interpretation or performance of the joint venture Agreement, Contract, or Articles of Association, the joint venture parties shall exert their greatest efforts to resolve them through friendly discussion or mediation. If friendly discussions or mediation are ineffective, disputes may be submitted to arbitration or the judiciary for resolution.

Article 110   Joint venture parties are to submit matters to arbitration according to relevant written arbitration agreements. Arbitration may be conducted before the Foreign Economic and Trade Arbitration Commission of the China Council for the Promotion of International Trade in accordance with the procedural rules for arbitration of the said Commission. If both parties agree, arbitration may also be conducted before an arbitration organ in the country of the defendant or in a third country, in accordance with the procedural rules for arbitration of the organ in question.

Article 111   If there is no written arbitration agreement between the joint venture parties, either party to a dispute that arises may file a lawsuit in the people's courts of China according to law.

Article 112   During periods when disputes are being resolved, with the exception of matters in dispute, the joint venture parties shall continue to perform all other provisions stipulated in the joint venture Agreement, Contract, and Articles of Association.

Chapter XVI Supplementary Provisions

Article 113   The Chinese organs in charge of visas may simplify procedures to convenience foreign staff and workers and Xianggang (Hong Kong) and Aomen (Macao) staff and workers of joint ventures (including their family members) who need to cross Chinese borders frequently.

Article 114   The department in charge of the enterprise is to be responsible for applying for and handling exit procedures for Chinese staff and workers of joint ventures, who, because of the requirements of work, go abroad for observation, business negotiations, study, or training.

Article 115   Foreign staff and workers and Xianggang (Hong Kong) and Aomen (Macao) staff and workers of joint ventures may bring in necessary means of transport and articles for office use, paying customs duty and industrial and commercial consolidated tax in accordance with stipulations.

Article 116   Joint ventures established in the special economic zones are to follow any separate stipulations of laws and regulations passed by the National People's Congress, the Standing Committee of the National People's Congress, or the State Council.

Article 117   The power of interpretation of these Regulations is vested in the Ministry of Foreign Economic Relations and Trade.

Article 118   These Regulations are to be implemented from the date of promulgation.

Appendix 1: Revision of Section 3 of Article 86 of the Implementing Regulations of the Law of the People's Republic of China on Joint Ventures Using Chinese and Foreign Investment

Revised by the State Council on 21 December 1986

The State Council issued a notice on 21 December 1986 on the revisions of Section 3 of Article 86 of the Implementing Regulations of the Law of the People's Republic of China on Joint Ventures Using Chinese and Foreign Investment.

The full text of the notice is as follows:

Section 3 of Article 86 of the Implementing Regulations of the Law of the People's Republic of China on Joint Ventures Using Chinese and Foreign Investment issued by the State Council on 20 September 1983, provides that:

> the actual amounts of exchange losses and gains caused by differences in exchange rates are to be recorded in the accounts as that year's losses and gains. Adjustments are not to be made for changes in exchange rates used for the keeping of accounts

or for remaining amounts on the books of various relevant foreign currency accounts.

The section shall be revised as:

The differences in the amounts of bookkeeping currencies caused by changes in exchange rates used for conversion shall be entered in the accounts as losses or gains. The changes in exchange rates used for bookkeeping and the book balances of all foreign currency accounts shall, for the purpose of account settlement at the end of a year, be dealt with according to the relevant laws of China and the regulations of financial accounting systems.

This Revision shall come into effect on the date of promulgation.

Appendix 2: Revision of Article 100 of the Implementing Regulations of the Law of the People's Republic of China on Joint Ventures Using Chinese and Foreign Investment

Revised by the State Council on 15 January 1986

Article 100 of the Implementing Regulations of the Law of the People's Republic of China on Joint Ventures Using Chinese and Foreign Investment, promulgated by the State Council on 20 September 1983, stipulates:

The term of a joint venture is to be discussed and decided by the joint venture parties according to the specific circumstances of different industries and projects. Joint venture terms for average projects in principle are from 10 to 30 years. Joint venture terms for projects with large investment, long construction periods, and low rates of return on capital may be more than 30 years.

This Article has now been revised as follows:

The term of a joint venture is to be discussed and decided by the joint venture parties according to the specific circumstances of different industries and projects. Joint venture terms for average projects are from 10 to 30 years. Joint venture terms for projects with large investment, long construction periods, and low rates of return on capital or having foreign partners who provide advanced or key technology to produce sophisticated or internationally competitive products may be extended to 50 years. Terms of such projects with the special approval of the State Council may be extended to more than 50 years.

This Revision shall come into effect on the date of promulgation.

3. Law of the People's Republic of China on Chinese–Foreign Cooperative Joint Ventures

Adopted at the First Session of the Seventh National People's Congress on 13 April 1988

Article 1   The Law is formulated in order to expand economic cooperation and technological exchange with foreign countries and to encourage, according to the principles of equality and mutual benefit, foreign enterprises and other economic organizations or individuals (hereafter referred to as the foreign cooperator) to establish with Chinese enterprises or other economic organizations (hereafter referred to as the Chinese cooperator) Chinese foreign cooperative joint ventures (hereafter referred to as cooperative joint ventures) within the territory of the People's Republic of China.

Article 2   In establishing a cooperative joint venture, the Chinese and foreign cooperators shall, in accordance with the provision of this Law, and the provisions of the investment or conditions for cooperation, determine the distribution of earnings or profits, the sharing of risks and losses, the manner of operation and management, and the disposal of property. The Chinese and foreign cooperators shall determine such distribution in advance with regard to the termination of the cooperative joint venture.

A cooperative joint venture which meets the conditions for being a legal person under Chinese law shall acquire the status of a Chinese legal person in accordance with the law.

Article 3   The state shall protect, according to law, the legitimate rights and interests of the cooperative joint venture and the Chinese and foreign cooperators.

The cooperative joint venture must abide by Chinese laws and regulations and must not injure the social and public interests of China.

The relevant state authorities shall exercise supervision over the cooperative joint venture according to law.

Article 4   The state shall encourage the establishment of productive cooperative joint ventures that are export oriented or technologically advanced.

Article 5   In applying for the establishment of a cooperative joint venture, such documents as the Agreement, the Contract, and the Articles of Association signed by both the Chinese and foreign cooperators shall be submitted for examination and approval to the department in charge of foreign economic relations and trade under the State Council (hereafter referred to as the Examination and Approval Authority). The Examination and Approval Authority shall, within 45 days of receipt of the application, decide whether to grant approval.

Article 6   When the application for the establishment of a cooperative joint venture is approved, the cooperators shall, within 30 days of receipt of the Certificate of Approval, apply to the Administrative Authority for Industry and Commerce for registration and obtain a Business License. The date of issuance of the Business License of a cooperative joint venture shall be the date of its establishment.

A cooperative joint venture shall, within 30 days of its establishment, register with the Tax Authority for tax registration.

Article 7   If, during the period of cooperation, the Chinese and foreign cooperators agree, after consultation, to make major modifications to the cooperative joint venture contract, they shall report to the Examination and Approval Authority for approval; and if the modifications are related to matters of statutory industrial and commercial registration or tax registration, they shall register the modifications with the Administrative Authority for Industry and Commerce or with the Tax Authority.

Article 8   The investment or requirements for cooperation contributed by the Chinese and foreign cooperators may be provided in cash, in kind, in the right to the use of land, industrial property rights, non-patent technology, and other property rights.

Article 9   The Chinese and foreign cooperators shall, in accordance with the law and regulations and the provisions in the cooperative joint venture Contract, duly fulfill their obligations of contributing the full investment and providing the requirements for cooperation. In case of failure to do so within the prescribed time, the Administrative Authority for Industry and Commerce shall set a time limit for fulfillment of those obligations; and if such obligations remain unfulfilled by the time limit, the matter shall be handled by the Examination and Approval Authority and the Administrative Authority for Industry and Commerce according to relevant state rules.

The investment or requirements for cooperation provided by the Chinese and foreign cooperators shall be verified by an accountant registered in China or a relevant authority, who shall provide a Verification Certificate.

Article 10   If the Chinese or foreign cooperator wishes to assign the whole or a part of its rights and obligations as prescribed in the cooperative joint venture Contract, it must have the consent of the other cooperator or cooperators, and report to the Examination and Approval Authority for approval.

Article 11   The cooperative joint venture shall conduct its operational and managerial activities in accordance with the approved Contract and the Articles of Association without interference in its autonomous right of operation and management.

Article 12   A cooperative joint venture shall establish a board or directors of a joint managerial organ which shall, according to the Contract or the Articles of Association of the cooperative joint venture, decide on major issues concerning the cooperative joint venture. If a Chinese or foreign cooperator assumes the chairmanship of the board of directors or the directorship of the joint managerial organ, the other cooperator shall assume the vice-chairmanship of the board or the deputy directorship of the joint managerial organ. The board of directors or the joint managerial organ may decide the appointment or employment of a general manager, who shall take charge of the routine operation and management of the cooperative joint venture. The general manager shall be responsible to the board of directors or the joint managerial organ.

If a cooperative joint venture, after its establishment, chooses to entrust a third party with its operation and management, it must obtain the unanimous agreement of the board of directors or the joint managerial organ, report to the Examination and Approval Authority for approval, and register the charge with the Administrative Authority for Industry and Commerce.

Article 13   The employment, dismissal, remuneration, welfare, labor protection, and labor insurance, etc. of the workers and staff of a cooperative joint venture shall be specified and provided for in contracts concluded in accordance with the law.

Article 14 The workers and staff of a cooperative joint venture shall, in accordance with the law, establish their trade unions to carry out trade union activities and protect their legal rights and interests.

A cooperative joint venture shall provide the necessary conditions for the venture's trade unions to carry out their activities.

Article 15 A cooperative joint venture must establish its account books within the territory of China, file its accounting statements according to accounting rules, and accept supervision by the financial and tax authorities.

If a cooperative joint venture violates the provisions of the preceding paragraph and fails to establish its account books within the territory of China, the financial and tax authorities may impose a fine, and the Administrative Authority for Industry and Commerce may order it to suspend its business operations or may revoke its Business License.

Article 16 A cooperative joint venture shall, on presentation of its Business License, open a foreign exchange account with a bank or any other financial institution which is permitted by the state exchange control authority to deal in foreign exchange.

Any matters concerning the foreign exchange of cooperative joint ventures shall be handled in accordance with the regulations of the state on foreign exchange control.

Article 17 A cooperative joint venture may obtain loans from financial institutions within the territory of China and also from those outside the territory of China.

Any loans to be used by the Chinese cooperator or the foreign cooperator as investment or as requirement for cooperation and any guarantees in relation to the loan shall be provided by the cooperator concerned on its own account.

Article 18 Each kind of insurance coverage of a cooperative joint venture shall be furnished by the insurance institutions within the territory of China.

Article 19 A cooperative joint venture may, within its approved scope of operation, import the materials it needs and export the produces. A cooperative joint venture may purchase, on both the domestic market and the world market, those raw materials, fuels, etc. falling under its approved scope of operation.

Article 20   A cooperative joint venture shall balance its own foreign exchange receipts and expenditures. If a cooperative joint venture is unable to balance expenditures, it may, in accordance with the state regulations, apply to the relevant authorities for assistance.

Article 21   A cooperative joint venture shall, in accordance with the state tax regulations, pay taxes, and may enjoy preferential treatment of tax reduction or exemption.

Article 22   The Chinese and foreign cooperators shall distribute earnings or profits, and undertake risks and losses in accordance with the provisions in the cooperative joint venture Contract.

If the Chinese and foreign cooperators agree in the cooperative joint venture Contract that the whole of the fixed assets of the cooperative joint venture shall be allocated to the ownership of the Chinese cooperative at the expiration of the cooperative joint venture, it may be agreed in the cooperative joint venture Contract that the foreign cooperator shall have its investment returned prior to the end of the period of cooperation. If the cooperative joint venture Contract provides that the foreign cooperator shall have its investment returned prior to the payment of income tax, application must be made to the financial and tax authorities, which shall examine and approve the application in accordance with the state regulations concerning tax.

If, according to the provisions in the preceding paragraph, the foreign cooperator has its investment returned prior to the end of the period of cooperation, the Chinese and foreign cooperators shall, in accordance with relevant laws and the provisions in the cooperative joint venture Contract, be liable for the debts of the cooperative joint venture.

Article 23   The profits received by the foreign cooperator after fulfillment of its obligations as required by the law and the cooperative joint venture Contract, and the other legitimate income and any funds it may receive after termination of the cooperative joint venture, may be remitted abroad according to law.

The wages, salaries, and other legitimate income earned by the foreign personnel of cooperative joint ventures may, after individual income tax has been paid, be remitted abroad according to law.

Article 24   Upon the expiration or early termination of the term of a cooperative joint venture, its assets, claims, and liabilities shall be liquidated according to legal procedure. The Chinese and foreign cooperators shall, in accordance with the provisions in the cooperative joint venture Contract, determine the ownership of the venture's properties.

A cooperative joint venture shall, upon the expiration or termination of its term, cancel its registration with the Administrative Authority for Industry and Commerce and the tax authorities.

Article 25 The period of cooperation of a cooperative joint venture shall be determined through consultation by the Chinese and foreign cooperators and shall be clearly specified in the cooperative joint venture Contract. If the Chinese and foreign cooperators agree to extend the period of cooperation, they shall apply to the Examination and Approval Authority 180 days prior to the expiration of the cooperation term. The Examination and Approval Authority shall, within 30 days of receipt of the application, decide whether to grant approval.

Article 26 Any dispute between the Chinese and foreign cooperators arising from performance of the Contract or the Articles of Association of a cooperative joint venture shall be settled through consultation or mediation. If the Chinese and foreign cooperators do not wish to settle a dispute through consultation or mediation, or if a dispute cannot be settled through consultation or mediation, the Chinese and foreign cooperators may submit the case to a Chinese arbitration institution or any other arbitration institution for arbitration in accordance with the arbitration clause in the cooperative joint venture Contract or a written agreement on arbitration concluded after occurrence of the dispute.

The Chinese or foreign cooperator may bring a suit in a Chinese court if no arbitration clause is provided in the cooperative joint venture Contract or if no written agreement on arbitration is concluded after occurrence of the dispute.

Article 27 The detailed rules for the implementation of this Law shall be formulated by the department in charge of foreign economic relations and trade under the State Council and be reported to the State Council for approval, and shall be effective after approval.

Article 28 This Law shall come into force on the day of promulgation.

4. Law of the People's Republic of China on Enterprises Operated Exclusively With Foreign Capital

Adopted at the Fourth Session of the Sixth National People's Congress on 12 April 1986

Article 1   With a view to expanding economic cooperation and technological exchange with other countries and promoting the development of its national economy, the People's Republic of China permits foreign firms, other economic entities, or individuals (hereafter referred to as foreign investors) to set up enterprises exclusively with foreign capital in China (hereafter referred to as wholly foreign-owned enterprises) and protects the lawful rights and interests of the enterprises so established.

Article 2   As referred to in the present Law, wholly foreign-owned enterprises are those established in China by foreign investors exclusively with their own capital in accordance with the relevant Chinese laws. The term does not include branches set up in China by foreign investors.

Article 3   Wholly foreign-owned enterprises shall be conducive to the development of China's national economy. Such enterprises shall use advanced technology and equipment or market all or most of their products outside China.

Provisions regarding the lines of business that the state forbids wholly foreign-owned enterprises to engage in or on which it places certain restrictions will be made by the State Council.

Article 4   The investments made by a foreign investor in China, the profits he earns, and his other lawful rights and interests shall be protected by Chinese laws.

The wholly foreign-owned enterprise must abide by Chinese laws and statutes and must do nothing detrimental to China's public interest.

Article 5   Except under special circumstances, the state shall not nationalize or expropriate wholly foreign-owned enterprises. Should it prove necessary to do so in the public interest, legal procedures will be followed, and reasonable compensation will be made.

Article 6   The application to establish a wholly foreign-owned enterprise shall be submitted for examination and approval by the department under the State Council, which is in charge of foreign economic relations and trade, or by other authorities entrusted with such powers by the State

Council. The department or said authorities shall, within 90 days from the date when such application is received, make a decision on whether to grant approval.

Article 7   Within 30 days after receiving a Certificate of Approval, the foreign investor should apply to the authorities in charge of the Administration of Industry and Commerce for Registration and a Business License. The date of issue of the Business License shall be deemed to be the date of establishment of the enterprise.

Article 8   The wholly foreign-owned enterprise, which meets the conditions for being a legal person under Chinese law, shall acquire the status of a Chinese legal person in accordance with the Law.

Article 9   The wholly foreign-owned enterprise must make investments in China within the period approved by the department in charge of examination and approval. If it fails to do so, the authorities in charge of the administration of industry and commerce may revoke the Business License.

The authorities in charge of the Administration of Industry and Commerce shall inspect and monitor the investment situation of a wholly foreign-owned enterprise.

Article 10   In the event of a separation, merger, transfer, or other major change, the wholly foreign-owned enterprise must report to and obtain approval from the authorities in charge of examination and approval and register the change with the authorities in charge of the Administration of Industry and Commerce.

Article 11   The production and business programs of the wholly foreign-owned enterprise shall be reported to the competent authorities for the record.

The enterprise shall be free from interference in its operations and management so long as these are conducted in accordance with the approved Articles of Association.

Article 12   The wholly foreign-owned enterprise shall employ Chinese workers and administrative staff under contracts concluded according to law. These contracts shall include provisions relating to employment, dismissal, remuneration, welfare, occupational safety, and workers' insurance.

Article 13   Workers and administrative staff in the employment of the wholly foreign-owned enterprise may set up trade unions in accordance with the law, and such unions may conduct activities to protect the lawful rights and interests of the employees.

The enterprise shall provide necessary facilities for the activities of the trade unions.

Article 14   The wholly foreign-owned enterprise shall set up account books in China, conduct independent auditing, and, in conformity with the regulations, submit its fiscal reports and statements to the financial and tax authorities for supervision.

If the enterprise refuses to maintain accounts books in China, the financial and tax authorities may impose a penalty on it, and the authorities in charge of the Administration of Industry and Commerce may order it to suspend operations or revoke its Business License.

Article 15   Within the scope of operations approved, the wholly foreign-owned enterprise may purchase, either in China or from the world market, raw and semifinished materials, fuels, and other materials it needs. When these are available from both sources, preference should be given to Chinese sources.

Article 16   The wholly foreign-owned enterprise shall apply to insurance companies in China for such kinds of insurance coverage as are needed.

Article 17   The wholly foreign-owned enterprise shall pay taxes in accordance with relevant state regulations. It may enjoy preferential treatment for reduction of taxes or exemption from them.

If the enterprise reinvests a portion of its after-tax profits in China, it may, in accordance with relevant state regulations, apply for a refund of the income tax paid on the reinvested amount.

Article 18   The wholly foreign-owned enterprise shall handle its foreign exchange matters in accordance with relevant state regulations.

The enterprise shall open an account with the Bank of China or with a bank designated by the Chinese authorities in charge of foreign exchange control.

The enterprise should take care to balance its foreign exchange receipts and payments. If, with the approval of the competent authorities, the enterprise markets its production in China and consequently experiences an imbalance in foreign exchange, the said authorities shall be responsible for helping it to eliminate the imbalance.

Article 19 The foreign investor may remit abroad profits legitimately earned from the enterprise, as well as other lawful earnings and any funds left over after the enterprise is liquidated.
Wages, salaries, and other legitimate income earned by foreign employees in the enterprise may be remitted abroad after the payment of personal income tax in accordance with Chinese Law.

Article 20 The foreign investor should apply for and secure approval of the duration of operations of its enterprise from the authorities in charge of examination and approval. When an extension of the duration of operations is desired, application must be made to the said authorities 180 days before the duration of operations expires. The authorities in charge of examination and approval shall, within 30 days from the date of receipt of such application, make a decision on whether to grant approval.

Article 21 When terminating operations, the wholly foreign-owned enterprise shall give timely notification and proceed with liquidation in accordance with relevant legal requirements.
Pending the completion of liquidation, a foreign investor may not dispose of the assets of the enterprise except for the purpose of liquidation.

Article 22 At the termination of operations the wholly foreign-owned enterprise should nullify its registration with the authorities in charge of the Administration of Industry and Commerce and return its Business License.

Article 23 In accordance with the present Law, the detailed rules and regulations for the implementation of this Law shall be formulated by the department under the State Council which is in charge of foreign economic relations and trade and shall go into effect after approval by the State Council.

Article 24 The present Law comes into force on the date of its promulgation.

5. Detailed Rules for the Implementation of the Law of the People's Republic of China on Wholly Foreign-Owned Enterprises

Approved by the State Council of the People's Republic of China on 28 October 1990
Promulgated by the Ministry of Foreign Economic Relations and Trade on 12 December 1990

Chapter I General Provisions

Article 1　The Detailed Rules are formulated in accordance with the provisions of Article 23 of the Law of the People's Republic of China on Wholly Foreign-Owned Enterprises.

Article 2　All wholly foreign-owned enterprises are subject to the jurisdiction and protection of Chinese laws.

Business activities conducted by a wholly foreign-owned enterprise within the territory of China must comply with Chinese law and regulations without injury to the social interests of China.

Article 3　Before a wholly foreign-owned enterprise can be established, it must be shown to be beneficial to the development of the Chinese national economy, be able to gain remarkable economic results, and meet at least one of the following requirements:

1. Using advanced technology and equipment which can help develop new products, save energy and raw materials, upgrade existing products, and substitute importation
2. Reaching 50% or more of the annual output value of the export product in the total output value of all products of that year with a balance or surplus in the foreign exchange receipt and expenditure

Article 4　The establishment of a wholly foreign-owned enterprise is prohibited in the following lines of business:

1. News, publishing, broadcasting, television, film production
2. Domestic commerce, foreign trade, insurance
3. Post and telecommunications
4. Any others prohibited by the provisions of the Chinese government

Article 5 The establishment of a wholly foreign-owned enterprise is restricted in the following lines of business:

1. Public utilities
2. Communications and transportation
3. Real estate
4. Trust investment
5. Leasing

An application for establishing a wholly foreign-owned enterprise in the lines of business described is subject to approval by the Ministry of Foreign Economic Relations and Trade of the People's Republic of China (hereafter referred to as Ministry of Foreign Economic Relations and Trade), unless otherwise stipulated in the Chinese laws and regulations.

Article 6 An application for establishing a wholly foreign-owned enterprise shall not be approved if the enterprise involves any of the following circumstances:

1. Detriment to China's sovereignty or public interests
2. Endangerment of the security of China
3. Violation of Chinese laws and regulations
4. Nonconformity with the requirements of the development of China's national economy
5. Possibility of environmental pollution

Article 7 A wholly foreign-owned enterprise, within the approved scope of operation, is entitled to do business independently without interference whatever.

Chapter II Establishment Procedures

Article 8 After the examination and approval of applications for the establishment of wholly foreign-owned enterprises by the Ministry of Foreign Economic Relations and Trade, Certificates of Approval shall be granted by the Ministry.

The State Council may authorize the people's governments in provinces, autonomous regions, municipalities directly under the central government, special cities with independent plans, and special economic zones to examine and approve the applications for establishing wholly foreign-owned enterprises under the following situations, and Certificates of Approval are granted by such people's governments after the approval.

1. The total amount of investment is within the authorization for approval as set by the State Council.
2. No allocations of raw materials by the state are required, and the national overall balance of energy resources, transportation, and quotas for export is not affected.

The approval of the establishment of a wholly foreign-owned enterprise by the people's governments in provinces, autonomous regions, municipalities directly under the central government, special cities with independent plans, and special economic zones within the authorization for approval set by the State Council shall be filed with the Ministry of Foreign Economic Relations and Trade within 15 days of approval. (The Ministry of Foreign Economic Relations and Trade and the people's governments in the provinces, autonomous regions, municipalities directly under the central government, special cities with independent plans, and special economic zones shall be hereafter referred to as the Examination and Approval Authority.)

Article 9   A wholly foreign-owned enterprise applying for the establishment shall, according to the authorization for approval, obtain the consent of the Department of Foreign Economic Relations and Trade in advance, if the products of such enterprise involve the export license, export quotas, or import license or are restricted for import by the state.

Article 10   Before applying for the establishment of a wholly foreign-owned enterprise, a foreign investor shall submit to the local people's government at county level or above where the enterprise will be located a report covering the following items: objective of the wholly foreign-owned enterprise to be established; scope and scale of operation; products; technology and equipment to be used; the anticipated sales ratio of products in domestic and international markets; acreage and other land requirements; conditions and quantity of required water, electric power, coal, gas or other energy resources; requirements for public facilities, etc.
    The local people's government at county level or above shall answer the foreign investor in written form within 30 days from the date of receiving the report submitted by the foreign investor.

Article 11   A foreign investor shall, through the local people's government at county level or above where the wholly foreign-owned enterprise will be established, submit the application for establishing the wholly foreign-owned enterprise with the following documents to the Examination and Approval Authority:

1. Application for establishing a wholly foreign-owned enterprise
2. Feasibility study report
3. Articles of Association of the enterprise
4. List of legal representatives of the enterprise (or the candidates for the board of directors)
5. Documents of testimonial and financial credit of the foreign investors
6. Written reply of the local people's government at county level or above where the wholly foreign-owned enterprise will be established
7. List of goods and materials needed to be imported
8. Other documents needed to be submitted

The documents in items 1 and 3 shall be written in Chinese, while documents in items 2, 4, and 5 may be written in foreign language with Chinese translation attached.

Where two or more foreign investors jointly apply for establishing a wholly foreign-owned enterprise, they shall submit the duplicate of the Contract signed between them to the Examination and Approval Authority for the record.

Article 12 The Examination and Approval Authority shall decide whether to approve or disapprove the application for the establishment of a wholly foreign-owned enterprise within 90 days from the date of receiving all the documents. Should anything imperfect or inappropriate be found in the aforementioned documents, the Examination and Approval Authority may demand a supplement or amendment to them within a limited period of time.

Article 13 After the application for establishing a wholly foreign-owned enterprise is approved by the Examination and Approval Authority, the foreign investor shall, within 30 days from the date of receiving the Certificate of Approval, apply to the Administrative Authority for Industry and Commerce for registration and a Business License. The date of issuance of the Business License for a wholly foreign-owned enterprise shall be the date of its establishment.

If the foreign investor fails to apply to the Administrative Authority of Industry and Commerce for registration after 30 days from the date of receiving the Certificate of Approval, the Certificate of Approval shall automatically become invalid.

The enterprise shall go through the formalities for tax registration with the Tax Authority within 30 days of its establishment.

Article 14   A foreign investor may entrust service organizations serving enterprises with foreign investment in China or serving enterprises with foreign investment in China or other economic organizations to handle the matters stipulated in Article 9, paragraph 1 of Article 10 and Article 11. A Contract of Mandate shall be signed between the foreign investor and the organizations above mentioned.

Article 15   The application for establishing a wholly foreign-owned enterprise shall include the following items:

1. Names, residence, places of registration of the foreign investors, and names, nationalities, and titles of the legal representatives
2. Name and legal address of the wholly foreign-owned enterprise to be established
3. Scope of operation, variety of products, and scale of production
4. Total amount of investment, registered capital, source of funds, ways and time limit of contribution to the wholly foreign-owned enterprise to be established
5. Form of organization or mechanism and legal representative of the enterprise
6. Main production equipment to be adopted and its present condition, production technology, level of process of technology, and their source of supply
7. Districts for sale, ways and means of selling products, and the sales ratio of products on the domestic and international markets
8. Arrangements for receipts and expenditures of foreign currency
9. Arrangements for staff and organization, employment, training, salaries and wages, welfare benefits, labor insurance, labor protection, and other matters of staff and workers
10. Possibility or degree of environmental pollution and the measures for solution
11. The choice and acreage of the land to use
12. Funds, energy, and raw materials necessary for capital construction and production and the measures for solution
13. The progress schedule of project
14. The duration of the enterprise to be established

Article 16   Articles of Association of a wholly foreign-owned enterprise shall include the following items:

1. Name and legal address of the wholly foreign-owned enterprise
2. Objective and scope of operation
3. Total amount of investment, registered capital and time limit of contribution
4. Form of organization
5. Internal organizations and their functions of the enterprise, and rules for handling routine affairs, the responsibility and authority of legal representative, general manager, general engineer, general accountant and other high-ranking management officers
6. Principles and systems governing finance, accounting, and auditing
7. Labor management
8. Duration, dissolution, and liquidation
9. Procedures for amendment of the Articles of Association

Article 17   The Articles of Association shall come into force after being approved by the Examination and Approval Authority. The same applies in the event of amendments.

Article 18   When a wholly foreign-owned enterprise is split up or merged with others or important changes take place on the capital for some reason, it shall apply to the Examination and Approval Authority for approval with a Certificate of Verification provided by an accountant registered in China. And then registration procedures for changes shall be followed at the Administrative Authority for Industry and Commerce.

Chapter III Form of Organization and Registered Capital

Article 19   A wholly foreign-owned enterprise shall take the form of a limited liability company. It may also with approval take other forms of organization.

Where a wholly foreign-owned enterprise is a limited liability company, the foreign investor shall be liable to the enterprise within the limit of the capital subscribed by it.

Where a wholly foreign-owned enterprise takes on other forms of organizations, the liability of the foreign investor to the enterprise shall be determined according to Chinese laws and regulations.

Article 20   The total amount of investment of a wholly foreign-owned enterprise refers to the sum of funds for operating the enterprise, meaning the sum total of capital construction funds and working capital necessary for reaching the production scale of the enterprise.

Article 21   The registered capital of a wholly foreign-owned enterprise refers to the total amount of capital registered at the Administrative Authority for Industry and Commerce when applying for the establishment of the enterprise, meaning all the capital subscribed by the foreign investor.

The registered capital of a wholly foreign-owned enterprise shall be appropriate to its business scale, and the ratio between its registered capital and total amount of investment shall be in conformity with the relevant provisions of China.

Article 22   A wholly foreign-owned enterprise shall not reduce its registered capital during its term of operation.

Article 23   Any increase in or assignment of the registered capital of a wholly foreign-owned enterprise shall be approved by the Examination and Approval Authority and then go through the procedures for alteration of registration with the Administrative Authority for Industry and Commerce.

Article 24   Where a wholly foreign-owned enterprise mortgages or assigns its property, or rights and interests, the enterprise shall submit it to the Examination and Approval Authority for approval and then file it with the Administrative Authority for Industry and Commerce for the record.

Article 25   A legal representative of a wholly foreign-owned enterprise is a person in charge who exercises his functions and powers on behalf of the enterprise in line with the enterprise's Articles of Association.

When the legal representative is unable to perform his functions and powers, he shall entrust in written form an agent to exercise his functions and powers.

Chapter IV Ways and Time Limit for Contributing Investment

Article 26   The investment contributed by a foreign investor may be provided in freely convertible foreign currency or by machinery, equipment, industrial property rights, and know-how, which are evaluated.

With the approval of the Examination and Approval Authority, a foreign investor may also contribute his profits in Renminbi yielded from his other enterprises operating in the territory of China.

Article 27   The machinery or equipment contributed as investment by a foreign investor shall meet the following requirements:

1. Necessary for the production of the wholly foreign-owned enterprise
2. Unable to be manufactured in China, or though able, their technical performance or time of supply does not meet the demand

The evaluation of such machinery or equipment shall not be higher than the normal price of similar machinery or equipment in the international market.

A detailed list of the evaluated machinery or equipment contributed as investment shall be made out, including items, assortments, quantity, and evaluation, and will be submitted as annex to the application for establishing a foreign-owned enterprise to the Examination and Approval Authority.

Article 28   The industrial property right or know-how contributed as investment by a foreign investor shall meet the following requirements:

1. It is owned by the foreign investor.
2. New products urgently needed in China or export products easily sold in the world market are able to be manufactured with such industrial property or know-how.

The evaluation of such industrial property right or know-how shall conform with the international evaluation principle, and its total evaluation shall be no more than 20% of the registered capital of the enterprise.

Detailed information shall be provided pertaining to the industrial property right or know-how contributed as investment, including copies of the ownership certificate, state of validity, technical characteristics, practice value, and the basis and standard on which the evaluation is made, and submitted as an annex to the application for establishing a wholly foreign-owned enterprise to the Examination and Approval Authority.

Article 29   When machinery or equipment contributed as investment arrives at a Chinese port, the wholly foreign-owned enterprise shall apply for inspection to the Chinese Commodity Inspection Organization, which will issue the inspection report to that effect.

Where the assortment, quality, and quantity of such machinery or equipment are inconsistent with those listed in the list of contributed investment which has been submitted to the Examination and Approval Authority, the authority has the power to require the foreign investor to make corrections within the given time.

Article 30   After the industrial property right or know-how contributed as investment is put into use, the Examination and Approval Authority has the power to make a check. If such industrial property right or know-how does not conform with the original document submitted by the foreign investor, the Examination and Approval Authority has the power to require the foreign investor to make corrections within the given time.

Article 31   The time limit for a foreign investor to subscribe the capital shall be stipulated in the application for establishing the wholly foreign-owned enterprise. The foreign investor may subscribe the capital by installments. However, the last installment shall be paid within three years from the date of the issuance of the Business License. The first installment by a foreign investor shall be no less than 15% of all of his capital subscribed and paid within 90 days from the date on which the enterprise's Business License is issued.

If a foreign investor fails to subscribe the first installment within the period stipulated in the preceding paragraph, the Certificate of Approval for a wholly foreign-owned enterprise will become invalid automatically. The enterprise shall then go through the procedures of nullifying its registration with the Administrative Authority for Industry and Commerce, and hand in its Business License for cancellation; in case a wholly foreign-owned enterprise fails to handle the procedures of nullification and cancellation, the Administrative Authority for Industry and Commerce shall withdraw the Business License of the enterprise and make an announcement.

Article 32   A foreign investor shall pay each of the installments on schedule after the first installment is made. If any installment is overdue by more than 30 days without appropriate reason, it shall be handled according to the provisions of paragraph 2, Article 31 of these Detailed Rules.

Where a foreign investor has appropriate reasons for the delay of its contribution, it shall, with the consent of the Examination and Approval

Authority, be submitted to the Administrative Authority for Industry and Commerce for the record.

Article 33 After each installment is paid by the foreign investor, the wholly foreign-owned enterprise shall hire an accountant registered in China for verification and a Report of Verification. The report shall be filed with the Examination and Approval Authority and the Administrative Authority for Industry and Commerce.

Chapter V Land Use and Fees

Article 34 The use of land by a wholly foreign-owned enterprise shall be reviewed and arranged by the people's government at county level or above according to the circumstances of its own district.

Article 35 A wholly foreign-owned enterprise shall with its Certificate of Approval and Business License handle the procedures with the land administrative department of the local people's government at county level or above where the enterprise is to be located and obtain a Certificate of Land within 30 days from the date of issuing its Business License.

Article 36 A Certificate of Land is a legal document against which the wholly foreign-owned enterprise is entitled to use the land. Without approval, the enterprise shall not assign the right to use the land during its term of operation.

Article 37 A wholly foreign-owned enterprise shall pay the land use fees to the department in charge of land in the locality at the time it receives the Certificate of Land.

Article 38 A wholly foreign-owned enterprise shall pay the land development fees if the land for which the enterprise is entitled to use has been developed.
The land development fees referred to in the preceding paragraph include expenses for requisition, demolition, and resettlement and expenses for infrastructure provided for the wholly foreign-owned enterprise. The land development fees may be charged in one lump sum or yearly by the land development unit.

Article 39 If the land to be used by a wholly foreign-owned enterprise is not developed, the enterprise may develop it by itself or entrust a relevant Chinese to do it. The construction for basic facilities shall be arranged under unified management of the people's government at county level or above where the enterprise is located.

Article 40   The standard for the land use fees and land development fees shall be fixed in accordance with the relevant provisions of China.

Article 41   The period for use of land by a wholly foreign-owned enterprise extends as long as its approved term of operation.

Article 42   A wholly foreign-owned enterprise may acquire the right to use the land according to either the provisions of the present Chapter or other laws and regulations of China.

Chapter VI Purchase and Sale

Article 43   A wholly foreign-owned enterprise shall make and implement its production and operation plan by itself. The plan shall be filed with the local department in charge of the enterprise's line of business.

Article 44   A wholly foreign-owned enterprise has the right to make decisions on its own to purchase machines, equipment, raw materials, fuel, parts, fittings, components, means of transport, stationery, etc. (hereafter referred to as goods and materials) for its own use.

In purchasing goods and materials in China, a wholly foreign-owned enterprise shall enjoy the same treatment as Chinese enterprises under like conditions.

Article 45   In selling products in the Chinese market, a wholly foreign-owned enterprise shall follow its approved sales ratio.

In case a wholly foreign-owned enterprise intends to sell more of its products than the approved sales ratio in the Chinese market, approval is required from the Examination and Approval Authority.

Article 46   A wholly foreign-owned enterprise has the right to export its own products by itself, and it may entrust a Chinese foreign trade corporation or corporation outside China with sales on commission.

A wholly foreign-owned enterprise has the right to sell its products by itself in China in line with the approved sales ratio or may entrust a Chinese commercial agency with sales on commission.

Article 47   For machinery or equipment contributed as investment by a foreign investor and for which the import license is required according to Chinese laws, the enterprise shall, with the list of export equipment and materials, which has been approved, apply to the Issuing Authority for an import license by itself or through an agency.

Within the approved scope of operation, a wholly foreign- owned enterprise shall make out an annual plan for import of goods and materials which are necessary for the production of the enterprise and if the import license for such goods and materials is required according to the provisions of China, and the enterprise shall apply for such license to the Issuing Authority every six months.

A wholly foreign-owned enterprise shall make out an annual plan for export products if the export license for such export products is required according to the provisions of China and shall apply for export license to the Issuing Authority every six months.

Article 48 Prices for goods, materials, technology, and service imported by a wholly foreign-owned enterprise shall not be higher than the normal price of similar goods, materials, technology, and service in the international market. The enterprise may decide the price of its products for export by itself with reference to the price in the international market, but the price shall not be lower than a reasonable price for export. If a wholly foreign-owned enterprise evades tax by means of import at higher price and export at lower price or other methods, the Tax Authority has the power to investigate according to tax laws.

The price for products sold in the Chinese market by a wholly foreign-owned enterprise in line with the approved sales ratio shall follow the provisions of the price control regulations in China.

The said price shall be filed with the Price Control Authority and Tax Authority, and is subject to their supervision.

Article 49 A wholly foreign-owned enterprise shall provide statistical information and submit statistical statements and reports in accordance with the Law of Statistics of the People's Republic of China and the provisions of statistical system concerning foreign investment in China.

Chapter VII Taxation

Article 50 A wholly foreign-owned enterprise shall pay taxes in accordance with the laws and regulations of China.

Article 51 Staff and workers in a wholly foreign-owned enterprise shall pay individual income tax in accordance with the provisions of Chinese laws and regulations.

Article 52   A wholly foreign-owned enterprise shall be exempted form customs duty and industrial and commercial consolidated tax for the following goods and materials imported by it:

1. Machinery, equipment, parts, building materials for the enterprise's construction, and materials required for installation and reinforcement of machinery which are contributed as investment by the foreign investor
2. Machinery, equipment, parts, means of transport for production, and equipment for production management imported by the enterprise for its own use with funds which are part of the total amount of investment
3. Raw materials, auxiliary materials, components, parts, and packing materials imported by the enterprise for production of export goods

Taxes shall be levied and pursued according to Chinese tax laws if the imported goods and materials mentioned in the preceding paragraph are approved for sale in China or for manufacturing products to be sold in China.

Article 53   Except for those restricted by China to be export, the export products of a wholly foreign-owned enterprise shall be exempted from customs duty and industrial and commercial consolidated tax in accordance with the tax laws of China.

Chapter VIII Foreign Exchange Control

Article 54   A wholly foreign-owned enterprise shall handle its foreign exchange transactions in accordance with the laws and regulations on exchange control of China.

Article 55   With the Business License issued by the Administrative Authority for Industry and Commerce, a wholly foreign-owned enterprise may open a foreign exchange account with a bank which is permitted to handle foreign exchange transactions in the territory of China, and the supervision of receipts and payments shall be carried out by the bank with which an account is opened.

The foreign exchange income of a wholly foreign-owned enterprise shall be deposited into the foreign exchange account in the bank with which an account is opened, and the expenditures in foreign exchange by the wholly foreign-owned enterprise shall be made out of the foreign exchange account.

Article 56 A wholly foreign-owned enterprise shall keep the balance of its foreign exchange receipts and expenditures by itself.

Where a wholly foreign-owned enterprise is unable to keep the balance of its foreign exchange revenue and expenditure by itself, the foreign investor shall state it expressly in its application for establishing the wholly foreign-owned enterprise, and put forward a concrete proposal of solution. The Examination and Approval Authority shall give a reply after consulting with the departments concerned.

Where it is stated expressly in the application that the wholly foreign-owned enterprise can keep the balance of its foreign exchange receipts and disbursements by itself, any governmental department will not be responsible for solving the matter on the balance of foreign exchange receipts and disbursements.

In case the products made by a wholly foreign-owned enterprise are needed urgently in China and are able to be used as import substitution, they can be sold in China with permission, and the foreign exchange may be collected upon the approval of the Authority for Exchange Control of China.

Article 57 If a wholly foreign-owned enterprise needs to open a foreign exchange account with a bank outside China as required for its production and operation, it shall obtain permission from the Authority for Exchange Control of China, and report regularly its foreign exchange receipts and payments with its bank statement according to the provisions of the Authority for Exchange Control.

Article 58 Staff and workers from foreign countries or from Hong Kong, Macao, or Taiwan engaged in a wholly foreign-owned enterprise may, after having paid income tax according to the tax laws of China, remit freely their salaries and wages and other legitimate income out.

Chapter IX Financial Affairs and Accounting

Article 59 A wholly foreign-owned enterprise shall, in accordance with Chinese laws, regulations, and provisions of the Finance Authority, set up its financial and accounting system and report it to the local finance and tax authorities for the record.

Article 60   The fiscal year of a wholly foreign-owned enterprise shall begin on 1 January and end on 31 December of the Gregorian calendar.

Article 61   The profit of a wholly foreign-owned enterprise after payment of income tax according to the tax laws of Chins shall be allocated for reserve funds, bonuses, and welfare funds for staff and workers. The proportion of allocation for reserve funds shall be no less than 10% of the profit after tax until the accumulative amount of allocation for reserve funds reaches 50% of the registered capital, and then no more allocation may be made. The proportion of allocation for bonuses and welfare funds for staff and workers shall be decided by the enterprise itself.

No profit shall be distributed unless losses suffered by a wholly foreign-owned enterprise from the previous accounting years are recovered; the profit retained by the enterprise and carried over from the previous accounting years may be distributed together with the distributable profit of the current accounting year.

Article 62   The accounting vouchers, books, statements, and financial reports prepared by a wholly foreign-owned enterprise shall be written in Chinese. If written in foreign languages, they shall be supplemented with Chinese translation.

Article 63   A wholly foreign-owned enterprise shall conduct independent accounting.

A wholly foreign-owned enterprise shall compile its annual accounting statement and statement on liquidation in accordance with the provisions of the finance and taxation authorities of China. A wholly foreign-owned enterprise using a foreign currency as its bookkeeping base shall compile not only the accounting statement in the foreign currency but also the separate accounting statement in Renminbi equivalent to the foreign currency.

A wholly foreign-owned enterprise shall engage an accountant registered in China to verify its annual accounting statement and statement on liquidation and render a Certificate of Verification.

The annual accounting statement and statement on liquidation of a wholly foreign-owned enterprise stipulated in the second and third paragraphs shall be, with the Certificate rendered by the accountant registered in China, submitted to the finance and tax authorities in the set time, as well as to the Examination and Approval Authority and the Administrative Authority for Industry and Commerce for the record.

Article 64   A foreign investor may engage a Chinese or foreign accountant to audit the account books of its enterprise. The expenses thereon shall be borne by the foreign investor.

Article 65   A wholly foreign-owned enterprise shall submit its annual balance sheet and its profit and loss statement to the finance and tax authorities as well as to the Examination and Approval Authority and the Administrative Authority for Industry and Commerce for the record.

Article 66   A wholly foreign-owned enterprise shall set an account book in its location, and accept the supervision of the finance and tax authorities.

In case that a wholly foreign-owned enterprise violates the aforesaid provisions, the finance and tax authorities may impose a fine on the enterprise, and the Administrative Authority for Industry and Commerce may order a suspension of business to the enterprise or revoke its Business License.

Chapter X Staff and Workers

Article 67   In the employment of staff and workers in the territory in China, a wholly foreign-owned enterprise shall sign labor contracts with its staff and workers according to the laws and regulations of China, and matters such as employment, dismissal, remuneration, welfare, labor protection, labor insurance, etc. shall be expressly stipulated in the contracts.

All wholly foreign-owned enterprises are prohibited from employing child labor.

Article 68   A wholly foreign-owned enterprise shall take the responsibility for professional and technical training of its staff and workers, and set up systems of examining its staff and workers, thus enabling them to meet the requirements of development in production and managerial skills.

Chapter XI Trade Unions

Article 69   Staff and workers in a wholly foreign-owned enterprise have the right to establish grassroots trade unions and carry out trade union activities in accordance with the Trade Union Law of the People's Republic of China (hereafter referred to as the Trade Union Law).

Article 70   The trade union as a representative of staff and workers in a wholly foreign-owned enterprise is empowered to sign labor contracts with the enterprise on behalf of the staff and workers and supervise the execution of those contracts.

Article 71   The basic tasks of the trade union in a wholly foreign-owned enterprise are to protect the lawful rights and interests of the staff and workers pursuant to the laws and regulations of China; to assist the enterprise in rational use of welfare and bonus funds; to organize political, professional, scientific, and technical studies and carry out literary, art, and sports activities for staff and workers; and to educate staff and workers to observe labor discipline and exert themselves to fulfill the productive tasks of the enterprise.

The representatives of the trade union have the right to attend as nonvoting members the meetings held by a wholly foreign-owned enterprise to decide matters concerning staff and workers on awards and penalties, salaries and wages, welfare benefits, labor protection, labor insurance, etc. A wholly foreign-owned enterprise shall pay attention to the opinions of the trade union for its cooperation.

Article 72   A wholly foreign-owned enterprise shall actively support the work of the trade union and provide necessary space and facilities for the trade union for the purpose of the office, meeting, and collective activities of welfare, culture, and sports in accordance with the provisions of the Trade Union Law.

A wholly foreign-owned enterprise shall allot monthly 2% of the total salaries and wages actually paid to its staff and workers as the trade union's funds. The funds shall be used by the trade union in that enterprise according to the relevant managerial rules for trade union funds formulated by the All-China Federation of Trade Union.

Chapter XII Duration, Termination, and Liquidation

Article 73   The term of operation of a wholly foreign-owned enterprise shall be, according to its particular line of business and its concrete conditions, stipulated by the foreign investor in its application for establishing the enterprise and approved by the Examination and Approval Authority.

Article 74   The term of operation of a wholly foreign-owned enterprise shall begin from the date on which the Business License of the enterprise is issued.

If an extension for term of operation is required upon the expiration, a wholly foreign-owned enterprise shall submit an application for extension of the term to the Examination and Approval Authority 180 days before the expiration. The Examination and Approval Authority shall decide the approval or disapproval within 30 days from the date of receiving the application for extension.

Upon the approval of extension of the term, the enterprise shall go through formalities for the alteration of registration with the Administrative Authority for Industry and Commerce within 30 days from the date of receiving the approval document.

Article 75   A wholly foreign-owned enterprise shall be terminated in any of the following situations:

1. Expiration of the term of operation
2. Dissolution decided by the foreign investor due to the poor operation and heavy losses
3. Inability to continue the operation due to heavy losses caused by *force majeure* such as natural calamity, war, etc.
4. Bankruptcy
5. Revocation made by the authorities concerned due to the violation of Chinese laws and regulations and harm to social and public interests
6. Occurrence of other reasons of dissolution stipulated in the Articles of Association of the enterprise

If a wholly foreign-owned enterprise is involved in the situations described in 2, 3, and 4 of the preceding paragraph, the enterprise shall submit an application for termination by itself to the Examination and Approval Authority for verifications and approval. The date of termination shall begin from the date of verification and approval by the Examination and Approval Authority.

Article 76   In case a wholly foreign-owned enterprise is terminated under the provisions of 1, 2, 3, and 6 in Article 75, the enterprise shall make a public announcement and notify the creditors within 15 days from the date of termination. It shall, within 15 days from the day on which the announcement of termination is issued, put forward the procedures and principles for liquidation, nominate the candidates for the liquidation committee, and submit them to the Examination and Approval Authority, and then carry out liquidation after the examination and verification by the authority.

Article 77   The liquidation committee shall be composed of the legal representative of a wholly foreign-owned enterprise and representatives of the creditors and the competent authorities concerned. It shall also engage an accountant registered in China and a lawyer as its members.

The liquidation expenses shall be paid first from the existing assets of the enterprise.

Article 78   The liquidation committee shall exercise its functions and powers as follows:

1. To convene the meeting of creditors
2. To take over and sort out the property of the enterprise, and work out a balance sheet and a list of property
3. To put forward a basis on which the property is evaluated and calculated
4. To formulate a liquidation program
5. To collect claims and clear debts
6. To recover the amount of money which should be but fail to be contributed by shareholders
7. To allocate the property left over after the clearance of all debts
8. To sue and be sued on behalf of the wholly foreign-owned enterprise

Article 79   Before the completion of the liquidation of a wholly-owned enterprise, the foreign investor shall not remit or carry the funds of the enterprise outside China and not dispose of the property of the enterprise by itself.

If the net assets and remaining property exceed the registered capital of a wholly foreign-owned enterprise upon its completion of the liquidation, the excess sum will be regarded as the profit on which income tax shall be levied in accordance with the tax laws of China.

Article 80   Upon the completion of liquidation of a wholly foreign-owned enterprise, the foreign investor shall go through the formalities for nullifying its registration and canceling its Business License with the Administrative Authority for Industry and Commerce.

Article 81   When a wholly foreign-owned enterprise is disposed of its property upon the liquidation, any Chinese-owned enterprises or other economic organizations have the priority of purchase under the like conditions.

Article 82   In case a wholly foreign-owned enterprise is terminated pursuant to 4 of Article 75, the liquidation shall be conducted with reference to the related laws and regulations of China.

In the event that a wholly foreign-owned enterprise is terminated according to 5 of Article 75, the liquidation shall be carried out in accordance with the relevant provisions of China.

Chapter XIII Supplementary Provisions

Article 83 All the insurance coverage of a wholly foreign-owned enterprise shall be furnished by insurance institutions within the territory of China.

Article 84 Economic Contract Law of the People's Republic of China shall apply to the economic contracts concluded between a wholly foreign-owned enterprise and any other Chinese-owned enterprises or economic organizations.

Foreign Economic Contract Law of the People's Republic of China shall apply to the economic contracts concluded between a wholly foreign-owned enterprise and a foreign company, enterprise or individual.

Article 85 If a company, enterprise, and other economic organization or individual in Hong Kong, Macao, and Taiwan and a Chinese citizen inhabits abroad establishes a wholly-owned enterprise by itself in the mainland, it shall be handled with reference to the present Detailed Rules.

Article 86 Staff and workers from foreign countries or Hong Kong, Macao, and Taiwan engaged in a wholly foreign-owned enterprise may bring in a rational number of self-use means of transport and articles for daily use through complying with the formalities for the importation according to the provisions of China.

Article 87 The Ministry of Foreign Economic Relations and Trade is responsible for the interpretation of the present Detailed Rules.

Article 88 The present Detailed Rules shall enter into force from the date of promulgation.

6. Provisions of the State Council of the People's Republic of China for the Encouragement of Foreign Investment

Promulgated on 11 October 1986

Article 1 These provisions are hereby formulated in order to improve the investment environment, facilitate the absorption of foreign investment, introduce advanced technology, improve product quality, and expand exports in order to generate foreign exchange and develop the national economy.

Article 2   The state encourages foreign companies, enterprises, and other economic entities or individuals (hereafter referred to as foreign investors) to establish Chinese–foreign equity joint ventures, Chinese–foreign cooperative ventures, and wholly foreign-owned enterprises (hereafter referred to as enterprises with foreign investment) within the territory of China. The state grants special preferences to the enterprises with foreign investment listed below:

1. Production enterprises whose products are mainly for export, which have a foreign exchange surplus after deducting from their total annual foreign exchange revenues the annual foreign exchange expenditures incurred in production and operation and the foreign exchange needed for the remittance abroad of the profits earned by foreign investors (hereafter referred to as export enterprises).
2. Production enterprises possessing advanced technology supplied by foreign investors which are engaged in developing new products, and upgrading and replacing products in order to increase foreign exchange generated by exports or for import substitution (hereafter referred to as technologically advanced enterprises).

Article 3   Export enterprises and technologically advanced enterprises shall be exempt from payment to the state of all subsidies to staff and workers, except for the payment of or allocation of funds for labor insurance, welfare costs, and housing subsidies for Chinese staff and workers in accordance with the provisions of the state.

Article 4   The site use fees for export enterprises and technologically advanced enterprises, except for those located in busy urban sectors of large cities, shall be computed and charged according to the following standards:

1. RMB 5–20 per square meter per year in areas where the development fee and the site use fee are computed and charged together
2. Not more than RMB 3 per square meter per year in site areas where the development fee is computed and charged on a one-time basis or areas developed by the above-mentioned enterprises themselves

Exemptions for specified periods of time from the fees provided in the foregoing provision may be granted at the discretion of local people's governments.

Article 5 Export enterprises and technologically advanced enterprises shall be given priority in obtaining water, electricity, and transportation services and communication facilities needed for their production and operation. Fees shall be computed and charged in accordance with the standards for local state enterprises.

Article 6 Export enterprises and technologically advanced enterprises, after examination by the Bank of China, shall be given priority in receiving loans for short-term revolving funds needed for production and distribution, as well as for other needed credit.

Article 7 When foreign investors in export enterprises and technologically advanced enterprises remit abroad profits distributed to them by such enterprises, the amount remitted shall be exempt from income tax.

Article 8 After the expiration of the period for the reduction or exemption of enterprise income tax in accordance with the provisions of the state, export enterprises whose value of export products in that year amounts to 70% or more of the value of their products for that year may pay enterprise income tax at one-half the rate of the present tax.

Export enterprises in the special economic zones and in the economic and technological development zones and other export enterprises that already pay enterprise income tax at a tax rate of 15% and that comply with the foregoing conditions, shall pay enterprise income tax at a rate of 10%.

Article 9 After the expiration of the period of reduction or exemption of enterprise income tax in accordance with the provisions of the state, technologically advanced enterprises may extend for three years the payment of enterprise income tax at a rate reduced by one-half.

Article 10 Foreign investors who reinvest the profits distributed to them by their enterprises in order to establish or expand export enterprises or technologically advanced enterprises for a period of operation of not less than five years, after application to and approval by the tax authorities, shall be refunded the total amount of enterprise income tax already paid on the reinvested portion. If the investment is withdrawn before the period of operation reaches five years, the amount of enterprise income tax refunded shall be repaid.

Article 11   Export products of enterprises with foreign investment, except crude oil, finished oil, and other products subject to special state provisions, shall be exempt from the consolidated industrial and commercial tax.

Article 12   Enterprises with foreign investment may arrange the export of their products directly or may also export by consignment to agents in accordance with state provisions. For products that require an export license, in accordance with the annual export plan of the enterprise, an application for an export license may be made every six months.

Article 13   Machinery and equipment, vehicles used in production, raw materials, fuel, bulk parts, spare parts, machine component parts, and fittings (including imports restricted by the state), which enterprises with foreign investment need to import in order to carry out their export contracts, do not require further applications for examination and approval and are exempt from the requirement for import licenses. The customs department shall exercise supervision and control, and shall inspect and release such imports on the basis of the enterprise Contract or the export contract.

The imported materials and items mentioned above are restricted to use by the enterprise and may not be sold on the domestic market. If they are used in products to be sold domestically, import procedures shall be handled in accordance with provisions, and the taxes shall be made up according to the governing sections.

Article 14   Under the supervision of the foreign exchange control departments, enterprises with foreign investment may mutually adjust their foreign exchange surpluses and deficiencies among each other.

The Bank of China and other banks designated by the People's Bank of China may provide cash security services and may grant loans in Renminbi to enterprises with foreign investment.

Article 15   The people's governments at all levels and relevant departments in charge shall guarantee the right of autonomy of enterprises with foreign investment and shall support enterprises with foreign investment in managing themselves in accordance with international advanced scientific methods.

With the scope of their approved contracts, enterprises with foreign investment have the right to determine by themselves production and operation plans, to raise funds, to use funds, to purchase production materials and to sell products, and to determine by themselves the wage levels, the forms of wages and bonuses, and the allowance system.

Enterprises with foreign investment may, in accordance with their production and operation requirements, determine by themselves their organizational structure and personnel system, employ or dismiss senior management personnel, increase or dismiss staff and workers. They may recruit and employ technical personnel, managerial personnel, and workers in the locality. The unit to which such employed personnel belong shall provide its support and shall permit their transfer. Staff and workers who violate the rules and regulations, and thereby cause certain bad consequences, may, in accordance with the seriousness of the case, be given differing sanctions, up to that of discharge. Enterprises with foreign investment that recruit, employ, dismiss, or discharge staff and workers shall file a report with the local labor and personnel department.

Article 16 All districts and departments must implement the Circular of the State Council concerning Firmly Curbing the Indiscriminate Levy of Charges on Enterprises. The people's governments at the provincial level shall formulate specific methods and strengthen supervision and administration.

Enterprises with foreign investment that encounter unreasonable charges may refuse to pay and may also appeal to the local economic committees up to the State Economic Commission.

Article 17 The people's governments at all levels and relevant departments in charge shall strengthen the coordination of their work, improve efficiency in handling matters, and promptly examine and approve matters reported by enterprises with foreign investment that require response and resolution. The Agreement, Contract, and Articles of Association of an enterprise with foreign investment shall be examined and approved by the departments in charge under the State Council. The Examination and Approval Authority must within three months from the date of receipt of all documents decide to approve or not to approve them.

Article 18 Export enterprises and technologically advanced enterprises mentioned in these provisions shall be confirmed jointly as such by the foreign economic relations and trade departments where such enterprises are located and the relevant departments in accordance with the enterprise Contract, and certification shall be issued.

If the actual results of the annual exports of an export enterprise are unable to realize the goal of the surplus in the foreign exchange balance that is stipulated in the enterprise Contract, the taxes and fees which have already been reduced or exempted in the previous year shall be made up in the following year.

Article 19   Except where these provisions expressly provide that they are to be applicable to export enterprises or technologically advanced enterprises, other articles shall be applicable to all enterprises with foreign investment.

These provisions apply from the date of implementation to those enterprises with foreign investment that have obtained approval for establishment before the date of implementation of these provisions and that qualify for the preferential terms of these provisions.

Article 20   For enterprises invested in and established by companies, enterprises, and other economic organizations or individuals from Hong Kong, Macao, or Taiwan, matters shall be handled by reference to these provisions.

Article 21   The Ministry of Foreign Economic Relations and Trade shall be responsible for interpreting these provisions.

Article 22   These provisions shall go into effect on the date of issue.

7. Regulations of the State Council on Encouraging Investment by Taiwanese Compatriot

Promulgated by the State Council on 25 June 1988

Article 1   These Regulations are formulated to promote economic and technological exchanges between the mainland and Taiwan region with a view to benefiting the mutual prosperity of both sides of the Taiwan Straits and to encourage companies, enterprises, and individuals of Taiwan (hereafter collectively referred to as the Taiwanese investors) to invest in the mainland.

Article 2   Taiwanese investors may invest in any province, autonomous region, municipality, and special economic zone of the mainland.

Taiwanese investors are encouraged to undertake land development and operation in Hainan Province and in the coastal areas in the provinces of Fujian, Guangdong, Zhejiang, and so on, where islands and areas are designated for such development.

Article 3 Taiwanese investors may invest in the mainland in the following forms:

1. In the establishment of enterprises with capital wholly owned by Taiwanese investors
2. In the establishment of equity joint ventures or cooperative joint ventures
3. By undertaking compensation trade, processing, or assembling with imported materials, coproduction
4. In the purchase of stocks and bonds of enterprises
5. In the purchase of houses and other real estate
6. By obtaining the right to use, develop, and operate land in accordance with the law
7. Other forms of investment permitted by law

Article 4 Taiwanese investors may invest in manufacturing, agriculture, service trades, and other industries which conform to the orientation of social and economic development. Taiwanese investors may select investment projects from those published by relevant authorities of the local people's government at all levels, or initiate their own investment intention and make applications to the foreign economic and trade departments of the proposed investment region or the examination and approval authorities designated by local people's government.

Article 5 In addition to the Regulations applicable to equity joint ventures, cooperative joint ventures, and wholly owned enterprises invested in and established by Taiwanese investors (hereafter collectively referred to as the Taiwanese Compatriots–Invested Enterprises) reference shall be made to relevant foreign economic laws and regulations of the state regarding the treatment granted to foreign investment enterprises, which treatment the Taiwanese Compatriots–Invested Enterprises shall enjoy correspondingly.

Dividends, interest, rentals, royalties, and other income derived from other forms of investment made by Taiwanese investors in the mainland or from other sources without permanent business establishments in the mainland, apart from being subject to the Regulations, shall also, with due reference, be subject to the foreign economic laws and regulations of the state.

Article 6   Taiwanese investors may make investments in free convertible currencies, machinery and equipment or other properties, industrial properties, and know-how.

Article 7   Investment in the mainland, properties purchase, industrial properties, profits from investment, and other lawful interests of Taiwanese investors shall be protected by law and can be transferred and inherited in accordance with law.

Article 8   The state shall not nationalize investments and other assets of Taiwanese investors.

Article 9   To meet the requirements of social and public interest, the state shall proceed, according to legal process, with any expropriation of the Taiwanese Compatriots–Invested Enterprises against appropriate compensation.

Article 10   All lawful profits, other lawful income, and money after liquidation received by Taiwanese investors may be remitted out of China in accordance with the law.

Article 11   All machinery and equipment, vehicles, and office appliances needed for production within the amount of total investment of the Taiwanese Compatriots–Invested Enterprises, and all articles and transportation vehicles for personal daily use and in reasonable quantity imported by individual Taiwanese compatriots during the operation of the enterprises shall be exempted from import duty, consolidated industrial and commercial tax, and from import license requirements.

All raw materials, fuels, bulk parts, parts, components, and accessories imported by Taiwanese Compatriots–Invested Enterprises for production of export products shall be exempted from import duty, consolidated industrial, and commercial tax, and from import license requirement, subject to supervision by the Customs. If the above-mentioned materials and parts are used in the production of goods to be sold within China, formalities and procedures for importation shall be completed in accordance with the relevant regulations of the state, and taxes shall be paid accordingly.

Export goods produced by Taiwanese Compatriots–Invested Enterprises, except those restricted by the state for export, shall be exempted from export duty and consolidated industrial and commercial tax.

Article 12   Taiwanese Compatriots–Invested Enterprises may borrow money from financial institutions on the mainland or from financial institutions outside China and may secure therefore with assets and interest therein by way of mortgage or guarantee.

Article 13   The duration of the enterprises wholly owned by Taiwanese investors shall be decided upon by the investors themselves; duration of equity joint ventures and cooperative joint ventures shall be decided upon by all parties through consultation. Taiwanese investors may also choose not to specify the duration.

Article 14   The composition of the board of directors and the appointment of chairman of the board of the equity joint ventures, composition of the board of directors or of the joint management organ, and appointment of chairman of the board or chairman of the joint management organ may be decided upon by parties to the equity or cooperative joint ventures through consultation and with reference to respective investment proportions and other conditions.

Article 15   The Taiwanese Compatriots–Invested Enterprises shall be managed and operated in accordance with the approved Contracts and Articles of Association. The autonomy of the enterprises shall not be interfered with.

Article 16   Individual Taiwanese compatriots and technical and managerial personnel employed by Taiwanese Compatriots–Invested Enterprises may apply for multientry documents.

Article 17   Taiwanese investors who invest in the mainland may appoint their relatives and friends on the mainland as their attorneys. Those attorneys shall hold legally valid power of attorney.

Article 18   In areas where there are large numbers of Taiwanese Compatriots–Invested Enterprises, Taiwanese investors may apply to the local people's government to establish an association of Taiwanese merchants.

Article 19   In the case of establishment of equity joint ventures and cooperative joint ventures with investment of Taiwanese investors, the mainland participants in the equity and cooperative joint venture shall be responsible for the application therefore. In the case of establishment of enterprises wholly owned by Taiwanese investors, the Taiwanese investors shall apply directly or entrust their relatives and friends or consulting services organization to make such application. Applications by

Taiwanese investors for investment and establishment of enterprises shall be handled by local foreign economic and trade departments or examining and approval authorities designated by the local people's government.

The examining and approval of Taiwanese Compatriots–Invested Enterprises shall be handled in accordance with the authorities specified by the State Council. Foreign economic and trade departments at all levels or examining and approval authorities designated by local people's governments shall, within 45 days of the receipt of all applications, decide whether to approve such application.

Applicants shall, within 30 days after the receipt of the letter of approval, apply to the Administration of Industry and Commerce for registration in accordance with the relevant provisions concerning business registration, and shall obtain a Business License.

Article 20   In the case of any dispute arising out of the execution of the Contracts or relating thereto which involves Taiwanese investors who invest in the mainland, the parties in dispute shall endeavor to resolve such disputes through consultation and conciliation.

If the parties in dispute are not willing to resolve their dispute through consultation and conciliation, or such dispute cannot be resolved through consultation and conciliation, they may submit the same to arbitration organizations of the mainland or in Hong Kong in accordance with the arbitration clause in the Contract or written arbitration agreement reached later.

If the parties have not included an arbitration clause in the Contract or reached a written arbitration agreement thereafter, they may bring an action in the people's court.

Article 21   The Ministry of Foreign Economic Relations and Trade shall be responsible for the interpretation of these Regulations.

Article 22   These Regulations come into effect on the date of promulgation.

8. Provisions of the State Council Concerning the Encouragement of Investments by Overseas Chinese and Compatriots From Hong Kong and Macao

Promulgated by Decree No. 64 of the State Council of the People's Republic of China on 9 August 1990 and effective as of the date of promulgation

Article 1   These Provisions are formulated with a view to promoting the economic development of our country and to encouraging overseas Chinese and compatriots from Hong Kong and Macao (hereafter referred to as overseas Chinese investors and those from Hong Kong and Macao) to make investments in China's inland areas.

Article 2   Overseas Chinese investors and those from Hong Kong and Macao can make investments in the various provinces, autonomous regions, municipalities directly under the Central government, and special economic zones in China's inland areas.

Overseas Chinese investors and those from Hong Kong and Macao are encouraged to engage themselves in business operations of land development in accordance with the pertinent regulations of the state.

Article 3   The investments made by the overseas Chinese investors and those from Hong Kong and Macao may take the following forms:

1. To establish enterprises with the capital wholly owned by the overseas Chinese investors and those from Hong Kong and Macao
2. To establish equity joint ventures and contractual joint ventures
3. To carry out compensation trade, to process supplied materials, to assemble supplied parts, and to carry out contractual production
4. To purchase shares and various bonds and debentures of existing enterprises
5. To purchase real estate
6. To obtain land use rights according to law and to engage in land development operation
7. To use other forms of investment permitted under the laws and regulations

Article 4   Overseas Chinese investors and those from Hong Kong and Macao can make investments in various trades in China's inland areas: in industries, in agriculture, in service trades, and in other trades that are in conformity with the orientation of social and economic development. Overseas Chinese investors and compatriots from Hong Kong and Macao may select their investment projects from the lists of projects made public by the departments concerned under various local people's governments; they may also put forward, of their own accord, proposals as to their investment intent and file their applications to the departments of foreign economic relations and trade or to the examining and approving organs designated by various local people's governments located in areas where they intend to make their investments.

The state encourages overseas Chinese investors and those from Hong Kong and Macao to make investments in the establishment of export-oriented enterprises and of technologically advanced enterprises, and gives corresponding preferential treatment to such enterprises.

Article 5 With respect to the various types of enterprises established with investments by overseas Chinese investors and those from Hong Kong and Macao—enterprises with the capital wholly owned by such investors equity, joint ventures, and contractual joint ventures (hereafter referred to as enterprises with investments by overseas Chinese and compatriots from Hong Kong and Macao)—they shall all be operated in accordance with these Provisions; in addition, they may also enjoy the corresponding preferential treatment as enjoyed by enterprises with foreign investment, in the light of the relevant provisions in the state laws, decrees, and regulations on external economic relations. Cases concerning other forms of investment made by such investors in China's inland areas, and concerning their dividends, interest, rental, royalties, and other income that come from China's inland areas without establishing business offices here, shall be handled in accordance with these Provisions, and, if need be, with reference to foreign-related economic laws, decrees, and regulations of the state.

Article 6 Overseas Chinese investors and those from Hong Kong and Macao may make their investments by using convertible currencies, machinery and equipment or other physical goods industrial property rights, and proprietary technology.

Article 7 The investment made in China's inland areas by overseas Chinese investors and those from Hong Kong and Macao, the assets they have purchased, their industrial property rights, the profits from their investments, and other lawful rights and interests shall be protected by state laws and may be transferred or inherited according to law. Overseas Chinese investors and those from Hong Kong and Macao shall abide by state laws and regulations in their activities in inland areas.

Article 8   The state shall not nationalize the investment made by overseas Chinese investors and compatriots from Hong Kong and Macao or other assets belonging to them.

Article 9   Where the state, in accordance with the needs of social and public interest, has to requisition the enterprises with investments by overseas Chinese investors and those from Hong Kong and Macao, the state shall handle the case according to the legal procedures, and the investors concerned shall be duly compensated.

Article 10   The lawful profits gained by overseas Chinese investors and those from Hong Kong and Macao from their investments, their other lawful incomes, and the funds after liquidation may be remitted out of China's inland areas according to law.

Article 11   Machinery and equipment imported to meet the needs of enterprises with investments by overseas Chinese and compatriots from Hong Kong and Macao and, included in the total amount of investment, motor vehicles for use in production, office equipment, as well as articles and means of communications for personal use and within reasonable quantities, imported by overseas Chinese and compatriots from Hong Kong and Macao during the period when they work in the aforesaid enterprises, shall be exempted from customs duties and consolidated industrial and commercial tax, and also from the application for import licenses.

The raw and processed materials, fuels, bulk parts, spare and component parts, primary parts, and fittings, which are imported by enterprises with investments by overseas Chinese and compatriots from Hong Kong and Macao for the production of export commodities, shall all be exempt from customs duties and consolidated industrial and commercial tax and also from the application for import licenses and placed under the supervision of the Customs. In case the aforesaid imported materials and parts are used for the production of commodities to be sold on China's inland markets, it is imperative to make up the procedures for importation and to pay taxes and duties according to the regulations.

The export commodities produced by the enterprises with investments by overseas Chinese and compatriots from Hong Kong and Macao shall, with the exception of those commodities the exportation of which is under restriction by the state, be exempt from customs duties on export goods and consolidated industrial and commercial tax.

Article 12   Enterprises with investments by overseas Chinese and compatriots from Hong Kong and Macao may obtain loans from financial institutions in China's inland areas; they may also obtain loans from financial institutions outside China's inland areas, and may use their assets as well as their rights and interests as mortgage or security.

Article 13 With respect to enterprises with the capital wholly owned by overseas Chinese investors and compatriots from Hong Kong and Macao, their period of operation shall be determined by the investors themselves; as to equity joint ventures and contractual joint ventures, their period of operation shall be determined, through consultation, by the various parties to the above-said joint ventures; they may also set no limit to the period of operation.

Article 14 The composition of the board of directors of joint ventures and the appointment of the chairman of the board of directors, the composition of the board of directors or of the joint management organs of contractual joint ventures, and the appointment of the chairman or the appointment of the director of the joint management organs shall be determined, through consultation, by the various parties to the equity joint ventures or to the contractual joint ventures in the light of the proportion of investments or the terms of contract.

Article 15 Enterprises with investments by overseas Chinese and compatriots from Hong Kong and Macao shall conduct their operational and management activities in accordance with the approved Contract or Articles of Association. The enterprises decision-making power for business operations and management shall not be interfered with.

Article 16 Overseas Chinese and compatriots from Hong Kong and Macao who have made investments in China's inland areas, and the technical and managerial personnel engaged from outside the boundaries of China's inland areas by enterprises with investments by overseas Chinese and compatriots from Hong Kong and Macao, may apply for multijourney travel documents.

Article 17 Overseas Chinese investors and those from Hong Kong and Macao who make investments in China's inland areas may appoint their relatives or friends residing in the inland areas as their agents. The agents should hold legally effective letters of authority.

Article 18 In areas where enterprises with investments by overseas Chinese and compatriots from Hong Kong and Macao are concentrated, overseas Chinese investors and those from Hong Kong and Macao may apply to the local people's government for the establishment of the Association of Overseas Chinese Investors and Investors from Hong Kong and Macao.

Article 19   With respect to equity joint ventures and contractual joint ventures to be established in China's inland areas, with the investments by overseas Chinese investors and those from Hong Kong and Macao, the application for the establishment of the aforesaid enterprises shall be filed by the inland party; as to the enterprises to be established with capital wholly owned by overseas Chinese investors and those from Hong Kong and Macao, the application shall be filed directly by such investor themselves, or they may entrust their relatives or friends residing in China's inland areas, or entrust the institution providing consultancy services with the application. Applications for the establishment of enterprises with investments by overseas Chinese and compatriots from Hong Kong and Macao shall be accepted and handled exclusively by the local department for foreign economic relations and trade, or by the examining and approving organs designated by the local people's government.

The examination and approval of the applications for the establishment of enterprises with investments from overseas Chinese and compatriots from Hong Kong and Macao shall be handled in accordance with the authorization by the State Council. Departments for foreign economic relations and trade at the various levels or the examining and approving organs designated by the local people's government shall, within 45 days of receipt of complete application documents, make the decision on whether the said application is approved or disapproved.

The applicant shall, within 30 days of receipt of the written approval, file an application to the Department for the Administration of Industry and Commerce, and, in accordance with the relevant procedures for registration and obtain the Business License.

Article 20   With respect to overseas Chinese investors and those from Hong Kong and Macao who have made investments in China's inland area, in case that a dispute arises during the execution of or in relation to a Contract, the parties concerned shall try their best to settle the dispute through consultation or mediation.

In case that the parties concerned are unwilling to settle the dispute through consultation or mediation, or the dispute cannot be settled through consultation or mediation, the parties concerned may, in accordance with the stipulations of the arbitration articles in the Contract, or in accordance with the written arbitration agreement reached by the parties concerned after the dispute has arisen, submit their dispute to the arbitration authorities in China's inland areas or elsewhere for settlement.

In the event that the parties concerned did not specify an arbitration article in their Contract, and no written arbitration agreement has been reached after the dispute occurs, then the dispute may be brought before the people's court.

Article 21   The right to interpret these Provisions rests with the Ministry of Foreign Economic Relations and Trade.

Article 22   These Provisions shall go into effect as of the date of promulgation.

9. Income Tax Law of the People's Republic of China for Enterprises With Foreign Investment and Foreign Enterprises

Promulgated on 9 April 1991

Article 1   Income tax shall be paid in accordance with the provisions of this Law by enterprises with foreign investment within the territory of the People's Republic of China on their income derived from production, business operations, and other sources.

Income tax shall be paid in accordance with the provisions of this Law by foreign enterprises on their income derived from production, business operations, and other sources within the territory of the People's Republic of China.

Article 2   Enterprises with foreign investment referred to in this Law mean Chinese–foreign equity joint ventures, Chinese-foreign contractual joint ventures, and foreign-capital enterprises that are established in China.

Foreign enterprises referred to in this Law mean foreign companies, enterprises, and other economic organizations which have establishments or places in China and engage in production or business operations and which, though without establishments or places in Chins, have income from sources within China.

Article 3   Any enterprise with foreign investment which establishes its head office in China shall pay its income tax on its income derived from sources inside and outside China. Any foreign enterprise shall pay its income tax on its income derived from sources within China.

Article 4   The taxable income of an enterprise with foreign investment and an establishment or a place set up in China to engage in production or business operations by a foreign enterprise shall be the amount remaining from its gross income in a tax year after the cost, expenses, and losses have been deducted.

Article 5   The income tax on enterprises with foreign investment and the income tax which shall be paid by foreign enterprises on the income of their establishments or places set up in China to engage in production or business operations shall be computed on the taxable income at the rate of 30%, and a local income tax shall be computed on the taxable income at the rate of 3%.

Article 6   The state shall, in accordance with the industrial policies, guide the orientation of foreign investment and encourage the establishment of enterprises with foreign investment which adopt advanced technology and equipment and export all or greater part of their products.

Article 7   The income tax on enterprises with foreign investment established in special economic zones, foreign enterprises which have establishments or places in special economic zones engaged in production or business operations, and enterprises with foreign investment of a production nature in economic and technological development zones shall be levied at the reduced rate of 15%.

The income tax on enterprises with foreign investment of a production nature established in coastal economic open zones or in the old urban districts of cities where the special economic zones or the economic and technological development zones are located shall be levied at the reduced rate of 24%.

The income tax on enterprises with foreign investment in coastal economic open zones, in the old urban districts of cities where the special economic zones or the economic and technological development zones are located, or in other regions defined by the State Council, within the scope of energy, communications, harbor, wharf, or other projects encouraged by the state, may be levied at the reduced rate of 15%. The specific rules shall be regulated by the State Council.

Article 8   Any enterprise with foreign investment of a production nature scheduled to operate for a period of not less than ten years shall, from the year beginning to make profit, be exempted from income tax in the first and second years and allowed a 50% reduction in the third to fifth years. However, the income tax exemption or reduction for enterprises with foreign investment engaged in the exploitation of resources such as petroleum, natural gas, rare metals, and precious metals shall be regulated separately by the State Council. Enterprises with foreign investment which actually operate for a period less than ten years shall repay the amount of income tax exempted or reduced.

The relevant regulations, promulgated by the State Council before the entry into force of this Law, which provide preferential treatment of exemption from or reduction of income tax on enterprises engaged in energy, communications, harbor, wharf, and other major projects of a production nature for a period longer than that specified in the preceding paragraph, or which provide preferential treatment of exemption from or reduction of income tax on enterprises engaged in major projects of a nonproduction nature, shall remain applicable after this Law comes into force.

Any enterprise with foreign investment which is engaged in agriculture, forestry, or animal husbandry and any other enterprise with foreign investment which is established in remote underdeveloped areas may, upon approval by the competent department for tax affairs under the State Council of an application filed by the enterprise, be allowed a 15% to 30% reduction of the amount of income tax payable for a period of another ten years following the expiration of the period for tax exemption and reduction as provided for in the preceding two paragraphs.

After this Law comes into force, any modification to the provisions of the preceding three paragraphs of this Article on the exemption or reduction of income tax on enterprises shall be submitted by the State Council to the Standing Committee of the National People's Congress for decision.

Article 9   The exemption or reduction of local income tax on any enterprise with foreign investment which operates in an industry or undertakes a project encouraged by the state shall, in accordance with the actual situation, be at the discretion of the people's government of the province, autonomous region, or municipality directly under the Central Government.

Article 10   Any foreign investor of an enterprise with foreign investment which reinvests its share of profit obtained from the enterprise directly into that enterprise by increasing its capital, or uses the profit as capital investment to establish other enterprises with foreign investment to operate for a period of not less than five years shall, upon approval by the tax authorities of an application filed by the investor, be refunded 40% of the income tax already paid on the reinvested amount. Where other preferential provisions are provided by the State Council, such provisions shall apply. If the investor withdraws its reinvestment before the expiration of a period of five years, it shall repay the refunded tax.

Article 11 Losses incurred in a tax year by any enterprise with foreign investment and by an establishment or a place set up in China by a foreign enterprise to engage in production or business operations may be made up by the income of the following tax year. Should the income of the following tax year be insufficient to make up for the said losses, the balance may be made up by its income of the further subsequent year, and so on, over a period not exceeding five years.

Article 12 Any enterprise with foreign investment shall be allowed, when filing a consolidated income tax return, to deduct from the amount of tax payable the foreign income tax already paid abroad in respect of the income derived from sources outside China. The deductible amount shall, however, not exceed the amount of income tax otherwise payable under this Law in respect of the income derived from sources outside China.

Article 13 The payment of receipt of charges or fees in business transactions between an enterprise with foreign investment, or an establishment or a place set up in China by a foreign enterprise to engage in production or business operations, and its associated enterprises, shall be made in the same manner as the payment or receipt of charges or fees in business transactions between independent enterprises. Where the payment or receipt of charges or fees is not made in the same manner as in business transactions between independent enterprises and results in a reduction of the taxable income, the tax authorities shall have the right to make reasonable adjustment.

Article 14 When an enterprise with foreign investment or an establishment or a place set up in China by a foreign enterprise to engage in production or business operations is established, moves to a new site, merges with another enterprise, breaks up, winds up, or makes a change in any of the main entries of registration, it shall present the relevant documents to and go through tax registration with, the local tax authorities after the relevant event is registered with or a change or cancellation in registration is made by the Administrative Agency for Industry and Commerce.

Article 15 Income tax on enterprises and local income tax shall be computed on an annual basis and paid in advance in quarterly installments. Such payments shall be made within 15 days from the end of each quarter, and the final settlement shall be made within five months from the end of each tax year. Any excess payment shall be refunded, and any deficiency shall be repaid.

Article 16   Any enterprise with foreign investment and any establishment or place set up in China by a foreign enterprise to engage in production or business operations shall file its quarterly provisional income tax return in respect of advance payments with the local tax authorities within the period for advance payment of tax, and it shall file an annual income tax return together with the final accounting statements within four months from the end of the tax year.

Article 17   Any enterprise with foreign investment and any establishment or place set up in China by a foreign enterprise to engage in production or business operations shall submit its financial and accounting systems to the local tax authorities for reference. All accounting records must be complete and accurate, with legitimate vouchers as the basis for entries.

If the financial and accounting bases adopted by an enterprise with foreign investment and an establishment or a place set up in China by a foreign enterprise to engage in production or business operations contradict the relevant tax provisions of the State Council, tax payment shall be computed in accordance with the relevant tax provisions of the State Council.

Article 18   When any enterprise with foreign investment goes into liquidation, and if the balance of its net assets or the balance of its remaining property after deduction of the enterprise's undistributed profit, various funds, and liquidation expenses exceeds the enterprise's paid-in capital, the excess portion shall be liquidation income on which income tax shall be paid in accordance with the provisions of this Law.

Article 19   Any foreign enterprise which has not establishment or place in China but derives profit, interest, rental, royalty, and other income from sources in China, or though it has an establishment or place in China, the said income is not effectively connected with such establishment or place shall pay an income tax of 20% on such income.

For the payment of income tax in accordance with the provisions of the preceding paragraph, the income beneficiary shall be the taxpayer, and the payer shall be the withholding agent. The tax shall be withheld from the amount of each payment by the payer. The withholding agent shall, within five days, turn the amount of taxes withheld on each payment over to the

State Treasury and submit a withholding income tax return to the local tax authorities.

Income tax shall be reduced or exempted on the following income:

1. The profit derived by a foreign investor from an enterprise with foreign investment shall be exempted from income tax.
2. Income from interest on loans made to the Chinese government or Chinese state banks by international financial organizations shall be exempted from income tax.
3. Income from interest on loans made at a preferential interest rate to Chinese state banks by foreign banks shall be exempted from income tax.
4. Income tax of the royalty received or the supply of technical know-how in scientific research, exploitation of energy resources, development of the communications industries, agricultural, forestry and animal husbandry production, and the development of important technologies may, upon approval by the competent department for tax affairs under the State Council, be levied at the reduced rate of 10%. Where the technology supplied is advanced or the terms are preferential, exemption from income tax may be allowed.

Where the preferential treatment of reduction and exemption of income tax on profit, interest, rental, royalty, and other income other than those provided for in this Article is required, it shall be regulated by the State Council.

Article 20   The tax authorities shall have the right to inspect the financial, accounting, and tax affairs of enterprises with foreign investment and establishments or places set up in China by foreign enterprises to engage in production or business operations, and have the right to inspect tax withholding of the withholding agent and its payment of the withheld tax into the State Treasury. The entities inspected must report the facts and provide relevant information. They may not refuse to report or conceal any facts.

When making an inspection, the tax officials shall produce their identity documents and be responsible for confidentiality.

Article 21   Income tax payable according to this Law shall be computed in terms of Renminbi (RMB). Income in foreign currency shall be converted into Renminbi according to the exchange rate quoted by the state exchange control authorities for purposes of tax payment.

Article 22   If any taxpayer fails to pay tax within the prescribed time limit, or if the withholding agent fails to turn over the tax withheld within the prescribed time limit, the tax authorities shall, in addition to setting a new time limit for tax payment, impose a surcharge for overdue payment, equal to 0.2% of the overdue tax for each day in arrears, starting from the first day the payment becomes overdue.

Article 23   The tax authorities shall set a new time limit for registration or submission of documents and may impose a fine of RMB 5,000 or less on any taxpayer or withholding agent which fails to go through tax registration or makes a change or cancellation in registration with the tax authorities within the prescribed time limit, fails to submit an income tax return, final accounting statements, or withholding income tax return to the tax authorities within the prescribed time limit, or fails to submit its financial and accounting systems to the tax authorities for reference.

Where the tax authorities have set a new time limit for registration or submission of documents, they shall impose a fine of RMB 10,000 or less on the taxpayer or withholding agent which again fails to meet the time limit for going through registration or making a change in registration with the tax authorities, or for submitting an income tax return, final accounting statements, or withholding income tax return to the tax authorities. Where the circumstances are serious, the legal representative and the person directly responsible shall be prosecuted for their criminal liability, by applying *mutatis mutandis* the provisions of Article 121 of the Criminal Law.

Article 24   Where the withholding agent fails to fulfill its obligation to withhold tax as provided in this Law, and does not withhold or withholds an amount less than that should have been withheld, the tax authorities shall set a time limit for the payment of the amount of tax that should have been withheld, and may impose a fine up to but not exceeding 100% of the amount of tax that should have been withheld.

Where the withholding agent fails to turn the tax withheld over the State Treasury within the prescribed time limit, the tax authorities shall set a time limit for turning over the taxes and may impose a fine of RMB 5,000 or less on the withholding agent; if it fails to meet the time limit again, the tax authorities shall pursue the taxes according to law and may impose a fine of RMB 10,000 or less on the withholding agent. If the circumstances are serious, the legal representative and the person directly responsible shall be prosecuted for their criminal liability by applying *mutatis mutandis* the provisions of Article 121 of the Criminal Law.

Article 25   Where any person evades tax by deception or conceal-ment or fails to pay tax within the time limit prescribed by this Law and, after the tax authorities pursued the payment of tax, fails again to pay it within the prescribed time limit, the tax authorities shall, in addition to re-covering the tax which should have been paid, impose a fine up to but not exceeding 500% of the amount of tax which should have been paid. Where the circumstances are serious, the legal representative and the per-son directly responsible shall be prosecuted for their criminal liability by applying the provisions of Article 121 of the Criminal Law.

Article 26   Any enterprise with foreign investment, foreign enter-prise, or withholding agent, in case of a dispute with the tax authorities on payment of tax, must pay tax according to the relevant regulations first. Thereafter, the taxpayer or withholding agent may, within 60 days from the date of receipt of the tax payment certificate issued by the tax au-thorities, apply to the tax authorities at the next higher level for reconsid-eration. The higher tax authorities shall make a decision within 60 days after receipt of the application for reconsideration. If the taxpayer or with-holding agent is not satisfied with the decision, it may institute legal pro-ceedings in the people's court within 15 days from the date of receipt of the notification on the decision made after reconsideration.

If the party concerned is not satisfied with the decision on punishment by the tax authorities, it may, within 15 days from the date of receipt of the notification on punishment, apply reconsideration to the tax authorities at the next higher level than that which made the decision on punishment. Where the party is not satisfied with the decision made after reconsidera-tion, it may institute legal proceedings in the people's court within 15 days from the date of receipt of the decision made after reconsideration. The party concerned may, however, directly institute legal proceedings in the people's court within 15 days from the date of receipt of the notification on punishment. If the party concerned does not apply reconsideration to the higher tax authorities or institute legal proceedings in the people's court within the time limit, and if the decision on punishment is not fulfilled, the tax authorities which made the decision on punishment may apply to the people's court for compulsory execution.

Article 27   Where any enterprise with foreign investment which was established before the promulgation of this Law would, in accordance with the provisions of this Law, otherwise be subject to higher tax rates or enjoy less preferential treatment of tax exemption or reduction than be-fore the entry into force of this Law, in respect to such enterprise, within its approved period of operation, the law and relevant regulations of the

State Council in effect before the entry into force of this Law shall apply. If any such enterprise has no approved period of operation, the laws and relevant regulations of the State Council in effect before the entry into force of this Law shall apply within the period prescribed by the State Council. Specific rules shall be regulated by the State Council.

Article 28   Where the provisions of the tax agreements concluded between the government of the People's Republic of China and foreign governments are different from the provisions of this Law, the provisions of the respective agreements shall apply.

Article 29   Rules for implementation shall be formulated by the State Council in accordance with this Law.

Article 30   This Law shall enter into force on 1 July 1991. The Income Tax Law of the People's Republic of China for Chinese–Foreign Equity Joint Ventures and the Income Tax Law of the People's Republic of China for Foreign Enterprises shall be annulled on the same date.

10. Detailed Rules for the Implementation of the Income Tax Law of the People's Republic of China for Enterprises With Foreign Investment and Foreign Enterprises

Promulgated on 30 June 1991

Chapter 1 General Provisions

Article 1   These Detailed Rules and Regulations are formulated in accordance with the provisions of Article 29 of the Income Tax Law of the People's Republic of China for Enterprises with Foreign Investment and Foreign Enterprises (hereafter referred to as the Tax Law)

Article 2   Income from production and business operations referred to in Article 1 paragraphs 1 and 2 of the Tax Law means income from production and business operations in manufacturing, mining, communications and transportation construction and installation, agriculture, forestry, animal husbandry, fishery, water conservancy, commerce, finance, service industry, exploration and exploitation, and other trades.

Income from other sources referred to in Article 1 paragraphs 1 and 2 of the Tax Law covers profit (dividend), interest income, rentals, income from alienation of property, income from provision or transfer of patents, know-how, trademark, copyright, and other nonbusiness income.

Article 3 Enterprises with foreign investment referred to in Article 2 paragraph 1 of the Tax Law, and foreign companies, enterprises, and other economic organizations which have establishments or places in China engaged in production and business operations referred to in Article 2 paragraph 2 of the Tax Law are generally referred to as Enterprise(s) in these Regulations unless particularly specified.

Establishments or places mentioned in Article 2 paragraph 2 of the Tax Law refer to management organizations, business organizations, representative offices and factories, places where natural resources are exploited, places where contracted projects of construction, installation, assembly, and exploration are operated, places where labor services are provided, and business agents.

Article 4 Business Agents mentioned in Article 3 paragraph 2 of these Regulations refer to any kinds of the following operating companies, enterprises, and other economic organizations or persons which are entrusted by foreign enterprises:

1. Represent the principal on a regular basis in sourcing, signing purchase contracts, and purchasing goods or commodities on the principal's behalf
2. Entering into an agency agreement or contract with the principal, storing the products or commodities owned by the principal on a regular basis, and delivering such products or commodities to other parties on the principal's behalf
3. Having the authority to represent the principal on a regular basis in signing sales contracts or accepting purchase orders

Article 5 Head Office mentioned in Article 3 of the Tax Law refers to the central organization of any enterprise with foreign investment formed in China as an independent legal entity pursuant to the laws of China that is in charge of the management, operation, and control of the enterprise.

The incomes derived from production, business operation, and other sources by the branches of an enterprise with foreign investment inside or outside China shall be consolidated by its head office in paying income tax.

Article 6 The income derived from sources inside China as mentioned in Article 3 of the Tax Law refers to:

1. The income derived from the production or business operation of enterprises with foreign investment and foreign enterprises which have establishments or places in China, and profits (dividends), interest, rentals, royalties, and other incomes derived inside or outside China that are actually related to those establishments or places.
2. The following income earned by foreign enterprises which have no establishments or places in China:
   a. Profits (dividends) earned by enterprises in China
   b. Interest on deposits or loans, on bonds, on payments made provisionally for others, and on deferred payments, derived inside China
   c. Rentals on properties rented to and used by persons in China
   d. Royalties obtained from the provision of patents, know-how, trademark and copyright, etc., for use in China
   e. Gains from the alienation of properties, such as house, buildings, structures, and their attached facilities located in China, or from the assignment of the right to the use of sites in China
   f. Other incomes derived in China and specified as taxable by the Ministry of Finance

Article 7 For Chinese–foreign cooperative joint ventures which do not constitute a legal entity, each partner may assess and pay its income tax separately in accordance with the relevant tax laws and regulations of the state. Otherwise, the enterprise may, upon approval by the local tax authorities of its application, consolidate the assessment and payment of income tax in accordance with the provisions of the Tax Law.

Article 8 The tax year referred to in Article 4 of the Tax law starts from 1 January and ends on 31 December under the Gregorian Calendar.

A foreign enterprise that has difficulty in computing its taxable income according to the tax year as stipulated in the Tax Law may apply to the local tax authorities for approval to use its own 12-month fiscal year as the tax year.

An enterprise which commences its business in the middle of the tax year, or has actually operated for less than 12 months in any tax year due to merger, close-down, etc., shall treat the actual operating period as the tax year.

An enterprise which goes through liquidation shall take the liquidation period as the tax year.

Article 9 The competent authority for tax affairs under the State Council, mentioned in Article 8 paragraph 3 and Article 19 paragraph 3 item 4 of the Tax Law and Article 72 of these Regulations, refers to the Ministry of Finance and the State Administration for Taxation.

Chapter II Computation of Taxable Income

Article 10   The taxable income referred to in Article 4 of the Tax Law shall be computed according to the following formulas:

1. Manufacturing industry:
   a. Taxable income = Product sales profit + profit from operations + nonbusiness income – nonbusiness expenditure
   b. Product sales profit = Net sales of the product sales costs – tax on product sales – (selling expenses + overhead expenses + financial expenses)
   c. Product net sales = Gross sales of the product – (sales returns + sales allowances)
   d. Product sales costs = Product costs of the period + product inventory at the beginning of the period – product inventory at the end of the period
   e. Product costs of the period = Production costs of the period + inventory of semifinished products and products in progress at the beginning of the period – inventory of the semifinished products and products in progress at the end of the period
   f. Production costs of the period = Direct material consumption in production of the period + direct wages + manufacturing expenses
2. Commerce:
   a. Taxable income = Sales profit + profit from other operations + nonbusiness income – nonbusiness expenditure
   b. Sales profit = Net sales – sales costs – tax on sales – (selling expenses + overhead expenses + financial expenses)
   c. Net sales = Gross sales – (sales return + sales allowance)
   d. Sales costs = Inventory of merchandise at the beginning of the period + [purchase of the period – (purchase returns + purchase allowances) + purchase expenses] – inventory of merchandise at the end of the period
3. Service industry:
   a. Taxable income = Net business income + nonbusiness income – nonbusiness expenditure;
   b. Net business income = Gross business income – (tax on business income + operating expenses + overhead expenses + financial expenses)

4. Other trades: Refer to the above-mentioned formulas for computation.

Article 11   The taxable income of an enterprise shall in principle be computed on an accrual basis.

The following operational and business incomes of an enterprise may be determined by stages and may be taken as the basis for computing taxable income:

1. Products or commodities sold under hire purchase may have the sales income realized according to the invoice date of the products or commodities being delivered. The sales income may also be realized according to the date of payment to be made by the buyer as stipulated in the contract.
2. For construction, installation, and assembly projects and provision of labor services that last beyond one year, the realization of the business income may be determined according to the progress of the contracted project or the amount of labor services completed.
3. For the processing or manufacturing of large machinery, equipment, and ships for other enterprises that lasts beyond one year, the realization of the income may be determined according to the progress or the amount of work completed.

Article 12   Partners of Chinese–foreign cooperative joint ventures operating on the basis of sharing products shall be considered as receiving incomes when they obtain their share of the products, and the amount of their income shall be computed according to the prices at which the products are sold to a third party, or with reference to the prevailing market prices of the products.

Enterprises engaged in cooperative exploration of petroleum resources shall be considered as receiving incomes when they receive their share of crude oil, and the amount of their income shall be computed according to the prices which are regularly adjusted with reference to the international market prices of crude oil of equal quality.

Article 13   In the case in which any income obtained by an enterprise is in the form of nonmonetary assets, or rights and interests, the income shall be computed or assessed with reference to the prevailing market prices.

Article 14   The exchange rates mentioned in Article 21 of the Tax Law refer to the buying rates quoted by the State Administration of Exchange Control.

Article 15   When paying the income tax in quarterly installments pursuant to Article 15 of the Tax Law, enterprises with income in foreign currencies shall convert the income into Renminbi in computing the taxable income, according to the exchange rates quoted by the State Administration of Exchange Control on the last day of the quarter. The final settlement can be made after the end of the tax year without reconverting the taxable foreign currency income, on which the tax has already been prepaid on a quarterly basis. Only the deficiencies to be made up on the taxable foreign currency income over the whole year shall be converted into Renminbi in assessment according to the exchange rates quoted by the State Administration of Exchange Control on the last day of the year.

Article 16   If an enterprise fails to provide complete and accurate evidence of costs and expenses and does not work out its taxable income correctly, the local tax authorities shall determine its profit rate with reference to the profit level of other enterprises of the same or similar trade and assess its taxable income. If an enterprise fails to provide complete and accurate evidence of receipts and does not report its income correctly, the local tax authorities shall assess its income by using the method of costs (expenses) plus reasonable profits, etc.

When the tax authorities assess the profit rate or income in accordance with the provisions of the preceding paragraph, whereas there are other provisions in the laws, regulations, and rules elsewhere, these other provisions shall be applicable.

Article 17   For foreign air transportation and ocean shipping enterprises engaged in international transportation and shipping business, the taxable income shall be assessed at 5% of the gross income generated from transport and shipping services for passengers and cargoes from China.

Article 18   For an enterprise with foreign investment investing in another enterprise inside China, the profits (dividends) obtained from the enterprise under investment may be excluded from the taxable income of the said enterprise with foreign investment. But the expenses and losses incurred in the above-mentioned investment shall not be deducted from the taxable income of the said enterprise.

Article 19   Unless otherwise provided the state, the following items shall not be listed as costs, expenses, or losses in computing the taxable income:

1. Expenditure on the acquisition or construction of fixed assets
2. Expenditure on the alienation or development of intangible assets
3. Interest on capital
4. Various income tax payments
5. Penalties on unlawful operations and losses sustained from confiscation of property
6. Various tax overdue surcharges and penalties
7. Losses from natural calamities or accidents covered by insurance indemnity
8. Donations and contributions other than those utilized in China for public welfare or relief purposes
9. Royalties paid to the head office
10. Other expenditure not related to production or business operation

Article 20   Reasonable overhead expenses that are relevant to production and business operation paid to the head office by a foreign enterprise which has establishment or places in China may be listed as expenses on the condition that the said expenses are backed up by supporting documents issued by the head office certifying the scope of overhead categorization, the total amount, the sharing basis and methods, together with a verification report signed by a certified public accountant, and examined and approved by the local tax authorities.

Enterprises with foreign investment shall share with their branches appropriate overhead expenses related to the production and business operation of the branches.

Article 21   Enterprises are permitted to list as expenses the reasonable interests actually incurred on loans related to production and business operation, provided that the loans and interest payments are supported by certifying documents and have been examined by the local tax authorities.

For the loans obtained by an enterprise to finance the expenditure on the acquisition or construction of fixed assets, or the alienation or development of intangible assets, the interest paid before the assets are put into use shall be included in the original value of the assets.

Reasonable interest mentioned in the first paragraph of this Article refers to interest computed at a rate not higher than the normal commercial lending rates.

Article 22   Entertainment expenses incurred in relation to production and business operation by an enterprise shall be backed up by reliable records or vouchers, and are permitted to be listed as expenses within the following respective limits:

1. For an enterprise with its annual net sales coming to RMB 15 million or less, the entertainment expenses shall not exceed 0.5% of the net sales; the entertainment expenses for the portion above the limit of RMB 15 million shall not exceed 0.3% of the said portion.
2. For an enterprise with its annual total business income coming to five million Renminbi or less, the entertainment expenses shall not exceed 1% of the total business income; for those with annual total business income coming to more than five million Renminbi, the entertainment expenses for the portion above the limit of five million Renminbi shall not exceed 0.5% of the said portion.

Article 23 Unless otherwise provided by the state, any exchange gain or loss incurred due to differences in exchange rates during an enterprise's preparatory or construction period, or during the period of production and business operation, shall be listed appropriately as profit or loss in the respective period.

Article 24 Wages, benefits, and allowances paid to employees can be listed as expenses by the enterprises upon the examination and approval of the pay scale and its supporting documents and information by the local tax authorities.

Enterprises shall not list as expenses any foreign social insurance premiums for employees working inside China.

Article 25 Enterprises engaged in the credit and leasing business may, according to their actual needs and after the approval of the local tax authorities, provide year by year for doubtful debts at not exceeding 3% of the year-end balances of their loans (not including interbank loans) or of their accounts receivable, bills receivable and other receipts, and deduct the provision from the taxable income of that year.

If the actual amount of bad debt expenses incurred by an enterprise runs in excess of the bad debt provision of the preceding year, the balance can be listed as bad debt expenses of the current year. The amount in deficiency of the provision of the preceding year shall be included in the taxable income of the current year.

Bad debt expenses incurred by an enterprise shall be reported to the local tax authorities for examination and confirmation.

Article 26   Bad debt expenses mentioned in Article 25 paragraph 2 of these Regulations refer to the following accounts receivable:

1. Because of the bankruptcy of the debtor, the amount due is not collectable even after its bankruptcy estates have been cleared off.
2. Due to the death of the debtor, the debtor's estate remains insufficient to repay the debts in full.
3. Because of the debtor's failure to repay the debts for over two years and the debt is still not collectable.

Article 27   Accounts receivable already itemized as bad debt expenses but recovered in full or in part by an enterprise in subsequent years shall be included in the taxable income of the recovering year.

Article 28   Unless otherwise provided by the state, foreign enterprise which have establishments or places in China may itemize as deductible expenses the foreign income tax already paid on the profits (dividends), interest, rentals, royalties, and other incomes sourced outside China, which are actually related to such establishments or places in China.

Article 29   Net assets or remaining property mentioned in Article 18 of the Tax Law refer to the balance of all assets or property upon the liquidation of an enterprise after deducting various liabilities and losses.

Chapter III Tax Treatment for Assets

Article 30   The fixed assets of enterprises refer to any houses, building, structures, machinery and other mechanical apparatus, means of transportation and other equipment, appliances and tools related to production and business operation with a useful life of one year or more, and articles which are not major equipment in production and business operation with a unit value of RMB 2,000 or less, or with a useful life of two years of less, may be itemized as expenses according to the actual amount used.

Article 31   Fixed assets shall be assessed according to their original value.

For purchased fixed assets, the original value shall be the purchase price plus freight, installation expense, and other related expenses incurred before they are put into use.

For self-made or self-built fixed assets, the original value shall be the actual expenditure incurred in the course of manufacture or construction.

For fixed assets treated as investments, the original value shall be the prices assessed according to the wear and tear condition, and the reasonable prices stipulated in the Contract, or with reference to the relevant market price information, plus the relevant expenses incurred before the fixed assets are put into use.

Article 32   Depreciation on the fixed assets of an enterprise shall be computed starting from the month following that in which the assets are put into use. Depreciation shall cease to be computed starting from the month following that month in which the fixed assets cease to be used.

For enterprises engaged in exploiting petroleum resources, all the investments made at the stage of exploration shall be accumulated and counted as capital expenditure with the oil (gas) field as a unit. Depreciation shall be computed starting from the month following that in which the oil (gas) field goes into commercial production.

Article 33   In computing depreciation on fixed assets, the residual value shall be assessed and deducted from the original value. The residual value shall not be less than 10% of the original value. Any need to retain a lower residual value or not to retain any residual value needs to be reported to local tax authorities for approval.

Article 34   Depreciation on fixed assets shall be computed by the straight-line method. In case of any need to use other depreciation methods, an application shall be made by the relevant enterprise to the local tax authorities for examination, which shall then be reported level by level up to the State Administration for Taxation for approval.

Article 35   The minimum depreciation periods for different kinds of fixed assets are as follows:

1. Premises, buildings, and structures: 20 years
2. Trains, ships, machinery, and other production equipment: ten years
3. Electronic equipment means of transportation other than trains and ships, as well as appliances, tools, and furniture related to production and business operation: five years

Article 36   Depreciation of fixed assets resulting from investments made by enterprises engaged in exploiting petroleum resources, during and after the stage of exploration, may be computed by a composite life method, without retaining the residual value, and the depreciation period shall not be less than six years.

Article 37   Premises, buildings, and structures referred to in Article 35 item 1 of these Regulations mean premises, buildings, and structures and their attached facilities used for production and operation or as living quarters or service centers for employees.

Premises and buildings include factory buildings, business centers, office buildings, storage, living quarters, canteens, other housing facilities, etc.

Structures include all kinds of towers, ponds, troughs, wells, racks, sheds (not including such simple facilities as makeshift work sheds, vehicle sheds, etc.), fields, roads, bridges, platforms, piers, docks, culverts, gas stations, and all kinds of pipes, chimneys, and enclosing walls etc. that are detached from buildings, machines, and equipment.

Facilities attached to premises, buildings, and structures refer to auxiliary facilities inseparable from premises, buildings, and structures, the value of which is not assessed separately, e.g., ventilation and drainage system, oil pipes, telecommunications and power transmission lines, escalators, elevators, and sanitary equipment in premises, buildings, and structures.

Article 38   The definition of trains, ships, machinery, and other production equipment as referred to in Article 35 item 2 of these Regulations are as follows:

- Trains include all kinds of locomotives, passenger coaches, foreign trains, and all kinds of auxiliary train facilities, the value of which is not assessed separately.
- Ships include different kinds of motor ships and auxiliary facilities on the ships, the value of which is not assessed separately.
- Machinery and other production equipment include all kinds of machines, mechanical equipment, machinery units, production lines and their accessory equipment, different kinds of power, transportation, transmission and conduction equipment, etc.

Article 39   The definitions of electronic equipment and means of transportation other than trains and ships as referred to in Article 35 item 3 of these Regulations are as follows:

- Electronic equipment means equipment mainly composed of integrated circuits, transistors, vacuum tubes, and other electronic component parts with the main function of bringing into play all kinds of electronic technology (including software), e.g., computers, computerized robots, numerical or program-controlled systems, etc.

* Means of transportation other than trains and ships include airplanes, motor vehicles, trains, tractors, motorcycles, motorboats, motor sailboats, junks, and other means of transportation.

Article 40 Where the period of depreciation on the fixed assets of an enterprise needs to be shortened due to special reasons, an application shall be made by the said enterprise to the local tax authorities for examinations which shall then be reported all the way up to the State Administration for Taxation for approval.

Fixed assets, the depreciation period of which needs to be shortened due to special reasons as mentioned in the preceding paragraph, include:

1. Machinery and equipment that are subject to strong corrosion by acid or alkali, and factory buildings and structures that are constantly subject to shakes or vibration
2. Machinery and equipment that are constantly running around-the-clock for the purpose of raising the utilization rate or increasing the intensity of usage
3. Fixed assets of a Chinese-foreign cooperative joint venture with the period of cooperation shorter than the depreciation periods as specified in Article 35 of these Regulations, which will be left with the Chinese party upon the termination of cooperation

Article 41 Used fixed assets acquired by an enterprise, with the remaining useful life shorter than the depreciation period specified in Article 35 of these Regulations, may be depreciated over the remaining useful life upon the examination and approval of the relevant supporting evidence by the local tax authorities.

Article 42 In the case where expenditures arise from expansion, replacement, renovation, and technical innovation of fixed assets in use result in the increase in their value, the original value of the fixed assets shall rise; for those fixed assets whose useful life can be prolonged, their depreciation periods shall be prolonged property, and the depreciation thereon shall be adjusted accordingly.

Article 43 No depreciation shall be allowed for fixed assets which remain in use after the full depreciation period.

Article 44   The balance of the proceeds from the alienation or disposal of a fixed asset by an enterprise, after deduction of the net undepreciated value or the residual value of the asset and the handling fees, shall be entered into the profit and loss account for the current year.

Article 45   Enterprises that have accepted any fixed asset as a gift may assess depreciation based on a reasonable valuation.

Article 46   Patents, know-how, trademark, copyright, right to the use of sites, and other intangible assets of enterprises shall be assessed according to the original value.

For an alienated intangible asset, the original value shall be the actual payment based on a reasonable price.

For a self-developed intangible asset, the original value shall be the actual expenditure incurred in the course of the development.

For an intangible asset put in as investment, the original value shall be the reasonable price stipulated in Agreement or Contract.

Article 47   Amortization of intangible assets shall be computed by the straight-line method.

Intangible assets, put in as investment or assigned with the right to use, may be amortized according to the stipulated time limit, if a time limit for the usage is provided for in the Agreement or Contract. Intangible assets without such a stipulated time limit, or being self-developed, shall be amortized over a period of not less than ten years.

Article 48   Reasonable exploration expenses incurred by an enterprise engaged in exploring petroleum resources may be amortized from the revenues generated from the oil (or gas) field that has gone into commercial production, but the amortization period shall not be less than one year.

If a foreign oil company terminated its operation in a contracted area owned by it due to its failure to find any oil (or gas), and if it does not continue to own such a contracted area for exploitation of oil (or gas) resources, or if it does not maintain any oil (or gas) exploitation operation or management organization or office in China, the reasonable exploration expenses already incurred in the terminated contracted area, upon the examination and confirmation of the expenses and after issuance of a certifying document by the relevant tax authorities, may be amortized from the production income generated from any newly owned contracted area, when a new oil (or gas) cooperative exploitation Contract is signed within ten years after the termination of the old Contract.

Article 49   Expenses incurred during the period of preparation for an enterprise to be established shall be amortized starting from the month following that in which it goes into production or business operation, but the amortization period shall not be less than five years.

The period of preparation mentioned in the preceding paragraph refers to the period starting from the date on which the preparation for the establishment of an enterprise is approved, up to the date when the enterprise goes into production or operation (including trial production or operation).

Article 50   Inventory of commodities, finished products, products in progress, semifinished products, and raw materials of an enterprise shall be priced according to the cost prices.

Article 51   For computation of the actual cost prices for delivery and acceptance of inventory, enterprises, may choose one of the following methods: first in; first out; moving average; weighted average; and last in, first out.

No change shall be made willfully once the method of inventory pricing is adopted. In case a change in the method of inventory pricing is truly necessary, it shall be reported to the local tax authorities for approval before the beginning of the next tax year.

Chapter IV Business Dealings Between Associated Enterprises

Article 52   Associated enterprises mentioned in Article 13 of the Tax Law refer to any company, enterprise, and other economic organization which has one of the following association with an enterprise:

1. An enterprise directly or indirectly owns or controls another enterprise in respect of capital, business operation, purchasing, selling, etc.
2. An enterprise and another enterprise are directly or indirectly owned or controlled by a third party.
3. Any other association with mutual benefits.

Article 53   Business transactions between independent enterprises mentioned in Article 13 of the Tax Law refer to business dealings between unrelated enterprises carried out according to the arm's-length prices and common business practice.

An enterprise is obligated to provide to the local tax authorities the relevant information on the business dealings between itself and its associated enterprises concerning prices, charge rates, etc.

Article 54   If the buying and selling between an enterprise and its associated enterprise is not priced at arm's length, the tax authorities may select an appropriate method according to the following sequence to make adjustment:

1. According to the pricing of the same or similar business activities among unassociated enterprises
2. According to the profit level obtainable from resale to unassociated third parties
3. According to the costs plus reasonable expenses and profit margin
4. According to any other appropriate methods

Article 55   For the interest paid or received on financing between an enterprise and its associated enterprises if the interest is higher or lower than the amount that can be agreeable between unassociated parties, or if the interest rate is higher or lower than the normal rate of similar lending business, the local tax authorities may adjust it according to the normal interest rates.

Article 56   In the case in which the labor services provided between an enterprise and its associated enterprise are not charged or paid according to the rates or business dealings between unassociated enterprise, the local tax authorities may make adjustment with reference to the normal charge rates of similar labor service activities between unassociated parties.

Article 57   In the case in which the alienation of property or the provision of property rights between an enterprise and its associated enterprises is not priced, charged, or paid according to the rates for business dealings between unassociated enterprises, the tax authorities may make adjustment with reference to the amount that may be agreeable between unassociated parties.

Article 58   An enterprise shall not list as expense management fees paid to its associated enterprises, except for the situation as provided for in Article 20 of these Regulations.

Chapter V Withholding at Source

Article 59   Profit, interest, rental, royalty, and other income referred to in Article 19 paragraph 1 of the Tax Law shall be assessed as income taxable on its full amount, unless otherwise provided by the state. The gross royalties obtained from the provision of patents and know-how include the drawings and information fee, technical service fee, personnel training fee, and other relevant fees in relation to the provision of patents and proprietary technology.

Article 60   Profit mentioned in Article 19 of the Tax Law refers to income derived according to the ratio of investment contributions or shares and other nondebt profit sharing rights.

Article 61   Other income referred to in Article 19 paragraph 1 and paragraph 4 of the Tax Law includes gains from alienation of properties including houses, buildings, structures, and their attached facilities located in China, or from the assignment of right to use of sites.

Gains from alienation of properties referred to in the preceding paragraph means the balance of the transfer value after deduction of the original value of the said property. In the event that proper evidence on the original value of the property cannot be provided by a foreign enterprise, the local tax authorities shall assess the original value of the property according to the specific conditions.

Article 62   The payment mentioned in Article 19 paragraph 2 of the Tax Law refers to payments in cash, by remittance, or through transfer accounts, as well as payment made in the forms of nonmonetary assets or rights and interests for an equivalent amount of money.

Article 63   Profit obtained by a foreign investor from an enterprise with foreign investment referred to in Article 19 paragraph 3 item 1 of the Tax Law means the profit made by an enterprise with foreign investment after deduction of the payment of income tax or the reduced income tax, or the profit which is exempted from the income tax, in accordance with the stipulations of the Tax Law.

Article 64   International financial organizations mentioned in Article 19 paragraph 3 item 2 of the Tax Law refer to financial institutions like the International Monetary Fund, the World Bank, the Asian Development Bank, the International Development Association, the International Fund for Agricultural Development, etc.

Article 65   Chinese state banks mentioned in Article 19 paragraph 3 item 2 and item 3 of the Tax Law refer to the People's Bank of China, the Industrial and Commercial Bank of China, the Agricultural Bank of China, the Bank of China, the People's Construction Bank of China, the Bank of Communications of China, the Investment Bank of China, and other financial institutions authorized by the State Council to be engaged in the business of foreign exchange deposits and loans, etc. for foreign clients.

Article 66   Reduction of or exemption from income tax on royalties as provided for in Article 19 paragraph 3 item 4 of the Tax Law is applicable to the following areas:

1. Royalties obtained from the provision of the following know-how technology in the production of farming, forestry, animal husbandry, and fishery:
   a. Technology provided to improve soil and grassland, to reclaim and develop barren hills, and to fully utilize the natural conditions;
   b. Technology to nurture new species and varieties of fauna and flora and to produce high-efficiency but low-toxic agricultural chemicals; and
   c. Technology to provide farming, forestry, animal husbandry, and fishery with scientific production and management, to preserve the ecological balance, and to increase the capability of fighting natural disasters.
2. Royalties obtained from the provision of know-how to academies of sciences, colleges and universities, and other institutions of higher learning and scientific research to conduct, or to cooperate in the conduct of, scientific research or scientific experiments.
3. Royalties obtained from the provision of know-how for the exploitation of energy resources and the development of communications and transportation.
4. Royalties obtained from the provision of know-how in energy conservation and the prevention and control of environmental pollution.
5. Royalties obtained from the provision of the know-how in the development of the following important fields of technology:
   a. Important advanced technology in the production of mechanical and electronic equipment;
   b. Nuclear power technology;
   c. Technology in the production of large-scale integrated circuits;

d. Technology in the production of photo-integration microwave semiconductors and microwave integrated circuits and microwave tubes;

e. Technology in the manufacturing of high-speed electronic computers and microprocessors;

f. Optical telecommunications technology;

g. Remote ultra-high-voltage direct current electricity transmission technology; and

h. Technology in the liquefaction, gasification, and integrated utilization of coal.

Article 67 For incomes earned by foreign enterprises engaged in projects in China, such as construction, installation, assembly, and exploration, and through provision of services, such as consultation, management, training, and other labor service, the tax authorities may appoint the payers of the contract sums or service fees to be income tax withholding agents.

Chapter VI Tax Preference

Article 68 Pursuant to Article 6 of the Tax Law enterprises with foreign investment encouraged by the state which request preferential treatment in relation to enterprise income tax shall be treated in accordance with the relevant laws and administrative regulations promulgated by the state.

Article 69 Special economic zones mentioned in Article 7 paragraph 1 of the Tax Law refer to the special economic zones in Shenzhen, Zhuhai, Shantou, and Xiamen and Hainan Special Economic Zone, established with the approval of the State Council. Economic and technological development zones mentioned in the same paragraph refer to the economic and technological development zones in the coastal port cities, established with the approval of the State Council.

Article 70 Coastal open economic zones mentioned in Article 7 paragraph 2 of the Tax Law refer to the cities, counties, and districts established as the coastal open economic zones with the approval of the State Council.

Article 71 Assessment of enterprise income tax at the reduced rate of 15% mentioned in Article 7 paragraph 1 of the Tax Law is limited to incomes obtained by the enterprises from production or business operation in the respective areas as specified in Article 7 paragraph 1 of the Tax Law.

Assessment of enterprise income tax at the reduced rate of 24% mentioned in Article 7 paragraph 2 of the Tax Law is limited to incomes obtained by the enterprise from production or business operation in the respective areas as specified in Article 7 paragraph 2 of the Tax Law.

Article 72   Productive enterprises with foreign investment mentioned in Article 7 paragraphs 1 and 2 and Article 8 paragraph 1 of the Tax Law refer to the enterprises with foreign investment engaged in the following industries:

1. Machine-building and electronics industries
2. Energy industries (not including oil and natural gas exploitation)
3. Metallurgical, chemical, and building material industries
4. Light, textiles, and packaging industries
5. Medical apparatus and pharmaceutical industries
6. Agriculture, forestry, animal husbandry, fishery, and water conservancy
7. Construction industry
8. Communications and transportation industries (not including passenger transportation)
9. Development of science and technology, geological survey, and industrial information consultancy that are directly at the service of production, and maintenance and repair service for production equipment and precision instruments
10. Other industries that are recognized by the taxation authorities under the State Council

Article 73   Assessment of enterprise income tax at the reduced rate of 15% mentioned in Article 7 Paragraph 3 of the Tax Law is applicable to the following projects:

1. Productive enterprises with foreign investment established in the coastal open economic areas, the special economic zones, or in the old urban districts of cities where the economic and technological development zones are located, and engaged in the following projects:
   a. Technology-intensive or knowledge-intensive projects;
   b. Projects with foreign investment of over US$30 million and more, and with long payback period; and
   c. Energy, transportation, and port construction projects.

2. Chinese–foreign equity joint ventures engaged in port and dock construction
3. Foreign banks, banks with Chinese and foreign joint investment, and other financial institutions established in the special economic zones and other areas approved by the State Council, with the capital contribution by the head office to their branches coming to ten million US dollars and more; and with the period of operation exceeding ten years
4. Productive enterprises with foreign investment established in the Shanghai Pudong New Area, and enterprises with foreign investment engaged in energy and transport construction projects, such as airport, port, railway, highway, and power station
5. Enterprises with foreign investment recognized as new or high-technology enterprises, which are established in the new and high-technology industrial development zones approved by the State council; and enterprises with foreign investment recognized as new-technology enterprises established in the Beijing new-technology industrial development experimental zones
6. Enterprises with foreign investment engaged in projects encouraged by the state and established in other areas designated by the State Council

Enterprises with foreign investment engaged in industries that fall under item 1 of this Article shall, after applying to the State Administration for Taxation for approval, pay enterprise income tax at the reduced rate of 15%.

Article 74   The period of operation mentioned in Article 8 paragraph 1 of the Tax Law refers to the period starting from the date an enterprise actually goes into production and operation to the date on which the enterprise terminates its production and operation.

An enterprise applying for exemption from a deduction in the enterprise income tax according to the provisions of Article 8 paragraph 1 shall file with the local tax authorities its line of business, the names of its major products, and the period of operation, for examination and approval. Prior to such examination and approval, no exemption or reduction of enterprise income tax shall be allowed.

Article 75   The relevant regulations promulgated by the State Council before the entry into force of this Law and shall remain applicable after this Law enters into force mentioned in Article 8 paragraph 2 of the Tax

Law refer to the following regulations concerning the exemption and reduction of enterprise income tax promulgated by the State Council:

1. Chinese–foreign equity joint ventures engaged in port and dock construction and with the operation period exceeding 15 years may, upon the approval of their applications by the tax authorities at the level of the province, autonomous region, or municipality directly under the administration of the central government in which the enterprises are located enjoy exemption from enterprise income tax from the first profit-making year to the fifth year, and reduction in enterprise income tax by 50% from the sixth to the tenth year.
2. Enterprises with foreign investment established in the Hainan Special Economic Zone and engaged in the construction of such infrastructure projects as port, dock, airport, highway, railway, power station, coal mine, water conservancy, etc., or in the development and operation of agriculture, and with the operation period exceeding 15 years may, upon approval of their applications by the Hainan Provincial Tax Authorities, enjoy exemption from enterprise income tax from the first profit-making year to the fifth year, and reduction in enterprise income tax by 50% from the sixth to the tenth year.
3. Enterprises with foreign investment established in the Shanghai Pudong New Area and engaged in the construction of such infrastructure projects as airport, port, railway, highway, and power station, etc., and with the operation period exceeding 15 years, may, upon approval of their applications by the Shanghai Municipal Tax Authorities, enjoy exemption from enterprise income tax from the first profit-making year to the fifth year, and reduction in enterprise income tax by 50% from the sixth to the tenth year.
4. Enterprises with foreign investment established in the special economic zones and engaged in service industries, and with the foreign investment exceeding five million US dollars and the operation period exceeding ten years may, upon approval of their applications by the relevant special economic zone tax authorities, enjoy exemption from enterprise income tax for the first profit-making year, and reduction in enterprise income tax by 50% for the second and third years.
5. Foreign banks, banks with Chinese and foreign joint investment, and other financial institutions established in the special economic zones and other areas approved by the State Council, with the capital put in by foreign investors, or the operating funds appropriated by the head offices of foreign banks to their branches,

exceeding ten million US dollars, and with the operation period lasting ten years and more may, upon approval of their applications by the relevant tax authorities, enjoy exemption from enterprise income tax for the first profit-making year and reduction in enterprise income tax by 50% for the second and third years.

6. Chinese–foreign equity joint ventures recognized as new or high-technology enterprises and established in new and high-technology industrial development zones approved by the State Council, with the operation period exceeding ten years may, upon approval of their applications by the local tax authorities, enjoy exemption from enterprise income tax for the first and second profit-making years. For enterprises with foreign investment established in the special economic zones and the economic and technological development zones, the preferential tax provisions of the special economic zones and the economic and technological development zones shall remain applicable. For enterprises with foreign investment established in the Beijing new-technology industrial development experimental zone, the preferential tax provisions of the Beijing new-technology industrial development experimental zone shall be applicable.

7. Export-oriented enterprises with foreign investment may, upon the expiration of the tax exemption and reduction period as provided for in the Tax Law, further enjoy a 70% reduction in enterprise income tax based on the rate stipulated by the Tax Law, if the value of their export products of the year exceeds 70% of the total value of products of the year. But for the special economic zones and the economic and technological development zones and other export-oriented enterprises which have already paid enterprise income tax at 15% and meet the above requirements, the enterprise income tax shall be levied at 10%.

8. Technologically advanced enterprises with foreign investment may, upon the expiration of the enterprise income tax exemption and reduction period as stipulated by the Tax Law further enjoy a 50% reduction in enterprise income tax for three years based on the rate stipulated by the Tax Law, if they remain technologically advanced enterprises.

9. Other regulations relating to the exemption and reduction of enterprise income tax having been promulgated, or having been approved to promulgate, by the State Council.

In applying for enterprise income tax exemption/reduction pursuant to the provisions of item 6, item 7, and item 8 of this Article, enterprises with foreign investment shall submit the relevant certifying documents issued by the department responsible for examination and confirmation to the local tax authorities for examination and approval.

Article 76   The first profit-making year mentioned in Article 8 paragraph 1 of the Tax Law and in Article 75 of these Regulations refers to the first profit-making tax year after an enterprise goes into production and operation. An enterprise sustaining losses in the initial stage of its operation may carry them over and make them up in the next year in accordance with the provisions of Article 11 of the Tax Law. Its first profit-making year may be the year in which the enterprise begins to make profit after the losses are made up.

The period of enterprise income tax exemption and reduction, as stipulated in Article 8 paragraph 1 of the Tax Law and Article 75 of these Regulations, shall be counted consecutively from the first profit-making year, and shall not be deferred due to losses incurred during the period.

Article 77   For an enterprise which goes into operation in the middle of the year, if it makes profit in the same year while the actual period of operation is less than six months, it may choose to take the following year as the year to start enjoying exemption from or reduction in enterprise income tax. However, income tax shall be levied in accordance with the Tax Law on the taxable income earned by the enterprise in that year.

Article 78   Unless otherwise provided by the State Council, the tax incentives of Article 8 paragraph 1 of the Tax Law are not applicable to enterprises engaged in the exploitation of such natural resources as petroleum, natural gas, rare metals, and precious metals.

Article 79   Enterprises that have enjoyed income tax exemption and reduction pursuant to the provision of Article 8 paragraph 1 of the Tax Law Article 75 of these Regulations, but whose actual operation falls short of the prescribed period, shall repay the exempted and reduced enterprise income tax, except from those having sustained huge losses caused by natural disasters or accidents.

Article 80   Reinvest its share of profit directly as referred to in Article 10 of the Tax Law means that the profits earned by a foreign investor before being drawn from an enterprise with foreign investment shall be used directly to increase the registered capital or to make direct capital investment in another enterprise with foreign investment after such profits are appropriated.

In assessing the refundable tax amount in accordance with the provisions of Article 10 of the Tax Law, the said foreign investor shall provide a supporting document certifying the attributable year of the profit used for reinvestment. In the case in which no supporting document can be provided, the local tax authorities shall calculate and determine the year by appropriate methods.

Foreign investors shall, within one year from the date the fund is actually injected, apply to the original tax collecting authorities for tax refund and submit a document certifying the amount and duration of the added or new capital investment.

Article 81   Where other preferential provisions are provided by the State Council, such provisions shall apply as mentioned in Article 10 of the Tax Law refers to the case in which a foreign investor who makes direct reinvestment in establishing or expanding an export-oriented enterprise or a technologically advanced enterprise in China or who reinvest profit from enterprise in Hainan Special Economic Zone directly into enterprise engaged in infrastructure and agriculture development in Hainan Special Economic Zone, may get a full refund of enterprise income tax paid on the reinvested amount, according to the relevant regulations of the State Council.

In applying for tax refund on reinvestment pursuant to the preceding paragraph, the said foreign investor shall, besides going through the procedures as provided for in Article 80 paragraphs 2 and 3 of these Regulations, submit a document issued by the relevant examination and confirmation department, certifying the relevant newly established or expanded enterprise as being an export-oriented or technologically advanced enterprise.

In the case in which the newly established or expanded enterprise, in which the said foreign investor makes reinvestment, fails to meet the standards of an export-oriented enterprise, or is no longer recognized as a technologically advanced enterprise within three years after it goes into production or operation, the said foreign investor shall pay back 60% of the tax refunded.

Article 82   Refund of the income tax paid on the reinvested amount mentioned in Article 10 of the Tax Law and Article 81 paragraph 1 of these Regulations shall be computed according to the following formula:

Tax refundable = Reinvested amount / (1 1 [the original enterprise income tax rate + local income tax rate applicable to the enterprise]) 2 original enterprise income tax rate applicable to the enterprise 2 refund rate.

Chapter VII Tax Credit

Article 83   The income tax paid abroad mentioned in Article 12 of the Tax Law refers to the income tax actually paid by an enterprise with foreign investment outside China on the income sourced outside China. It does not include any tax paid but later compensated or any tax borne by others.

Article 84   The income tax payable under this law in respect of the income derived from sources outside China, as mentioned in Article 12 of the Tax Law, refers to the tax payable computed based on the taxable income arrived at from the income derived outside China by the enterprise with foreign investment after deduction of the costs, expenses, and losses allowed in accordance with the relevant provisions of the Tax Law and these Regulations that are attributable to the obtaining of the income. That tax payable shall be credit amount and shall be computed country by country but not item by item. The computation formula is as follows:

$$\begin{array}{l}\text{Credit limit}\\\text{for tax on}\\\text{income derived}\\\text{from sources}\\\text{outside China}\end{array} = \begin{array}{l}\text{Total tax}\\\text{sourced inside}\\\text{and outside}\\\text{China computed}\\\text{in accordance}\\\text{with the Tax Law}\end{array} \times \frac{\text{Income sourced from a foreign country}}{\text{Total income sourced inside and outside China}}$$

Article 85   When the income tax actually paid on the income derived outside China by an enterprise with foreign investment is less than the credit limit computed pursuant to Article 84 of these Regulations, the foreign income tax actually paid outside China can be credited against the tax payable. If it exceeds the credit limit, the exceed portion shall not be allowed as credit against the tax payable nor shall it be listed as expense, but the balance of the foreign tax paid may be utilized to offset against the tax payable in subsequent years. The carryover shall not exceed five years at the maximum.

Article 86   The provisions of Articles 83 to 85 of these Regulations shall be applicable only to enterprises with foreign investment which have their head offices established in China. Enterprises with foreign investment applying tax credit pursuant to Article 12 of the Tax Law shall submit the original tax payment certificates of the same year issued by the relevant tax authorities outside China. Duplicates, or tax payment certificates of different tax years, shall not be acceptable as supporting documents for tax credit.

Chapter VIII Tax Administration

Article 87   Enterprises shall go to the local tax authorities for tax registration within 30 days after the completion of their registration with the State Administration for Industry and Commerce. When an enterprise with foreign investment establishes or terminates a branch outside China, it shall make supplementary tax registration, change of registration, or deregistration with the local tax authorities within 30 days after the establishment or termination.

In going through the registration mentioned in this Article, the enterprises shall submit the relevant documents, licenses, and information.

Article 88   Enterprises that experience change of address, restructuring, merger, spin-off, termination, or change in capital sum and in scope of business, etc., shall go to the local tax authorities for change of registration, or deregistration, and shall submit the relevant approval documents within 30 days after the completion of change of registration, or before deregistration, with the State Administration for Industry and Commerce.

Article 89   Foreign enterprises which have two or more business establishments set up in China may select one establishment for consolidated tax filing and payment. However, that establishment shall meet the following requirements:

1. It shall assume the supervisory and management responsibility over the business of other establishments.
2. It shall keep complete accounting records and vouchers that correctly reflect the income, costs, expenses, profits, and losses of other business establishments.

Article 90   For a foreign enterprise which chooses to consolidate its income tax filing and payment pursuant to Article 89 of these Regulations, application shall be made by a business establishment selected by it to the local tax authorities for examination and then submitted for approval according to the following provisions:

1. If all the business establishments involved in the consolidated tax filing are located in the same province, autonomous region, or mu-

nicipality directly under the administration of the central government, the application is subject to approval by the tax authorities
of that province, autonomous region, or municipality.

2. If they are located in two or more different provinces, autonomous
    regions, or municipalities directly under the administration of the
    central government, the application is subject to approval by the
    State Administration for Taxation.

Once the consolidated tax filing of a foreign enterprise is approved, any establishment of new business organizations, merger,
change of address, termination, close-down, etc., shall be reported by
the business establishment in charge of consolidated tax in advance of
the occurrence of any of the above situations, to the local tax authorities. Any change in the business establishments involved in the consolidated tax filing shall be treated in accordance with the provisions of
the preceding paragraph.

Article 91   When different tax rates are applicable to different business establishments of a foreign enterprise involved in consolidated tax
filing, the taxable income of different establishments shall be computed
separately on a reasonable basis, and income tax shall be paid according
to the different rates.

When both profit and loss were incurred in the different business establishments mentioned in the preceding paragraph and there is a net
profit after the profits and losses are offset against each other, income tax
shall be levied at a rate applicable to the profit-making establishments.
For those establishments sustaining losses, income tax shall be levied at a
rate applicable to such establishments when they become profitable after
the losses have been made up against the income in subsequent years. Income tax on the amount of losses which have been made upon shall be
levied at a rate applicable to those establishments, which help the loss establishments to make up losses.

Article 92   Notwithstanding the provisions of Article 91 of these
Regulations, when a business establishment in charge of consolidated tax
filing cannot compute the taxable income of different establishments appropriately on a separate basis, the local tax authorities may make a reasonable apportionment of the taxable income amount of these business
establishments, with reference to their respective proportion of business
income, costs and expenses, assets, and the number of staff and workers,
or the amount of wages.

Article 93 Enterprises with foreign investment which have branches in China shall handle their joint tax filing with reference to the provisions of Article 91 and Article 92 of these Regulations.

Article 94 Some provisional income tax to be paid by enterprises in quarterly installments as stipulated in Article 15 of the Tax Law shall be paid according to the actual profit for that quarter. Enterprises that have difficulty in assessing the provisional income tax based on the actual quarterly profit may pay the tax based on one-fourth of the taxable income of the preceding year or by adopting other formulas approved by the local tax authorities.

Article 95 Enterprises shall file their income tax returns and final accounting statements with the local tax authorities within the time limit as prescribed in Article 16 of the Tax Law, irrespective of making profits or sustaining losses in the tax year. Unless otherwise provided, enterprises shall submit at the same time audit reports signed by a certified public accountant registered in China upon submission of the final accounting statement.

In the event that an enterprise cannot submit the income tax returns and the final accounting statements within the time limit prescribed by the Tax Law due to special reasons, an application shall be made to the local tax authorities within the filing time limit for approval of appropriate extension.

Article 96 Branches or business establishments under an enterprise shall submit a copy of their final accounting statements to the local tax authorities at the same time as they submit them to their respective head office, or to the business establishment in charge of consolidated tax filing.

Article 97 An enterprise which is merged, spinned off, or terminated during the year shall settle the income tax liability for that period with the local tax authorities, within 60 days from the cease of operations with the excess payment refunded or deficiency made good.

Article 98 In the case in which an enterprise, which converted its foreign currency into Renminbi according to the official exchange rate in paying tax, has excess tax refundable, it shall convert the refundable Renminbi tax amount into the original foreign currency according to the exchange rate of the day when the tax was first paid, and then convert the sum back to Renminbi, according to the exchange rate of the day when the tax refund voucher is issued. In the case where there is balance of tax payable, the balance of tax payable shall be converted into Renminbi according to the exchange rate of the date when the tax payment certificate is issued.

Article 99   When an enterprise with foreign investment goes through liquidation, it shall file its income tax return with the local tax authorities prior to its deregistration with the State Administration for Industry and Commerce.

Article 100   Unless otherwise provided by the state, enterprises shall keep inside China their account books and accounting records and other supporting documents that enable proper computation of taxable income.

Account books, accounting statements, and other accounting supporting documents of the enterprises shall be completed in Chinese language or in both Chinese and foreign languages.

Enterprises using electronic computers for bookkeeping shall treat the accounting records in computer storage or output as account books. Magnetic tapes and diskettes shall be kept properly before hard copies are printed.

Accounting supporting documents, account books, and accounting statements of the enterprises shall be kept for at least 15 years.

Article 101   Sales invoices and business receipts of the enterprises shall be submitted to the local tax authorities for approval before they are printed and put into use.

The controlling mechanism over the printing and use of sales invoice and business receipts shall be formulated by the State Administration for Taxation.

Article 102   All enterprise income tax returns and tax payment certificates shall be printed by the State Administration for Taxation.

Article 103   If the final due dates for tax filing and tax payment of enterprises fall upon Sunday or an official public holiday, the day following the public holiday shall be treated as the final due date.

Article 104   The relevant tax authorities may pay to tax withholding agents, as provided for in Article 19 paragraph 2 of the Tax Law and Article 67 of these Regulations, withholding handling fees computed at a certain percentage of the tax withheld. Detailed procedures shall be formulated by the State Administration for Taxation.

Article 105 In the event that any taxpayer or withholding agent fails to accept the examination of the tax authorities in accordance with the relevant provisions, or fails to pay the late-payment penalty within the time limit prescribed by the tax authorities, the local tax authorities may, according to the seriousness of the case, impose a penalty of not more than RMB 5,000.

Article 106 In the event that any enterprise violates the provisions of Article 87, Article 90 Paragraph 2, Article 95, Article 96, Article 97, Article 99, Article 100, or Article 101 of these Regulations, the tax authorities may, according to the seriousness of the case, impose a penalty of RMB 5,000 or less.

Article 107 Tax evasion mentioned in Article 25 of the Tax Law refers to unlawful activities deliberately carried out by a taxpayer in violation of the provisions of the Tax Law, such as altering, forging or destroying bills, accounting documents, or account books; falsifying or overstating costs and expenses; concealing or understating the amount of taxable income or revenue; dodging tax payments; or defrauding back the paid taxes.

Article 108 The tax authorities shall serve notices of contravention on the relevant parties for cases involving penalty in accordance with the relevant provisions of the Tax Law and these Regulations.

Article 109 All units and individuals have the right to provide information and assistance to report offenders or offenses against the Tax Law. The tax authorities shall keep confidential the identities of the informers and rewarding them according to the relevant regulations.

Chapter IX Supplementary Rules

Article 110 Enterprises with foreign investment which were registered with the State Administration for Industry and Commerce before the promulgation of the Tax Law shall pay income tax at the rates stipulated in the Tax Law. If their actual tax liabilities are higher than those incurred before the enforcement of the Tax Law, the original applicable tax rates may be adopted during the approved operation period. If there is no agreed period of operation, the original tax rate will apply within five years. However, if the tax liability of a particular year during the aforesaid period is higher than that assessed at the rate stipulated in the Tax Law, the tax rate stipulated in the Tax Law shall be adopted starting from that tax year.

Article 111   Enterprises with foreign investment, which were registered with the State Administration for Industry and Commerce before the promulgation of the Tax Law but have enjoyed the preferential treatment of income tax exemption and reduction pursuant to the laws and regulations before the enforcement of the Tax Law, may continue to enjoy the preferential treatments until the expiration of the tax exemption and reduction period.

Enterprises with foreign investment, which were registered with the Administration for Industry and Commerce before the enforcement of the Tax Law, but have not yet started to make profit, or have become profit making for less than five years, shall be granted income tax exemption and reduction for a due period pursuant to Article 8 paragraph 1 of the Tax Law.

Article 112   Enterprises with foreign investment registered with the State Administration for Industry and Commerce after the promulgation and before the enforcement of the Tax Law may refer to the provisions of Article 110 and Article 111 of these Regulations for application.

Article 113   The authority of interpretation of these Regulations shall rest with the Ministry of Finance and the State Administration for Taxation.

Article 114   These Regulations shall come into force on the date of enforcement of the Income Tax Law of the People's Republic of China for Enterprises with Foreign Investment and Foreign Enterprises. The Detailed Rules and Regulations for the Implementation of the Income Tax Law of the People's Republic of China Concerning Joint Ventures with Chinese and Foreign Investment and the Detailed Rules and Regulations for the Implementation of the Income Tax Law of People's Republic of China Concerning Foreign Enterprises shall be abrogated at the same time.

11. Provisional Regulations Governing Development and Operation of Tracts of Land With Foreign Investment

Promulgated on 19 May 1990

Article 1   With a view to attracting foreign investment to develop and operate tracts of land (hereinafter referred to as development of tracts of land) in order to strengthen the construction of public facilities, improve the investment environment, absorb foreign investment in setting up technologically advanced and export enterprises, and develop an export-oriented economy, hereof the Regulations are stipulated.

Article 2 The development of tracts of land as referred to in these Regulations denote in accordance with plans of the tracts of land after state-owned land use right is obtained, leveling the land and construction of public facilities such as water supply, sewage, electricity and heat supply, roads and telecommunications, making the land usable for industry and other constructions and then the transfer of the land use right and operations of the public facilities, or construction of universal factory premises and auxiliary production and services facilities and transfer or leasing of the buildings on the ground.

Development of tracts of land should have clear aims and clear intentions for the construction projects on the developed land.

Article 3 People's governments at municipal and county levels should draw up proposals (or preliminary feasibility study reports) on items of tracts of land to be developed with foreign investment.

Proposals on the use of a piece of farmland under 66 hectares and of land for other purposes under 133 hectares and proposals on land-comprehensive development projects with an investment within the authorization of approval by provincial, autonomous regional, and municipal people's governments (including the people's government or administrative committee of the special economic zone) submitted to them for examination and approval.

Proposals on the use of farmland larger than 66 hectares and of land for other purposes bigger than 133 hectares and proposals on land development projects with an investment beyond the authorization of approval by provincial, autonomous regional, and municipal people's governments should be forwarded by such people's government to the State Planning Commission for examination and overall study and submitted to the State Council for final examination and approval.

Article 4 Foreign investors who intend to develop and operate tracts of land should establish Chinese–foreign equity joint ventures, or Chinese–foreign contractual joint ventures, or wholly foreign-owned enterprises (hereafter referred to as development enterprises), respectively in line with the Law of the People's Republic of China on Chinese–Foreign Equity Joint Ventures, the Law of the People's Republic of China on Chinese–Foreign Contractual Joint Ventures, and the Law of the People's Republic of China on Wholly Foreign-Owned Enterprises.

The development enterprises are subjected to the jurisdiction and protected by Chinese laws, and all their activities should be in accordance with the laws and regulations of the People's Republic of China.

The development enterprises enjoy autonomy in operation and management according to law, but they have no administrative power in the development areas. The relationship between the development enterprises and other enterprises is a commercial one.

The state encourages state-owned enterprises to set up development enterprises with foreign business people, with the state-owned land use right as their investment or conditions for cooperation.

Article 5   The development enterprises should acquire the state-owned land use right over the areas to be developed in accordance with Chinese laws.

When granting the state-owned land use right for valuable consideration to the development enterprises, people's governments at the municipal or county levels in development areas should, in accordance with laws and administrative regulations on state-owned land administration, define the area, purpose, and terms for the granting, land utilization fees and other conditions, sign contracts on the grant of the state-owned land use right for valuable consideration, and submit them to relevant authorities for approval.

Article 6   After the state-owned land use right is granted for valuable consideration, resources and buried objects still belong to the state. If they need to be developed, relevant laws and administrative regulations should be observed.

Article 7   The development enterprises should work out programs or feasibility study reports on the development of tracts of land, defining the objectives for the general development and different stages of development, the details of the implementation of the development, and the plans for the developed land.

A land development program or feasibility study report should be examined by a government at a city or county level and then submitted to a people's government at the provincial, autonomous regional, or municipal level for approval. Departments for examining such programs and reports should coordinate work of relevant governing departments on construction and management of public facilities.

Article 8   All development construction must conform and be subject to city planning requirements and management if the land for development is within the area of city planning.

The various kinds of construction projects in the developed areas must conform to laws, administrative regulations, and standards relating to environmental protection.

Article 9 The development enterprises must accomplish the programs for the development of tracts of land and reach the conditions as stipulated in the contracts on granting state-owned land use right for valuable consideration before they transfer the state-owned land use right. No development enterprise is allowed to transfer the land use right to others if it fails to invest in land development according to contracts on granting the state-owned land and as required by programs for land development.

Laws and administrative regulations on management of state-owned land should be observed when the development enterprises and other enterprises transfer or mortgage the state-owned land use right and when the state-owned land use right is terminated.

Article 10 The development enterprises can attract investors to development areas to be granted with the state-owned land use right for valuable consideration and set up enterprises in development areas. Foreign investment enterprises should be established according to the Laws of the People's Republic of China on Chinese–Foreign Equity Joint Ventures, the Law of the People's Republic of China on Chinese–Foreign Contractual Joint Ventures, and the Law of the People's Republic of China on Wholly Foreign-Owned Enterprises.

The establishment of enterprises in development areas should be in keeping with relevant state investment policies, which encourage establishment of technologically advanced enterprises and export enterprises.

Article 11 The post and telecommunications facilities in development areas should be put under unified planning, construction, and operation by post and telecommunications departments or approved at the provincial, autonomous regional or municipal level. Post and telecommunications facilities can be constructed with investment from land development enterprises or from both the enterprises and post and telecommunications departments as a joint venture, and the facilities shall be operated by post and telecommunications departments after their completion, and, in accordance with the bilateral contract, the development enterprises shall be economically compensated.

Article 12 The development enterprises which invest in the construction of production-related public facilities such as power stations, heat supply centers, and waterworks in development areas can operate power, water, and heat supply businesses in the development areas or transfer them to local public facility enterprises for operation.

If the development enterprises find their public facilities have a surplus for other areas or wish to have them connected with systems outside the development area, they should sign contracts with local public facility enterprises according to relevant state laws and proceed with the business in accordance with the conditions as stipulated in the contracts.

Local public facility enterprises should operate businesses that divert water or electricity from other areas to the development areas.

Article 13   For areas to be developed at coastal areas, harbors, or rivers to become harbor construction sites, the shoreline will be under state unified development planning and control. The development enterprises may build or operate special ports and wharves under unified plans by state communications departments.

Article 14   Businesses and social activities in violation of state laws and regulations are prohibited in developed areas.

Article 15   If the development areas where export-led processing enterprises have a concentrated need to practice special measures in import and export and customs control, they must report to the State Council for approval, and relevant state departments will work out detailed measures in this regard.

Article 16   Administration, judicial affairs, ports, and customs in development areas are managed, respectively, by relevant government departments, local people's governments, and judicial organs within their jurisdiction powers.

Article 17   These Regulations are applicable as a measure of reference to firms, enterprises, and other economic organizations or individuals from Hong Kong, Macao, and Taiwan, which intend to develop the tracts of land.

Article 18   These Regulations shall go into effect in China's special economic zones, coastal cities opened to foreign investors, and coastal economic development zones on the date of promulgation.

12. The Notice of the State Council on Relevant Issues Concerning the Provisional Regulations on Value-Added Tax, Excise Tax, Business Tax, and Other Taxes Applicable to Foreign-Invested Enterprises and Foreign Enterprises

The People's Government of Each Province, Autonomous Region, and Municipality Directly Under the Central Government, Each Ministry and Committee of, and Each Department Directly Under the State Council:

According to the Decision of the Standing Committee of the National People's Congress for the Provisional Regulations on Value-Added Tax, Excise Tax, Business Tax and Other Taxes Applicable to Foreign-Invested Enterprises and Foreign Enterprises (hereafter referred to as Decision) discussed and approved by the Fifth Session of the Standing Committee of the Eighth National People's Congress, some relevant issues concerning sorts of taxation, etc. applicable to foreign invested enterprises and foreign enterprises are to be notified as follows:

I. Issues Concerning Sorts of Taxation Applicable to Foreign-Invested Enterprises and Foreign Enterprises

In accordance with the provisions of the Decision, besides the Provisional Regulations on Value-Added Tax of the People's Republic of China, the Provisional Regulations on Excise Tax of the People's Republic of China, the Provisional Regulations on Business Tax of the People's Republic of China, and the Law of Foreign-Invested Enterprises and Foreign Enterprises Income Tax of the People's Republic of China, the following provisional regulations shall be applied to foreign invested enterprises and foreign enterprises as well:

1. Provisional Regulations for Value-Added Tax on Land of the People's Republic of China, promulgated by the State Council on 31 December 1993
2. Provisional Regulations on Resource Tax of the People's Republic of China, promulgated by the State Council on 25 December 1993
3. Provisional Regulations on Stamp Duty of the People's Republic of China, promulgated by the State Council on 6 August 1988
4. Provisional Regulations on Butchery Duty, promulgated by the Government Administration Council of the Central People's Government on 19 December 1950
5. Provisional Regulations on Urban Real Estate Tax, promulgated by the Government Administration Council of the Central People's Government on 8 August 1951

6. Provisional Regulations on Vehicle and Boat License Duty, promulgated by the Government Administration Council of the Central People's Government on 13 September 1951

7. Provisional Regulations on Deed Tax, promulgated by the Government Administration Council of the Central People's Government on 3 April 1950

During the process of tax reforms, the State Council will, in succession, modify and formulate several new provisional regulations on tax, which foreign-invested enterprises and foreign enterprises shall implement accordingly.

II. Issues Concerning Resolution to the Added Tax Burden of Foreign-Invested Enterprises After Alteration of the Value-Added Tax, Excise Tax, and Business Tax Levied upon

1. Foreign-invested enterprises approved and established by 31 December 1993, which have got the tax burden added due to the alteration of value-added tax, excise tax, and business tax levied upon, may submit their application to the tax authority. The tax authority may, within their business period approved, ratify to repay the added taxation to foreign-invested enterprises due to their added tax burden, but the expiration shall not exceed 5 years; if the business period is not provided for, the added taxation mentioned above shall be refunded to foreign-invested enterprises, by which the application shall be submitted to and approved by the tax authority, within the period of not exceeding five years.

2. If both value-added tax and excise tax are levied upon foreign-invested enterprises, the part which exceeds the original tax burden among the sum having been paid shall be returned respectively in accordance with the ratio of the value-added tax and excise tax having been paid.

3. Foreign-invested enterprises, whose products are produced directly for export or sold to export enterprises for export, may, according to the Provisional Regulations on Value-Added Tax of the People's Republic of China, handle the taxation fund once for all against the Sheet of Customs Declaration for Export and Tax Paid Certificate.

4. Foreign-invested enterprises may, in principle, handle the taxation fund applied for due to the added tax burden once for all at the end of a year; if the added tax burden is a relatively large amount,

they may apply for pre-fund once a quarter of a year and clear off the balance at the end of a year.

5. Issues concerning refund of value-added tax and excise tax shall be exclusively conducted and undertaken by the National Taxation Bureau. The national treasuries of all levels shall conscientiously verify and strictly check on all the items. The calculation of taxation fund, the procedures of application for and approval of tax refund are to be separately formulated by the National Taxation Bureau.

6. Issues concerning refund of business tax will be provided for by the people's government of each province, autonomous region, and municipality directly under the Central Government.

III. Issues Concerning Taxation on Sino-Foreign Cooperatively Exploiting Oil Resource

Value-added tax at the rate of 5% shall be levied upon the crude oil and natural gas in kind exploited through Sino-foreign cooperation, together with the charge for the utility of mineral zone in accordance with the present regulations. Resources tax, however, shall not be levied for the time being. The value-added tax when being levied shall not be credited to taxation upon purchased items. And the taxation shall not be repaid when the crude oil and natural gas is exported.

The provisions regulated above shall be applicable, mutatis mutandis, to the offshore oil fields independently operated by the China National Offshore Oil Corporation.

The present notice shall be implemented from the date of 1 January 1994.

13. Regulations Governing Financial Institutions With Foreign Capital in the People's Republic of China

Promulgated on 25 February 1994

Chapter I General Principles

Article 1   These Regulations are formulated in order to meet the needs of opening to the outside world and economic development and strengthen and improve the management of financial institutions with foreign capital.

Article 2   Financial institutions with foreign capital mentioned in these Regulations refer to the following financial institutions that are established and operate in China upon approval in accordance with the relevant laws and regulations of the People's Republic of China:

1. Subsidiary banks incorporated by foreign capital whose head offices are in China (hereafter referred to as foreign banks)
2. Branches of foreign banks in China (hereafter referred to as foreign bank branches)
3. Banks incorporated jointly by foreign and Chinese equity institutions (hereafter referred to as equity joint venture banks)
4. Finance companies incorporated by foreign capital whose head offices are in China (hereafter referred to as foreign finance companies)
5. Finance companies incorporated jointly by foreign and Chinese financial institutions (hereafter referred to as equity joint venture finance companies)

The State Council determines the locations that are open to financial institutions with foreign capital.

Article 3   Financial institutions with foreign capital shall abide by the laws and regulations of the People's Republic of China, and shall not engage in activities that harm the social and public interests of the People's Republic of China.

The legitimate business operation and lawful rights and interests of the financial institutions with foreign capital shall be protected by the laws of the People's Republic of China.

Article 4   The People's Bank of China is the sole regulatory authority responsible for the regulation and supervision of the financial institutions with foreign capital; the branches of the People's Bank of China exercise routine regulation and supervision of the financial institutions with foreign capital in their jurisdiction.

Chapter II Establishment and Registration

Article 5   The minimum registered capital for a foreign bank and an equity joint venture bank shall be in the amount of a freely convertible currency equivalent to RMB 300 million yuan; and that for a foreign finance company and an equity joint venture finance company shall be in the amount of a freely convertible currency equivalent to RMB 200 million yuan, of which, the paid-up capital shall not be below 50% of the registered capital.

The head office of a foreign bank branch shall allocate a working capital in a freely convertible currency equivalent to not less than RMB 100 million yuan to its branches without any repayment or recompense.

Article 6 The applicant for the establishment of a foreign bank or a foreign finance company is subject to the following conditions:

1. The applicant is a financial institution.
2. The applicant has maintained a representative office in China for two years or longer.
3. The total assets of the applicant at the end of the year prior to its application shall not be below US$ 10 billion.
4. There is a sound system for financial regulation and supervision in the home country or region of the applicant.

Article 7 To establish a foreign bank branch, the applicant is subject to the following conditions:

1. The applicant has maintained a representative institution in China for two years or longer.
2. The total assets of the applicant at the end of the year prior to the application shall not be below US$20 billion.
3. There is a sound system for financial regulation and supervision in the home country or region of the applicant.

Article 8 To establish an equity joint venture bank or an equity joint venture finance company, the applicant is subject to the following conditions:

1. Each partner to the joint venture shall be a financial institution.
2. The foreign partner has a representative institution in China.
3. The total assets of the foreign partner at the end of the year prior to the application shall not be below US$10 billion.
4. There is a sound system for financial regulation and supervision in the home country or region of the applicant.

Article 9 The applicant for the establishment of a foreign bank or a foreign finance company shall submit to the People's Bank of China a written application together with the following documents:

1. A letter of application specifying: the name of the foreign bank or finance company to be set up, the registered capital and paid-up capital, the intended business activities, etc.
2. A feasibility study
3. The Articles of Association of the intended foreign bank or finance company
4. A photocopy of the business license issued by the relevant regulatory authorities of the country or region in which the applicant is incorporated
5. The annual reports of the applicant for the last three years
6. Other documents required by the People's Bank of China

Article 10   To establish a foreign bank branch, the head office of the foreign bank shall submit to the People's Bank of China a written application together with the following documents:

1. The application signed by the legal representative specifying: the name of the branch to be set up by the foreign bank, the amount of working capital free from repayment allocated by the parent company, the intended business activities, etc.
2. A photocopy of the business license issued by the relevant regulatory authorities of the country or region in which the applicant is incorporated
3. The annual reports of the applicant for the last three years
4. Other documents required by the People's Bank of China

Article 11   To establish an equity joint venture bank or a finance company, the partners to the equity joint venture shall submit to the People's Bank of China a jointly written application together with the following documents:

1. The application for the establishment of an equity joint venture bank or a finance company specifying: the name of the intended equity joint venture bank or finance company to be set up, the name of all the partners to the joint venture, the amount of the registered capital and paid-up capital, the proportion of the capital contributions of all parties to the joint venture, the intended business activities, etc.
2. A feasibility study
3. The Contract for the equity joint venture and the Articles of Association of the joint venture bank or finance company to be set up
4. A photocopy of the business licenses issued by the relevant regula-

tory authorities of the country or region in which the applicants are incorporated
5. The annual reports of the applicants for the last three years
6. Other documents required by the People's Bank of China

Article 12 Except the annual reports, all documents required in Article 9, Article 10, and Article 11 hereof, if written in a foreign language, shall have a Chinese translation attached.

Article 13 The applicant shall be given a formal application form when the People's Bank of China approves the application for the establishment of a financial institution with foreign capital after preliminary examination. The applicant shall be considered rejected if the applicant fails to receive the formal application form within 90 days from the date of application.

Article 14 The applicant shall, within 60 days from the date of receiving the formal application form, present to the People's Bank of China the completed form and the following documents for ratification:

1. A list of the key executives of the intended financial institution with foreign capital and their resumés
2. A power of attorney granted to the key executive officer of the intended financial institution with foreign capital
3. In case of applying for setting up a foreign bank branch, a letter of guarantee from the head office specifying the responsibility for the tax and debt obligations incurred by the foreign bank branch
4. Other documents required by the People's Bank of China

Article 15 The financial institution with foreign capital shall, within 30 days from the date of receiving the approval document of the People's Bank of China, raise and transfer to China the required paid-up capital or working capital, and then register with the industry and commerce administration authorities in accordance with law after the transferred capital is verified by a certified public accountant registered in China. It shall also register with a taxation office, in accordance with law, within 30 days from the date it enters into operation.

Article 16 The financial institution with foreign capital shall apply to the State Administration of Exchange Control for the issuance of the Foreign Exchange Operation License within 30 days from the date of approval by the People's Bank of China.

Chapter III Scope of Business

Article 17   Subject to approval by the People's Bank of China, a foreign bank, foreign bank branch, or equity joint venture bank shall be allowed to conduct some or all of the following business activities:

1. Foreign currency deposit taking
2. Foreign currency lending
3. Foreign currency bill discounting
4. Approved foreign exchange investment
5. Foreign exchange remittance
6. Foreign exchange guarantee
7. Import and export settlement
8. Foreign currency dealing and brokerage
9. Exchange of foreign currencies and bills denominated in foreign currency
10. Foreign currency credit card payment
11. Custody and safe-deposit box service
12. Credit verification and consultation
13. Approved business activities in domestic currency and other foreign currencies

Article 18   Subject to approval by the People's Bank of China, a foreign finance company or equity joint venture finance company shall be allowed to conduct some or all of the following business activities:

1. Foreign currency deposit of US$10,000 in minimum for each deposit with a maturity of three months or longer
2. Foreign currency lending
3. Foreign currency bill discounting
4. Approved foreign exchange investment
5. Foreign exchange guarantee
6. Foreign currency dealing and brokerage
7. Credit verification and consultation
8. Foreign exchange trust business
9. Approved business activities in domestic currency and other foreign currencies

Article 19   The foreign currency deposit taking specified in this chapter refers to the following deposits denominated in foreign currencies:

1. Interbank deposits both in China and abroad
2. Deposits taken from the nonbank clients located outside China

3. Deposits taken from foreigners in China
4. Deposits taken from overseas Chinese and compatriots from Hong Kong, Macao, and Taiwan
5. Deposits taken from enterprises with foreign investment in China
6. Redeposits as occurred as a result of lending by financial institutions with foreign capital to nonenterprises with foreign investment
7. Other approved foreign exchange deposits

Article 20   The foreign exchange remittance specified in this chapter refers to the inward remittance from abroad and the outward remittance by enterprises with foreign investment, foreigners, overseas Chinese, and compatriots from Hong Kong, Macao, and Taiwan on the mainland of China.

Article 21   The import and export settlement specified in this chapter refers to such business as the import and export settlement of enterprises with foreign investment, the export settlement of approved nonenterprises with foreign investment, and the import settlement occurred as a result of their lending conducted by foreign banks, foreign bank branches, and equity joint venture banks.

Chapter IV Supervision and Administration

Article 22   The deposit and lending rates as well as various types of fees charged by a financial institution with foreign capital shall be determined by itself in accordance with the relevant rules and regulations of the People's Bank of China.

Article 23   To conduct deposit-taking business, a financial institution with foreign capital is required to deposit reserves with a local branch of the People's Bank of China. The reserve ratio shall be determined, and adjusted when necessary, by the People's Bank of China. The deposit reserves are free of interest.

Article 24   Thirty percent of the working capital of a foreign bank branch shall be maintained in the form of interest-bearing assets designated by the People's Bank of China, including the deposits held with the banks designated by the People's Bank of China.

Article 25   The total assets of a foreign bank, an equity joint venture bank, a foreign finance company, or an equity joint venture finance company shall not exceed twenty times the sum of its paid-up capital plus reserves.

Article 26   The loans granted to an enterprise and its related enterprises by a foreign bank, an equity joint venture bank, a foreign finance company, or an equity joint venture finance company shall not exceed 30% of the sum of its paid-up capital plus reserves, except those specially approved by the People's Bank of China.

Article 27   The gross investment of a foreign bank, an equity joint venture bank, a foreign finance company, or an equity joint venture finance company shall not exceed 30% of the sum of its paid-up capital plus reserves, with the exception of that made to a financial institution and approved by the People's Bank of China.

Article 28   The fixed assets maintained by a foreign bank, an equity joint venture bank, a foreign finance company, or an equity joint venture finance company shall not exceed 40% of the sum of its paid-up capital plus reserves.

Article 29   A financial institution with foreign capital shall ensure the liquidity of its assets. The specific requirements to financial institutions with foreign capital on their assets liquidity shall be made separately by the People's Bank of China.

Article 30   Deposits taken from within the territory of the People's Republic of China by a financial institution with foreign capital shall not exceed 40% of its total assets.

Article 31   A financial institution with foreign capital shall make provisions fund for nonperforming (bad) assets in accordance with the relevant procedures as stipulated by the state.

Article 32   A foreign bank, an equity joint venture bank, a foreign finance company, or an equity joint venture finance company whose paid-up capital is below the level of its registered capital, shall supplement the paid-up capital by transferring 25% of its post-tax profit each year until the sum of the paid-up capital plus reserves equals to the registered capital.

Article 33   A financial institution with foreign capital shall employ at least one Chinese citizen as its senior executive.

Article 34 A financial institution with foreign capital shall employ certified public accountants registered in China. Such employment shall be subject to the confirmation by the relevant local branch of the People's Bank of China.

Article 35 A financial institution with foreign capital shall gain approval from the People's Bank of China and conduct the related registration with an industry and commerce administration department in accordance with the law in any of the following cases:

1. Establishment of an affiliate
2. Adjustment or transfer of registered capital, increase or decrease of working capital
3. Change of the institution's name or business address
4. Replacement of senior executives

Article 36 A financial institution with foreign capital shall submit to the People's Bank of China and its related branches financial statements and other relevant data.

Article 37 The People's Bank of China and its branches have the right to examine and audit the operational management and financial situation of a financial institution with foreign capital.

Chapter V Dissolution and Liquidation

Article 38 In case of a self-termination of its business activities, a financial institution with foreign capital shall submit a written application to the People's Bank of China 30 days before the termination, and will be dissolved and liquidated after the Bank's examination and approval.

Article 39 The People's Bank of China may order a financial institution with foreign capital which is unable to meet its liabilities to cease operation and make repayment within a limited period of time. If it has recovered redeemability and wants to resume business within the time limit, it shall apply to the People's Bank of China for resuming business; if it fails to recover redeemability beyond the time limit, it shall enter into liquidation.

Article 40 In case of the termination of a financial institution with foreign capital due to dissolution, cancellation under the law, or because of the declaration of bankruptcy, matters concerning its liquidation shall be handled under the stipulations of relevant Chinese laws and regulations.

Article 41   Upon the completion of liquidation, a financial institution with foreign capital shall deregister itself at the original registration agency within the legal time limit.

Chapter VI Penalties

Article 42   In case of a financial institution with foreign capital established in violation of the stipulations of Chapter II hereof and without approval, the People's Bank of China shall outlaw it, confiscate its illegal gains, and may, together, fine an amount of foreign exchange equivalent to RMB 50,000–100,000 yuan.

Article 43   In case of a financial institution with foreign capital conducting business activities beyond its approved business scope and in violation of the stipulations of Chapter III hereof, the People's Bank of China or its relevant branch institutions shall order it to cease those business activities which are beyond its approved business scope and confiscate its illegal receipts from the nonapproved business activities, and a penalty of an amount of foreign currency equivalent to RMB 10,000–50,00 shall also be imposed.

Article 44   In case of a financial institution with foreign capital conducting business activities in violation of the relevant stipulations of Chapter IV hereof, the People's Bank of China or its relevant branches are entitled to order it to rectify, readjust its business, or supplement sufficient funds accordingly, and a penalty of an amount of foreign currency equivalent to RMB 5,000–30,000 yuan shall also be imposed.

Article 45   In case of a failure of a financial institution with foreign capital to render financial statements and related data in violation of the relevant stipulations of Chapter IV hereof, the People's Bank of China or its relevant branches shall serve a warning, circulate a notice, and demand the submission of them within a time limit, and a penalty of an amount of foreign currency equivalent to RMB 3,000–20,000 yuan shall also be imposed.

Article 46   In case of a failure to comply with these regulations, a financial institution with foreign capital shall not only be penalized under the relevant stipulations of Article 43, Article 44, and Article 45 of this

Chapter, but it may also be ordered to cease operation, and even have its business license suspended by the People's Bank of China where serious offenses are committed.

Article 47 In case of breach of other laws and regulations of the People's Republic of China, a financial institution with foreign capital shall be penalized by the relevant authorities according to law.

Chapter VII Supplementary Provisions

Article 48 These Regulations are also applicable to the financial institutions established and operated on the mainland of China by financial institutions from such regions as Hong Kong, Macao, and Taiwan.

Article 49 The regulatory procedures for representative offices established in China by financial institutions with foreign capital are to be formulated separately by the People's Bank of China.

Article 50 The People's Bank of China shall be responsible for the interpretation of these Regulations and for the formulation of the detailed rules for the implementation of these Regulations.

Article 51 These Regulations are effective as of 1 April 1994. The Regulations Governing Foreign Banks and Sino–Foreign Equity Joint Venture Banks in the Special Economic Zones of the People's Republic of China promulgated by the State Council on 2 April 1995 and the Procedures Regulating Financial Institutions with Foreign Capital and Sino–Foreign Equity Joint Venture Financial Institutions in Shanghai ratified by the State Council on 7 September 1990 and issued by the People's Bank of China on 8 September 1990 are to be abolished simultaneously.

14. Arbitration Law of the People's Republic of China

Adopted on 31 August 1994 by the Ninth Session of the Standing Committee of the Eighth National People's Congress and promulgated on 31 August 1994

Chapter I General Provisions

Article 1 This Law is formulated in order to ensure that economic disputes shall be impartially and promptly arbitrated, to protect the legitimate rights and interests of the relevant parties, and to guarantee the healthy development of the socialist market economy.

Article 2   Disputes over contracts and disputes over property rights and interests between citizens, legal persons, and other organizations as equal subjects of law may be submitted to arbitration.

Article 3   The following disputes shall not be submitted to arbitration:

1. Disputes over marriage, adoption, guardianship, child maintenance, and inheritance
2. Administrative disputes falling within the jurisdiction of the relevant administrative organs according to law

Article 4   The parties adopting arbitration for dispute settlement shall reach an arbitration agreement on a mutually voluntary basis. An arbitration commission shall not accept an application for arbitration submitted by one of the parties in the absence of an arbitration agreement.

Article 5   A people's court shall not accept an action initiated by one of the parties if the parties have concluded an arbitration agreement, unless the arbitration agreement is invalid.

Article 6   The arbitration commission shall be selected by the parties by agreement.

The jurisdiction by level system and the district jurisdiction system shall not apply in arbitration.

Article 7   Disputes shall be fairly and reasonably settled by arbitration on the basis of facts and in accordance with the relevant provisions of law.

Article 8   Arbitration shall be conducted in accordance with the law, independent of any intervention by administrative organs, social organizations, or individuals.

Article 9   The single ruling system shall be applied in arbitration. The arbitration commission shall not accept any application for arbitration, nor shall a people's court accept any action submitted by the party in respect of the same dispute after an arbitration award has already been given in relation to that matter.

If the arbitration award is canceled or its enforcement has been disallowed by a people's court in accordance with the law, the parties may, in accordance with a new arbitration agreement between them in respect of the dispute, reapply for arbitration or initiate legal proceedings with the people's court.

Chapter II Arbitration Commissions and Arbitration Association

Article 10 Arbitration commissions may be established in the municipalities directly under the Central Government, in the municipalities where the people's governments of provinces and autonomous regions are located, or, if necessary, in other cities divided into districts. Arbitration commissions shall not be established at each level of the administrative divisions.

The people's governments of the municipalities and cities specified in the above paragraph shall organize the relevant departments and the Chamber of Commerce for the formation of an arbitration commission.

The establishment of an arbitration commission shall be registered with the judicial administrative department of the relevant province, autonomous region, or municipalities directly under the Central Government.

Article 11 An arbitration commission shall fulfill the following conditions:

1. It must have its own name, domicile, and Articles of Association.
2. It must possess the necessary property.
3. It must have its own members.
4. It must have arbitrators for appointment.

The Articles of Association of an arbitration commission shall be formulated in accordance with this Law.

Article 12 An arbitration commission shall comprise a chairman, two to four vice-chairmen, and seven to eleven members.

The chairman, vice-chairmen, and members of an arbitration commission must be persons specialized in law, economic, and trade and persons who have actual working experience. The number of specialists in law, economic, and trade shall not be less than two-thirds of the members of an arbitration association.

Article 13 The arbitration commission shall appoint fair and honest persons as its arbitrators.

Arbitrators must fulfill one of the following conditions:

1. They have been engaged in arbitration work for at least eight years.
2. They have worked as a lawyer for at least eight years.
3. They have been a judge for at least eight years.
4. They are engaged in legal research or legal teaching and in senior positions.
5. They have legal knowledge and are engaged in professional work relating to economics and trade, and in senior positions or of the equivalent professional level.

The arbitration commission shall establish a list of arbitrators according to different professionals.

Article 14   Arbitration commissions are independent of administrative organs and there are no subordinate relations with any administrative organs or between the different arbitration commissions.

Article 15   The China Arbitration Commission is a social organization with the status of a legal person. Arbitration commissions are members of the China Arbitration Association. The Articles of Association of the China Arbitration Association shall be formulated by the national general meeting of the members.

The China Arbitration Association is an organization in charge of self-regulation of the arbitration commissions. It shall conduct supervision over the conduct (any breach of discipline) of the arbitration commissions and their members and arbitrators in accordance with its Articles of Association.

The China Arbitration Association shall formulate Arbitration Rules in accordance with this Law and the Civil Procedure Law.

Chapter III Arbitration Agreement

Article 16   An arbitration agreement shall include the arbitration clauses provided in the contract and any other written form of agreement concluded before or after the disputes providing for submission to arbitration.

The following contents shall be included in an arbitration agreement:

1. The expression of the parties' wish to submit to arbitration
2. The matters to be arbitrated
3. The arbitration commission selected by the parties

Article 17 An arbitration agreement shall be invalid under any of the following circumstances:

1. Matters agreed upon for arbitration are beyond the scope of arbitration prescribed by law
2. Arbitration agreements concluded by persons without or with limited capacity for civil acts
3. Arbitration agreements if signed by a party under duress

Article 18 If the arbitration matters or the arbitration commission are not agreed upon by the parties in the arbitration agreement, or if the relevant provisions are not clear, the parties may supplement the agreement. If the parties fail to agree upon the supplementary agreement, the arbitration agreement shall be invalid.

Article 19 An arbitration agreement shall exist independently. Any changes to, rescission, termination, or invalidity of the contract shall not affect the validity of the arbitration agreement.
An arbitration tribunal has the right to rule on the validity of a contract.

Article 20 If the parties object to the validity of the arbitration agreement, they may apply to the arbitration commission for a decision or to a people's court for a ruling. If one of the parties submits to the arbitration commission for a decision, but the other party applies to a people's court for a ruling, the people's court shall give the ruling.
If the parties contest the validity of the arbitration agreement, the objection shall be made before the start of the first hearing of the arbitration tribunal.

Chapter IV Arbitration Procedure

Section 1 Application and Acceptance for Arbitration

Article 21 The parties applying for arbitration shall fulfill the following conditions:

1. They must have an arbitration agreement.
2. They must have a specific claim with facts and argument on which the claim is based.
3. The arbitration must be within the jurisdiction of the arbitration commission.

Article 22   The party applying for arbitration shall submit to an arbitration commission the arbitration agreement, an application for arbitration, and copies thereof.

Article 23   An arbitration application shall state clearly the following:

1. The name, sex, age, occupation, work unit, and address of the party; the name, address, and legal representative of the legal person or other organization; and the name and position of its person in charge.
2. The arbitration claim and the facts and argument on which the claim is based.
3. Evidence and the source of evidence; the name and address of the witness(es).

Article 24   Within 5 days from the date of receiving the arbitration application, the arbitration commission shall notify the parties that it considers the conditions for acceptance have been fulfilled, and that the application is accepted by it. If the arbitration commission considers that the conditions have not been fulfilled, it shall notify the parties in writing of its rejection, stating its reasons.

Article 25   Upon acceptance of an arbitration application, the arbitration commission shall, within the time limit provided by the Arbitration Rules, serve a copy of the Arbitration Rules and the list of arbitrators on the applicant, and serve a copy of the arbitration application, the Arbitration Rules, and the list of arbitrators on the respondent.

Upon receipt of a copy of the arbitration application, the respondent shall, within the time limit prescribed by the Arbitration Rules, submit its defense to the arbitration commission. Upon receipt of the defense, the arbitration commission shall, within the time limit prescribed by the Arbitration Rules, serve a copy of the reply on the applicant. The failure of the respondent to submit a defense shall not affect the proceeding of the arbitration procedures.

Article 26   Where the parties had agreed on an arbitration agreement but one of the parties initiates an action before a people's court without stating the existence of the arbitration agreement, the people's court shall, unless the arbitration agreement is invalid, reject the action if the other party submits to the court the arbitration agreement before the first hearing of the case. If the other party fails to object to the hearing by the people's court before the first hearing, the arbitration agreement shall be considered to have been waived by the party, and the people's court shall proceed with the hearing.

Article 27 The applicant may abandon or alter his arbitration claim. The respondent may accept the arbitration claim or object to it. It has a right to make a counterclaim.

Article 28 A party may apply for property preservation if, as the result of an act of the other party or for some other reasons, it appears that an award may be impossible or difficult to enforce.

If one of the parties applies for property preservation, the arbitration commission shall submit to a people's court the application of the party in accordance with the relevant provisions of the Civil Procedure Law.

If a property preservation order is unfounded, the applicant shall compensate the party against whom the order was made for any losses sustained as a result of the implementation of the property preservation order.

Article 29 The parties and their legal representatives may appoint lawyers or engage agents to handle matters relating to the arbitration. In the event that a lawyer or an agent is appointed to handle the arbitration matters, a letter of authorization shall be submitted to the arbitration commission.

Section 2 Composition of the Arbitration Tribunal

Article 30 An arbitration tribunal may comprise three arbitrators or one arbitrator. If an arbitration tribunal comprises three arbitrators, a presiding arbitrator shall be appointed.

Article 31 If the parties agree to form an arbitration tribunal comprising three arbitrators, each party shall select or authorize the chairman of the arbitration commission to appoint one arbitrator. The third arbitrator shall be selected jointly by the parties or be nominated by the chairman of the arbitration commission in accordance with a joint mandate given by the parties. The third arbitrator shall be the presiding arbitrator.

If the parties agree to have one arbitrator to form an arbitration tribunal, the arbitrator shall be selected jointly by the parties or be nominated by the chairman of the arbitration commission in accordance with a joint mandate given by the parties.

Article 32 If the parties fail, within the time limit prescribed by the Arbitration Rules, to select the form of the constitution of the arbitration tribunal or fail to select the arbitrators, the arbitrators shall be appointed by the chairman of the arbitration commission.

Article 33   After the arbitration tribunal is constituted, the arbitration commission shall notify the parties in writing of the composition of the arbitration tribunal.

Article 34   In any of the following circumstances, an arbitrator must withdraw from the arbitration, and the parties shall have the right to apply for his withdrawal if he:

1. is a party or a close relative of a party or of a party's representative.
2. is interested in the case.
3. has some other relationship with a party to the case or with a party's agent which could possibly affect the impartiality of the arbitration.
4. meets a party or his agent in private, accepts an invitation for dinner by a party or his representative, or accepts gifts presented by any of them.

Article 35   When applying for the withdrawal of an arbitrator, the petitioning party shall state his reasons and submit a withdrawal application before the first hearing. A withdrawal application may also be submitted before the conclusion of the last hearing if reasons for the withdrawal only became known after the start of the first hearing.

Article 36   Whether an arbitrator is withdrawn or not shall be determined by the chairman of the arbitration commission. If the chairman is serving as an arbitrator, the withdrawal or not shall be determined collectively by the arbitration commission.

Article 37   If an arbitrator is unable to perform his duties as an arbitrator as a result of the withdrawal or any other reasons, another arbitrator shall be selected or appointed in accordance with the provisions of this Law.

After a replacement arbitrator has been selected or appointed following the withdrawal of an arbitrator, the parties may apply to resume the arbitration procedure. The arbitration tribunal shall determine whether the resumption of the procedure may be allowed. The arbitration tribunal may determine on its own whether the arbitration procedure shall be resumed.

3

Article 38   An arbitrator involved in one of the circumstances described in Item 4, Article 34, if it is serious, or those described in Item 6, Article 58, such arbitrator shall be legally liable in accordance with the law. The arbitration commission shall remove his name from the list of arbitrators.

Section 3 Hearing and Arbitral Awards

Article 39   An arbitration tribunal shall hold a tribunal session to hear an arbitration case. If the parties agree not to hold a hearing, the arbitration tribunal may render an award in accordance with the arbitration application, the defense statement, and other documents.

Article 40   An arbitration shall not be conducted in public. If the parties agree to a public hearing, the arbitration may proceed in public, except those concerning state secrets.

Article 41   The arbitration commission shall notify the two parties within the time limit provided by the Arbitration Rules of the date of the hearing. Either party may request to postpone the hearing within the time limit provided by the Arbitration Rules if there is a genuine reason. The arbitration tribunal shall decide whether to postpone the hearing.

Article 42   If the applicant for arbitration who has been served with a notice in writing does not appear before the tribunal without good reasons, or leaves the tribunal room during a hearing without the permission of the arbitration tribunal, such applicant shall be deemed to have withdrawn his application.

If the party against whom the application was made was served with a notice in writing but does not appear before the tribunal without due reasons or leaves the tribunal room during a hearing without the permission of the arbitration tribunal, an award by default may be given.

Article 43   The parties shall produce evidence in support of their claims.

An arbitration tribunal may collect on its own evidence it considers necessary.

Article 44   For specialized matters, an arbitration tribunal may submit for appraisal to an appraisal organ agreed upon by the parties or to the appraisal organ appointed by the arbitration tribunal if it deems such appraisal to be necessary.

According to the claim of the parties or the request of the arbitration tribunal, the appraisal organ shall appoint an appraiser to participate in the hearing. Upon the permission of the arbitration tribunal, the parties may question the appraiser.

Article 45   Any evidence shall be produced at the start of the hearing. The parties may challenge the validity of such evidence.

Article 46   In the event that the evidence might be destroyed or if it would be difficult to obtain the evidence later on, the parties may apply for the evidence to be preserved. If the parties apply for such preservation, the arbitration commission shall submit the application to the basic-level people's court of the place where the evidence is located.

Article 47   The parties have the right to argue during an arbitration procedure. At the end of the debate, the presiding arbitrator or the sole arbitrator shall ask for the final opinion of the parties.

Article 48   An arbitration tribunal shall make a written record of the hearing. If the parties or other participants to the arbitration consider that the record has omitted a part of their statement or is incorrect in some other respect, they shall have the right to request correction thereof. If no correction is made, the request for correction shall be noted in the written record.

The arbitrators, recorder, parties, and other participants to the arbitration shall sign or affix their seals to the record.

Article 49   After the submission of an arbitration application, the parties may settle the dispute among themselves through conciliation. If a conciliation agreement has been reached, the parties may apply to the arbitration tribunal for an award based on the conciliation agreement. They may also withdraw the arbitration application.

Article 50   If the parties fall back on their words after the conclusion of a conciliation agreement and the withdrawal of the arbitration application, application may be made for arbitration in accordance with the arbitration agreement.

Article 51   Before giving an award, an arbitration tribunal may first attempt to conciliate. If the parties apply for conciliation voluntarily, the arbitration tribunal shall conciliate. If conciliation is unsuccessful, an award shall be made promptly.

When a settlement agreement is reached by conciliation, the arbitration tribunal shall prepare the conciliation statement or the award on the basis of the results of the settlement agreement. A conciliation statement shall have the same legal force as that of an award.

Article 52   A conciliation statement shall set forth the arbitration claims and the results of the agreement between the parties. The conciliation statement shall be signed by the arbitrators, sealed by the arbitration commission, and served on both parties.

A conciliation statement shall have legal effect once signed and accepted by the parties.

If the parties fall back on their words before the conciliation statement is signed and accepted by them, an award shall be made by the arbitration tribunal promptly.

Article 53   An award shall be based on the opinion of the majority arbitrators. The opinion of the minority arbitrators shall be recorded in writing. If an opinion of the majority arbitrators cannot be constituted at the tribunal, the award shall be given according to the opinion of the presiding arbitrator.

Article 54   The arbitration claims, the matters in dispute, the grounds upon which an award is given, the results of the judgment, the responsibility for the arbitration fees, and the date of the award shall be set forth in the award. If the parties agree not to include in the award the matters in dispute and the grounds on which the award is based, such matters may not be stated in the award. The award shall be signed by the arbitrators and sealed by the arbitration commission. The arbitrator who disagrees with the award may select to sign or not to sign it.

Article 55   During the course of arbitration by an arbitration tribunal, where a part of facts has been made clear, a partial award may first be given in relation to that part.

Article 56   The parties may, within 30 days of the receipt of the award, request the arbitration tribunal to correct any typographical errors, calculation errors, or matters which had been awarded but omitted in the award.

Article 57   An award shall be legally effective on the date it is given.

Chapter V Application for Cancellation of an Award

Article 58   The parties may apply to the intermediate people's court at the place where the arbitration commission is located for cancellation of an award if they provide evidence proving that the award involves one of the following circumstances:

1. There is no arbitration agreement between the parties.
2. The matters of the award are beyond the extent of the arbitration agreement or not within the jurisdiction of the arbitration commission.
3. The composition of the arbitration tribunal or the arbitration procedure is in contrary to the legal procedure.
4. The evidence on which the award is based is falsified.
5. The other party has concealed evidence which is sufficient to affect the impartiality of the award.
6. The arbitrator(s) has (have) demanded or accepted bribes, committed graft, or perverted the law in making the arbitral award.

The people's court shall rule to cancel the award if the existence of one of the circumstances prescribed in the preceding clause is confirmed by its collegiate bench.

The people's court shall rule to cancel the award if it holds that the award is contrary to the social and public interests.

Article 59   If a party applies for cancellation of an award, an application shall be submitted within 6 months after receipt of the award.

Article 60   The people's court shall, within 2 months after receipt of the application for cancellation of an award, render its decision for cancellation of the award or for rejection of the application.

Article 61   If the people's court holds that the case may be rearbitrated by the arbitration tribunal after receipt of the application for cancellation of an award, the court shall inform the arbitration tribunal of rearbitrating the case within a certain period of time and rule to suspend the cancellation procedure. If the arbitration tribunal refuses to rearbitrate, the people's court shall rule to resume the cancellation procedure.

Chapter VI Enforcement

Article 62   The parties shall execute an arbitration award. If one party fails to execute the award, the other party may apply to a people's court for enforcement in accordance with the relevant provisions of the Civil Procedure Law, and the court shall enforce the award.

Article 63   A people's court shall, after examination and verification by its collegiate bench, rule not to enforce an award if the party against whom an application for enforcement is made provides evidence proving that the award involves one of the circumstances prescribed in Clause 2, Article 217 of the Civil Procedure Law.

Article 64   If one party applies for enforcement of an award while the other party applies for cancellation of the award, the people's court receiving such application shall rule to suspend enforcement of the award.

If a people's court rules to cancel an award, it shall rule to terminate enforcement. If the people's court overrules the application for cancellation of an award, it shall rule to resume enforcement.

Chapter VII Special Provisions on Foreign-Related Arbitration

Article 65   The provisions of this Chapter shall apply to all arbitration of disputes arising from foreign economic, trade, transportation, or maritime matters. In the absence of provisions in this Chapter, other relevant provisions of this Law shall apply.

Article 66   A foreign arbitration commission may be organized and established by the China International Chamber of Commerce.

A foreign arbitration commission shall comprise one chairman, several vice-chairmen, and several committee members.

The chairman, vice-chairmen, and committee members may be appointed by the China International Chamber of Commerce.

Article 67   A foreign arbitration commission may appoint foreigners with professional knowledge in such fields as law, economic and trade, science, and technology as arbitrators.

Article 68   If the parties to a foreign-related arbitration apply for evidence preservation, the foreign arbitration commission shall submit their applications to the intermediate people's court in the place where the evidence is located.

Article 69   The arbitration tribunal of a foreign arbitration commission may record the details of the hearing in writing or record the essentials of the hearing in writing. The written record of the essentials shall be signed or sealed by the parties and other participants in the arbitration.

Article 70 A people's court shall, after examination and verification by its collegiate bench, rule to cancel an award if a party to the case provides evidence proving that the arbitration award involves one of the circumstances prescribed in Clause 1, Article 260 of the Civil Procedure Law.

Article 71 A people's court shall, after examination and verification by its collegiate bench, rule not to enforce an award if the party against whom an application is made provides evidence proving that the arbitration award involves one of the circumstances prescribed in Clause 1, Article 260 of the Civil Procedure Law.

Article 72 Where the party subject to enforcement or its property is not within the territory of the People's Republic of China, a party applying for the enforcement of a legally effective arbitration award shall apply directly to the foreign court having jurisdiction for recognition and enforcement of the award.

Article 73 Foreign arbitration rules may be formulated by the China International Chamber of Commerce in accordance with this Law and the relevant provisions of the Civil Procedure Law.

Chapter VIII Supplementary Provisions

Article 74 If the law has stipulated a time limitation of arbitration, such provisions of the law shall apply. If the law has not stipulated a time limitation of arbitration, the provisions on the limitation of actions shall apply.

Article 75 The arbitration commission may formulate provisional arbitration rules in accordance with this Law and the relevant provisions of the Civil Procedure Law before the formulation of the arbitration rules by the China Arbitration Association.

Article 76 The parties shall pay arbitration fees in accordance with the relevant provisions.

The methods for the collection of arbitration fees shall be submitted to the commodity prices administration department for approval.

Article 77 Arbitration of labor disputes and disputes over contracts for undertaking agricultural projects within agricultural collective economic organizations shall be separately stipulated.

Article 78 In the event of conflict between the provisions on arbitration formulated before the coming into effect of this Law, the provisions of this Law shall prevail.

Article 79 Arbitration organs established before the coming into effect of this Law in the municipalities directly under the Central Government, in the municipalities where people's governments of the provinces or autonomous regions, and in other cities divided into districts must be reorganized in accordance with the relevant provisions of this Law. The arbitration organs which are not reorganized shall be terminated at the expiration of one year after the date of effectiveness of this Law.

All other arbitration organs established before the implementation of this Law and not conforming to the provisions of this Law shall be terminated on the date of effectiveness of this Law.

Article 80 This Law shall be effective as of 1 September 1995.

APPENDIX TWO

China's Foreign Investment Laws and Regulations

1. Law on Civil Procedure of the People's Republic of China (Promulgated on 9 April 1991)
2. The Company Law of the People's Republic of China (Promulgated on 29 December 1993)
3. Law of the People's Republic of China on Bankruptcy of Enterprises (Trial Implementation) (Promulgated in December 1986)
4. Provisional Regulations of the People's Republic of China on Private Enterprises (Promulgated by the State Administration for Industry and Commerce in 1988)
5. Measures for the Implementation of the Provisional Regulations of the People's Republic of China on Private Enterprises (Promulgated by the State Administration for Industry and Commerce on 16 January 1989)
6. Customs Law of the People's Republic of China (Adopted and promulgated at the 19th Session of the Standing Committee of the Sixth National People's Congress on 22 January 1987)
7. Law of the People's Republic of China on Import and Export Commodity Inspection (Promulgated on 21 February 1989)
8. Implementing Rules to the Law of the Inspection of Import and Export Commodities of the People's Republic of China (Promulgated by the Standing Administration for the Inspection of Import and Export Commodities on 23 October 1992)
9. Rules of the People's Republic of China on Origin of Export

Goods (Adopted at the Standing Conference of the State Council on 28 February 1992)

10. Measures for the Implementation of the Rules of the People's Republic of China on Origin of Export Goods (Promulgated by the Ministry of Foreign Economic Relations and Trade on 1 April 1992)

11. Checklist of the People's Republic of China on Main Procedures for Manufacture and Processing of Origin Criterion of Goods with Import Elements (Promulgated by the Ministry of Foreign Economic Relations and Trade on 1 April 1992)

12. Regulations on the Administration of Technology Import Contracts of the People's Republic of China (Promulgated by the State Council on 24 May 1985)

13. Detailed Rules for the Implementation of the Regulations on the Administration of Technology Import Contracts of the People's Republic of China (Approved by the State Council on 30 December 1987 and promulgated by the Ministry of Foreign Economic Relations and Trade on 20 January 1988)

14. Taxation Management Law of the People's Republic of China (Adopted at the 27th Session of the Standing Committee of the Seventh National People's Congress on 4 September 1992)

15. Provisional Regulations of the People's Republic of China on Value-Added Tax (13 December 1993)

16. Detailed Implementing Rules to the Provisional Regulations of the People's Republic of China on Value-Added Tax (Promulgated by the Ministry of Finance on 25 December 1993)

17. Provisional Regulations of the People's Republic of China on Consumption Tax (Promulgated by the Ministry of Finance on 13 December 1993)

18. Detailed Implementing Rules to the Provisional Regulations of the People's Republic of China on Consumption Tax (Promulgated by the Ministry of Finance on 25 December 1993)

19. Provisional Regulations of the People's Republic of China on Business Tax (Promulgated by the Ministry of Finance on 13 December 1993)

20. Detailed Implementing Rules to the Provisional Regulations of the People's Republic of China on Business Tax (Promulgated by the Ministry of Finance on 25 December 1993)

21. Patent Law of the People's Republic of China (Adopted at the Fourth Session of the Standing Committee of the Sixth National People's Congress on 12 March 1984)

22. Implementing Regulations of the Patent Law of the People's Re-

public of China (Approved by the State Council and Promulgated by the Patent Office of the People's Republic of China on 21 December 1992)

23. Trademark Law of the People's Republic of China (Adopted at the 24th Session of the Standing Committee of the Fifth National People's Congress on 23 August 1982)

24. Law of the People's Republic of China on Economic Contracts Involving Foreign Investments (Adopted at the 10th Session of the Standing Committee of the Sixth National People's Congress on 21 March 1985)

25. Rules of the Procedure of Arbitration of the China International Economic and Trade Arbitration Commission (Amended and adopted at the First Session of the Standing Committee of the Second China Council for the Promotion of International Trade and the China International Chamber of Commerce on 17 March 1994)

26. Regulations of the People's Republic of China for Controlling the Registration of Enterprises as Legal Persons (Promulgated by the State Administration for Industry and Commerce on 13 June 1988)

27. Detailed Rules for the Implementation of the Regulations of the People's Republic of China for Controlling the Registration of Enterprises as Legal Persons (Enforced from 1 December 1988)

28. Regulations of the People's Republic of China on Granting and Transfer of Land Use Rights for Valuable Consideration in Cities and Towns (Promulgated on 19 May 1990)

29. Individual Income Tax Law of the People's Republic of China (Promulgated on 10 September 1980)

30. Implementing Regulations of the Individual Income Tax Law of the People's Republic of China (Promulgated by the State Council on 28 January 1994)

31. Accounting Regulations of the People's Republic of China for Foreign-Funded Enterprises (Promulgated on 24 June 1992)

32. Provisions of the People's Republic of China on Financial Management of Foreign-Funded Enterprises (Promulgated on 24 June 1992)

33. Provisional Regulations of the Ministry of Foreign Economic Relations and Trade on Management of Export Goods (Issued by the Ministry of Foreign Economic Relations and Trade in December 1992)

34. Provisions of the Ministry of Foreign Economic Relations and Trade and the State Administration for Industry and Commerce

on Contract for and Management of Sino-Foreign Joint Ventures (Issued by the Ministry of Foreign Economic Relations and Trade on 13 September 1990)

35. Interpretation by the Ministry of Foreign Economic Relations and Trade on Certain Articles of Detailed Implementing Rules to the Law of the People's Republic of China on Foreign-Funded Enterprises (Issued by the Ministry of Foreign Economic Relations and Trade on 5 December 1991)

36. Implementation Rules of the Ministry of Foreign Economic Relations and Trade Concerning the Verification and Determination of Export-Oriented Enterprises and Technologically Advanced Enterprises with Foreign Investment (Promulgated by the Ministry of Foreign Economic Relations and Trade on 27 January 1987)

37. Supplementary Provisions for the Implementation Rules of the Ministry of Foreign Economic Relations and Trade Concerning the Verification and Determination of Export-Oriented Enterprises and Technologically Advanced Enterprises with Foreign Investment (Promulgated by the Ministry of Foreign Economic Relations and Trade on 2 February 1992)

38. Implementing Rules of the Ministry of Foreign Economic Relations and Trade Concerning Application for Import and Export Licenses by the Foreign Investment Enterprises (Promulgated by the Ministry of Foreign Economic Relations and Trade on 5 December 1991)

39. Interim Provisions on the Term of Joint Ventures of Chinese-Foreign Equity Joint Ventures (Approved by the State Council on 30 September 1990 and Promulgated by the Ministry of Foreign Economic Relations and Trade on 22 October 1990)

40. Rules of the Customs of the People's Republic of China for the Control of the Import of Materials and Parts Required by Foreign Investment Enterprises for the Fulfillment of Export Contracts (Promulgated by the Customs General Administration on 24 November 1986)

41. Provisional Rules of the People's Bank of China Concerning Renminbi Loans Against Mortgage on Foreign Exchange by Enterprises with Foreign Investment (Published by the Xinhua News Agency on 12 December 1986)

42. Provisional Rules of the People's Bank of China Concerning the Provisions of Foreign Exchange Guarantees by Organizations within Chinese Territory (Promulgated by the People's Bank of China on 20 February 1987)

43. Provisional Regulations Concerning the Ratio Between the Registered and the Total Investment of Chinese–Foreign Equity Joint Ventures (Promulgated by the State Administration for Industry and Commerce on 1 March 1987)

44. Rules of the Bank of China on Loans for Foreign Investment Enterprises (Approved by the State Council on 7 April 1987 and promulgated by the Bank of China on 26 April 1987)

45. Provisions on the Contributions Made by the Parties to Joint Ventures Using Chinese and Foreign Investment (Approved by the State Council on 23 December 1987 and promulgated by the Ministry of Foreign Economic Relations and Trade and the State Administration for Industry and Commerce on 1 January 1988)

46. Provisions of the Ministry of Labor and Personnel of the People's Republic of China on Autonomous Rights of Enterprises with Foreign Investment in the Hiring of Personnel and on Salaries and Wages, Insurance and Welfare Expenses (Promulgated by the Ministry of Labor and Personnel on 26 November 1986)

47. Labor Law of the People's Republic of China (Adopted at the Eighth Session of the Standing Committee of the Eighth National People's Congress on 5 July 1994)

48. Foreign Trade Law of the People's Republic of China (Adopted at the Seventh Session of the Standing Committee of the Eighth National People's Congress on 12 May 1994)

49. Provisional Regulations on the Guidance of Foreign Investment Orientation (Promulgated by Xinhua News Agency on 27 June 1995)

50. Directory of Industries for the Guidance of Foreign Investment Orientation (Promulgated by Xinhua News Agency on 27 June 1995)

The English text of all legislation is an unofficial translation only, and the Chinese should be regarded as definitive in case of any divergence.

Index

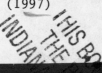

INDIANAPOLIS-MARION COUNTY
PUBLIC LIBRARY

offers you:	MAGAZINES	PAMPHLETS
BOOKS	MAPS	PICTURES
RECORDS	FRAMED ART	PROGRAMS
FILMS	VIDEOTAPES	FOR ADULTS
MUSIC	AUDIOCASSETTES	AND CHILDREN

Other borrowers will appreciate the prompt return of this book.

A CHARGE IS MADE FOR OVERDUE MATERIALS

GAYLORD